Return to My Father's House

RETURN TO

MY

FATHER'S HOUSE

A Charter Member of the American Communist Party Tells Why He Joined—And Why He Later Left to Fight Communism

----

MAURICE L. MALKIN

EDITED BY
CHARLES W. WILEY

ARLINGTON HOUSE   *New Rochelle, New York*

Library of Congress Catalog Card Number 72-189373

ISBN 0–87000–144–2

MANUFACTURED IN THE UNITED STATES OF AMERICA

DEDICATION

To my father and mother for their sacrifices and wise guidance in leading me to a return.

To my wife Laura and our daughters Arlene and Lana for the help and happiness they have given me.

ACKNOWLEDGEMENTS

My deep gratitude to Eugene Lyons and Newton Fulbright for their encouragement and help in the publication of this book.

My sincere thanks to Grace Poggi for her assistance in preparing the manuscript.

"Labor is Entitled to All it Produces"

No money should be received without acknowledgment in this book. Members must see that the Financial Secretary places a stamp in the book for each month for which Dues or Assessments are paid.

Name *M. Malkin*

Initiated by *Lee Chumley*

M. & M. W. I. U. Union No. 300

Organizer Branch No.

June 22 1915.

METAL & MACHINERY
Department
Industry

Student Workers
Occupation

Ledger_____ Page_____

R. Thomas Fin. Secy.

Gen. No. 516489

WORKERS (COMMUNIST) PARTY OF AMERICA
American Section of the Communist International

Name *M. L. Malkin*

Admitted *Charter Member*

District Organizer

No. **B**

District 2 City N.Y.C.
Section 2 Sub Sec. B
Shop Nucleus
Street Nucleus 2 5

MEMBERSHIP
1928—CARD—1928
This card expires Dec. 31, 1928.

Issued by the CENTRAL EXECUTIVE COMMITTEE

From my Industrial Workers of the World membership card.

Certification that I was a charter member of the Workers Party of America.

AIMS

The W.I.R. is a workers' SELF-HELP organization—aid from workers for workers, distinct and apart from capitalist charity. Its function shall be to promote international working-class help and raise the spirit of SOLIDARITY among all workers; those who give, and those who receive.

It shall render assistance wherever the laboring masses are menaced by suffering, and where reactionary forces are prepared to make use of the distress of the workers to weaken their powers of resistance—whether this suffering and distress be the result of strikes, lock-outs, or mass-unemployment, or of natural catastrophes.

It shall administer relief with impartiality, render assistance without discrimination as to party, religion or race.

It shall especially concern itself with the welfare of workers' children, aiming to win them and their parents away from the various bourgeois charity organizations where hatred against the working class is fostered and encouraged, and where capitalism, taking advantage of the workers' need, turns our children and their parents into beggars unfit for the class struggle.

The W.I.R. shall give full consideration to the struggles of the Negro masses in their fight against discrimination, and foster the spirit of solidarity between white and Negro workers.

The W.I.R. shall in no way act as a substitute for, or in opposition to, any section of the labor, trade union, or cooperative movements, but shall act as an auxiliary organization in cooperation with them in relief work.

The W.I.R. shall aid the workers in their struggles in all ways possible within the present system, at the same time pointing out that COMPLETE EMANCIPATION OF THE WORKING CLASS CANNOT BE ACHIEVED WITHIN THE CAPITALIST SYSTEM.

Not Charity—But Solidarity

Workers International Relief
United States Section

Non-Political, Non-Sectarian, Non-Partisan
BUT ALWAYS FOR THE WORKERS

Name *Maurice L. Malkin*

Initiated *St. C. 10 St. City*

Beatrice Carlin
Local Secretary

131 W. 28 St.
Address of Local

City *New York City*

Branch *Down Town*

Membership Card
Issued by
NATIONAL OFFICE OF THE
Workers International Relief
949 Broadway, Room 512, New York

Front and back of my WIR membership card.

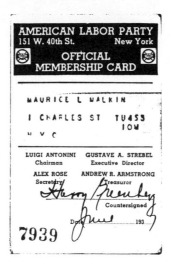

Cover page of my ALP card. The ALP was the
forerunner of the Liberal Party in New York.

COMMUNIST PARTY OF THE U.S.A.

1 9 3 **7**
Membership
Book   № 80965

Name ...*Maurice Malkin*......

State ...*New York*.... District...**2**...

County ...*New York*... City ...*N.Y.*

Section (A.D. or Ward)...*1*...Branch...*4*....

issued on *Jan. 27, 1937.*
                      (date)

Signature of State or District
Chairman or Secretary of Party

No Party Membership Book is valid unless it has the
Party Seal affixed thereon.

CONSTITUTION
Preamble

The Communist Party of the United States of America
is a working class political party carrying forward today
the traditions of Jefferson, Paine, Jackson, and Lincoln,
and of the Declaration of Independence; it upholds the
achievements of democracy, the right of "life, liberty,
and the pursuit of happiness," and defends the United
States Constitution against its reactionary enemies who
would destroy democracy and all popular liberties; it is
devoted to defense of the immediate interests of workers,
farmers, and all toilers against capitalist exploitation,
and to preparation of the working class for its historic
mission to unite and lead the American people to extend
these democratic principles to their necessary and logi-
cal conclusions;

By establishing common ownership of the national economy, through a government of the people, by the people,
and for the people; the abolition of all exploitation of
man by man, nation by nation, and race by race, and
thereby the abolition of class divisions in society; that is,
by the establishment of socialism, according to the scientific principles enunciated by the greatest teachers of
mankind, Marx, Engels, Lenin, and Stalin, embodied in
the Communist International; and the free cooperation of
the American people with those of other lands, striving
toward a world without oppression and war, a world
brotherhood of man.

To this end, the Communist Party of the United States
of America establishes the basic laws of its organization
in the following Constitution.

ARTICLE I
Name

The name of this organization shall be the COMMU-
NIST PARTY OF THE UNITED STATES OF AMERICA.

ARTICLE II
Emblem

The emblem of the Party shall be the crossed hammer
and sickle, representing the unity of worker and farmer.

9

Pages from my Party book, my proof that I was
a member of the Communist Party, U.S.A.
When a Communist is expelled from the
Party, his Party book is seized. The Party can
then disclaim any knowledge of the ex-mem-
ber, in case he wishes to testify against the
Party. I refused to give up my book. The signature is Israel Amter's.

CHAPTER I

I was born in the town of Petrikov, in Minsk province of the old Polish sector of the expanded Russian Empire—amid the historical Pripet Marshes, a region trampled and fought over by the armies of East and West since time immemorial. The date was November 10, 1900 and I was the second youngest of eleven children.

My Father and brothers had refused to serve in the armies of the Czar because the Jews in Russia, since the ascension of Alexander III in 1881, had been reduced to a mere animal existence. As punishment, my family had been deprived of all civil rights. We were outcasts, denied any protection under the law. Had a bully taken the notion, in broad daylight, to put a bullet through one of us, he would probably never have been brought to trial.

Most of the Jews in the region had come originally on the invitation of early Polish princes. The Tartars, during their last devastating invasion in the 13th Century, had slaughtered the inhabitants and laid bare the country until it was depopulated. The Polish rulers had invited the Germans to settle in the area, with special inducements extended to artisans, and the Jews had responded. Denied the privilege of owning land in Germany or elsewhere in Europe, the Jews had turned to craft-metallurgy, leather making, tailoring, etc. My family had always been carpenters.

The Malkins had originally immigrated to Russia from England. It is the original family name and was never changed. *Malkin* is found in Chaucer's *Canterbury Tales* and in *Knights of the Round Table*.

The comparatively happy life under Polish rule had ended with a series of partitions that began in 1772 and ended with the division of Poland among Russia, Prussia, and Austria—with Russia getting the larger share.

The Malkins were third generation Petrikov residents. My great, great grandfather had migrated from a town named Malkin, in honor of his father, by Czar Nicholas I, in recognition of his outstanding military service. The town of Malkin, like Petrikov, was in the State of Minsk. My great, great grandfather left because of the extreme anti-semitism there. He had no birth certificate or other legal identification papers. After settling in Petrikov, none of my family served in the Czar's armies and we never had any legal rights of any kind.

Jews in Russia, after Alexander III, were denied travel permits and restricted to their native towns and villages. Even Jews who in better times had found their way to St. Petersburg (now Leningrad), Moscow and other large cities were treated similarly. Only the very wealthy Jews, those able to loan large sums to the Czar, were exempt from the stringent regulations.

It was stamped on the birth certificates, passports and other legal papers of this tiny "elite" section of Russian Jews, about one per cent of the total, that they were privileged members of their race. They were bankers, industrialists, importers and exporters, medical specialists who had graduated from West European universities, etc. Only these Jews were allowed to live in main cities and travel. Ninety-nine percent of the Jewish population, about 3½–4 million, had stamped on all their identity papers in large letters *Gdye Yevreyi nye dozvolno zhit* (Where Jews are not allowed to live). These Jews were not even allowed to send their children to universities in large cities in spite of the fact that they were all subject to the military draft.

The one per cent privileged Jews were an eyesore to the others because they helped to create propaganda for the anti-semites—the Black Hundred Society and other extremists (similar to the Ku Klux Klan, but even more fanatical)—that all Jews were shylocks and money grabbers. The slogan *"Biy zhidov e Spasay Rosiyu!"* ("Kill the Jews and Save Russia!") harmed the 99 percent much more than the one percent.

Petrikov was a typical Russian *Mestechko* (small town). There were between 750 and 800 families, with a total population of about 4,000. Fully 3,000 were Jews, most of them small businessmen and artisans. The merchants traded with the peasants and with businessmen in the neighboring villages. The town doctor, Dr. Shapiro, was a friend of my family who had come to Petrikov to practice medicine after graduating from medical school in Minsk.

The Russians in Petrikov were officials, barge builders, dock workers, fishermen and peasants who lived on the outskirts of town.

12

We had no railroad, the nearest was at Kapetkevitch, but the Pripet River was navigable, after the winter ice had melted in late spring, until the middle of November. Two steamers, old-fashioned sidewheelers, the *Litvinka* and *Catherina*, would stop regularly at a wooden wharf down a slope from town. Those with free time would stroll down to see the loading and unloading of passengers, horses, cows and pigs. They would stand and watch the boats depart, backing into the stream with clouds of black smoke rolling from the white and red smoke stacks.

Around the town were forests, a source of logs for building houses and other structures and firewood for heating. The peasants sold wood for two or three rubles for each wagonload.

Denied regular employment because of his outlaw status, Father depended on odd jobs of carpentry for a living. Sometimes a merchant in town would need some carpentry done—fixing windows, doors or similar small jobs. But most of the time he worked on their farms for the peasants, who would pay him with potatoes or other foods.

One of my earliest memories is of a cold winter night when Father came home with nothing for us to eat. Mother, after thoughtful silence, got up from her chair near the stove and started to boil some water in which she put a few leaves of cabbage. We called it soup.

After that I went to bed hungry many nights. We seldom had enough to eat. We shivered—always, it seemed—from the winter cold and from fear of the soldiers and drunken peasants in the town square and on the streets.

I remember our home, a one-room log house in the hilly northwest section of the town, above the river and the marshes where the village cattle and goats were gathered in summer by a peasant herdsman. I remember the sound of winter wind slipping through the chinks between the logs, through the holes where the caulking had dried and dropped out. A Russian-style brick oven stove *(pechka)* was in one corner of the room. When the temperature dropped to 40 degrees below zero, we children were glad to sleep on the stove to keep from freezing.

One- and two-story log structures, with an occasional brick facade for the stores and shops, lined the main street of Petrikov. The plaza, or town square, was the center of activity. It served as a market place, meeting ground and leisure area. Around it were stores, such as the

13

barber and butcher shops, and, near the only hotel, horse and buggies could be rented. In the center of the square stood the town hall, a red brick building. It looked something like the court house in a county-seat town in the United States of 100 years ago.

An important building on the square was the fire house, a big barnlike structure used for entertainment when a circus or theatrical troupe visited the town. The fire department was a volunteer organization with manually operated equipment, some of it horse drawn. Serving as fire chief was Doctor Barsky, the village dentist, a knock-kneed little man with a reedy voice. He used to lead all the parades in his uniform and I still smile at the memory of Dr. Barsky wearing his mounted brass hat with the painted eagle of the Czar, a tight pair of trousers and a long blue and red overcoat with brass buttons that dragged behind his heels. A graduate of the Imperial Dental College in Minsk, he was Fire Chief because his office was next to the firehouse. The most important man in town—and the most feared—was Michael Shtupak, the *Uradnik* (Chief of Police), a great hulking, dull witted man who frequently lurched drunkenly about the streets watching for girls. He usually forced himself on Jewish women because Russians would have shot him for his behavior. Shtupak commanded an eight-man staff, with headquarters in the town hall. His home, with inside wood panelling, stood on the square at the foot of Main Street, the most imposing two-story log house in town. He augmented his small salary with what he could squeeze from the merchants, and it was impossible to conduct any sort of business without paying bribes to this bullying official.

Shtupak's usual greeting was "Dirty Damn Jews!" and I would dart around corners and cut across vacant lots to keep out of his way. He survived the disaster of the Russo-Japanese War, the Revolution of 1905, and was still in Petrikov until at least January, 1914.

The first real tragic experience in my childhood was the death of my 14-year old sister, Rachael Leah, when I was three. She died of malnutrition and pneumonia—cut down by the cold wind slashing across the frozen marshes, in March, 1904, after a long severe winter. My sisters, Bertha and Elsie, ages eight and six, my baby brother Solomon and I were sent to stay with an aunt during the funeral. At home that evening, Mother was red-eyed from weeping and Father and my brothers were strangely silent. They sat on the floor with their shoes off in the orthodox custom of mourning, the *Shiva*. Be-

14

cause it was Friday, Mother lit the candles after sundown and Father left for the synagogue.

We younger children huddled near the stove while my brothers blamed the terrible conditions in which we lived on a system of government that fostered brutal injustices. Mother began preparing food for the Sabbath. My brothers, especially Joseph, had turned from religion to embrace a new revolutionary movement. They had joined the Bolsheviks, who were against religion and God, but promised that once the Czar was deposed, men would be able to create a heaven on earth and eliminate all injustices. Father had always questioned this theory and predicated that nothing but evil and sorrow would come from it.

Father returned and, as was his usual custom, began to pray: "The Sixth Day: Thus the heaven and the earth were finished . . ." He faltered—and Harry, my oldest brother, finished the prayer: . . . "And all the host of them: And on the Seventh Day God finished His work which He had made."

After we ate white bread, the *Challah*, I suddenly missed Rachael and asked where she was. Mother said she had gone on a trip and would be away for a long time. There was complete silence, then Father began to speak: "God has punished us because of our sins." For a long time he had talked of making a pilgrimage to Palestine, to the Holy places. Now he was firmly resolved to go. He would sell the house, and with part of the money he and Abraham, his third son and a devout Zionist, would make the trip. Surely, God would then relieve the suffering that fell so heavily on our house.

The plan was carried through in the spring and the rest of us moved in with Father's sister, a widow with two daughters. Father and Abraham set out without the identity papers necessary to get them past the Czar's police. Since they couldn't have obtained such documents, their only hope was to elude the authorities. As with most such attempts, they were caught and arrested while attempting to cross into Austria—near Brody, at the Russian border town of Radzivil. They were forced to walk home, a distance of 800 miles, as part of a convoy of similar prisoners escorted by soldiers. At night they were put in the jails of the towns that they passed through.

Back in Petrikov they were released with a warning: "*Never* stray from the area again!"

Father bought a new house, a dilapidated and abandoned log shack near the center of town. All of us pitched in, cutting new logs and pressing clay and moss between the chinks. The shack was converted into a comparatively comfortable one-room home.

Life continued as usual. Father tramped the country looking for work. Sometimes he would be gone for a week. He would return with bread and potatoes—and, occasionally, there would be a few rubles for herring or a piece of meat. Mother would sometimes work at stalls in the open market to help out. She sold candy and *Kvas,* a Russian type of cold drink; a mixture of saccharin, red coloring, water and a few lemons in a big ten-gallon jug.

When it rained, the unpaved streets became a quagmire of knee deep mud, and in winter heavy snows blocked the streets and roads. Winter began in September and rarely ended before May.

Shortly before the cold set in, we children cut firewood in the nearby forest. Occasionally, we were able to borrow a wagon and team and in two days could bring home enough wood to last all winter. But usually we had to carry the wood on our backs.

Clothing was always a problem. I wore hand-me-downs, which Mother had patched and repatched and mended in a dozen places. In the summer we went barefooted and in the winter we wrapped our feet in potato sacks or, if we were lucky enough to have any, in felt.

Despite Czarist persecutions there were four synagogues in our town. (Today under communism, I doubt that there are that many in the entire State of Minsk.) Each temple maintained its own parochial school because only ten percent of the Jews in any one town or village were permitted to attend public school. The one in Petrikov was a red brick building in the better section. It was attended by Russians and a handful of children from the "better" Jewish families.

Because we were political outcasts, nobody in my family could even attend a Jewish parochial school. All the Malkin boys were taught, whenever possible, by private tutors at night.

Joseph and Nathan had joined the Bolshevik Party and meetings were held in our house, always when Father was away from home. Eventually, the Petrikov unit had located its headquarters with us and a supply of arms and ammunition was hidden under the wooden flooring of our house.

I understood little of what went on and my first recollections are of strange young men and women quietly coming and going. Eventually, many became very familiar. They followed the leadership of George Plekhanov, the father of Russian Marxism, and Nikolai Lenin. Their prophet was Karl Marx, whose works had been translated into Russian. (Marx, a German Jew, had renounced his religion to marry into a well known German family, and he himself became one of history's worst anti-semites.)*

To Joseph and Nathan, and the young men and women who met with them, "Scientific Socialism" and the "Intellectual Dictatorship of the Proletariat" were the answers to all the problems of the world. They believed that the unhappy fate of the Jews was the fate of all working class people and could be relieved only by a revolution that would sweep capitalism from the earth. Standing with the capitalists, the owners and the bosses, were brutal hirelings such as Shtupak, the Petrikov Chief of Police.

One of the group which came to the house was a woman whose name was Hannah Garelick. One day she came into the house when Father was home. She ran to the chicken coop, which was located under the brick stove in the house, and, with a yell, opened it and let out the few chickens. She screamed *"Freiheit! Freiheit far ale-men!"* ("Freedom! Freedom for all!"). My father grabbed her by the scruff of the neck and threw her bodily out of the house.

(The next time I saw this woman was in 1935 when she was playing a leading role in the American Communist Party as a Jewish lecturer on Marxism. The Party's Control Commission had heard that Hannah was making wild statements, and sent me to check up. When I heard her speak, she left the impression that she still didn't know that Karl Marx was not related to Groucho, Chico and Harpo!)

The Jews were told that their future was in the ranks of the revolutionary proletariat and they were wooed with special attention by the clever Bolsheviks. They recruited people who had little or nothing to lose from revolution. Special agents were trained to enlist Jews and train them in Marxism. Slogans were coined. The appeal was to an abused minority who were urged to join the movement against oppression.

The Jews were scapegoats for everything that went wrong in Imperial Russia. The police and, frequently, members of the Orthodox Clergy incited riots which were bloody and terrible beyond descrip-

*See *Selected Essays of Karl Marx*, especially on the Jewish Question

17

tion. To defend themselves, the *Boyevoiotriad* (Mutual Defense League) was created as protection against attacks from mobs, drunken peasants and bullying soldiers. The Bolsheviks were the top echelon, and in Petrikov several non-Jewish Russians were members.

There was particular need for protection in Petrikov. The town had four saloons and they all did a thriving business. Most of the villagers were content to buy a bottle of Vodka and take it home, but the peasants who came to town to sell their produce often stayed to get drunk. Their drinking bouts would generally lead to a free-for-all fight that ended in the street. Usually, the combatants would adjust their differences and go off together in quest of a Jewish victim.

Things grew worse with the Russo-Japanese War. A wave of nationalism swept Russia and "Kill the Jews and Save Russia!" became a popular slogan. The lurching police chief Shtupak became even more vicious, especially to the Malkin family. We were "Socialists!" as well as "Jewish Bastards!" and "Enemies of the State!" He became so vile towards my mother and sisters, that my brother Abraham, a husky young man, decided to take drastic action. He stopped Shtupak one night when he saw him alone, picked the petty tyrant up by the scruff of the neck and warned him that if he didn't let up on us, he would regret it. There were no witnesses to the threat, and even in Imperial Russia an entire Jewish family couldn't be thrown in jail at the whim of a small town police chief. He had no way of knowing what might happen to him some dark night, and being a bully and a coward, and knowing that the Malkins could take pretty good care of themselves, he left us in peace after that—until Harry and Abraham left for the United States.

This occurred one night after a troop of Cossacks arrived in town to round up recruits for the army. Harry had just been married and his father-in-law gave him money for forged passports and travel papers. He and Abraham slipped out of town and managed to escape across the border.

Two days later we were visited by Cossacks who literally tore the house apart, tapping walls and ripping the flooring. The search continued for two hours. I saw Mother and Father struck and Joseph and Nathan beaten and kicked. We younger children, cowering like frightened animals, sought refuge behind the stove. Fortunately, the searchers failed to probe beneath the sub-flooring of logs covered by a layer of loose, dry dirt. They didn't find the secret door and the hidden arms. The Cossacks finally left, but warned that next time things would not be so easy for us.

This was one of the many such raids, with blows and curses, that I witnessed in our home.

CHAPTER II

———————————————————————————

The Russo-Japanese War broke out on January 6, 1904, when Tokyo suddenly broke off diplomatic relations. Two days later, without a formal declaration of war, an attack was made on the Russian fleet at Port Arthur. The news fired patriotic feelings in Russia. Crowds gathered to cheer the soldiers as they marched in the streets, and the popular opinion was that the shooting would stop the moment the Japanese "monkeys" saw the caps of the Czar's brave troops.

The resulting disaster was a shock to the country. Then came fury —and "vengeance" against the Jews, who were somehow blamed for the defeat.

The shots fired in far-off Port Arthur reverberated with tragic consequences in the muddy streets of Petrikov.

The war came to us with a military inspector who headed a troop of Cossacks. He opened headquarters in town hall and immediately assumed the duties of an all-powerful military governor. His first act was to summon the heads of the town's civic, social and religious organizations, and demand an immediate census of the population. The head of each organization was required to submit a list of his membership, with ages, addresses and occupations. All males between 17 and 23 were ordered to report for physical examinations. The order was greeted with anguish in almost every home in the village. Men called away for military service, it was believed, seldom came back—and were never the same if they did. Soldiers fortunate enough not to be killed in battle, frequently died of minor wounds because of infection or neglect. Plague and pestilence claimed others. Orthodox Jews crowded the synagogues, praying that their sons might be spared.

Petrikov was placed under martial law, and most Jews feared to venture into the streets, where more than 200 Cossacks were turned loose. In succeeding months, as news of defeats filtered back, attacks became a common occurrence. The nights rang with the shouts and laughter of the soldiers staggering from the saloons and lurching along the streets. Discipline was a travesty; there never was any to speak of in the Russian army. The soldiers ravished their own towns and their own women as they did those of an invaded country. The people of Petrikov were helpless. Doors of homes were broken down and young girls were raped before the eyes of their parents. Many were dragged from their homes and disappeared, some of them forever, carried off by troops on the move.

Joseph and Nathan, along with the other Bolsheviks, opposed the war from the beginning. They were teen-aged boys, too young for the army, but they were not too young to agitate against the war. They surreptitiously circulated literature—labeling the effort an act of imperialist aggression, and of absolutely no concern to the working class.

Nathan reached military age but escaped service by joining a traveling theatrical group that provided entertainment for the troops. At the war's end, it was stranded in the south Ukraine and broke up. Nathan made his way home with returning troops. Some of the soldiers were pitiful sights, lurching with missing legs or frozen toes. Some were walking skeletons, devoured by dysentery. The villagers, who could do little to help, watched these glum and silent men pass through Petrikov. There was not enough food for the townspeople, almost everybody was hungry.

The only cheerful people were Communists and other radicals, rejoicing in misfortune. This was the situation that they had hoped for. Total confusion and the breakdown of imperialist institutions would give them the opportunity, they told themselves, to establish the new Marxian socialist order.

And so Russia had the revolution of 1905. Radical forces of every stripe and hue, of which Russia was liberally supplied, joined the fray. The fighting was far away, in St. Petersburg and the larger cities, but we in Petrikov heard about it.

Since local Bolshevik headquarters was in our one-room log house, home became a beehive of activity the moment Father was away. Young men would gather, but never more than ten at one time, and sit with Joseph and Nathan in one corner discussing the latest Party orders or literature while Mother and we younger children huddled

21

near the stove. While a lookout at the door kept a sharp watch, the conspirators would lift the floor boards, brush away the layer of dirt, and remove the trap door in the sub-flooring. They would take out the revolvers and rifles, oil and polish the mechanisms with loving tenderness, then put them back in the hiding place.

Mother, a very religious, honest woman, was deeply troubled, I later realized, by these revolutionary and secret activities that involved her home and her sons. While Bolsheviks discussed their affairs, she would sit cleaning goose feathers for bedding to earn a little money to augment Father's meager income. The guns which she saw tended with such care might be the instruments of terrible and shocking murder, and, if discovered by the police or Cossacks, would mean prison for all of us. Although basically a believer in non-violence, Mother could not help feeling that Nathan and Joseph had a right to take up arms against a government that blamed its mistakes on helpless Jews. Sometimes the group would sing Bolshevik songs that roused new dedication to the cause of revolution:

> On the barricades, on the barricades
> Wound for wound
> Hell for hell
> Bullet for bullet
> To struggle we shall go
>
> With plows and hoe
> With knife and steel
> We will make them feel
> The misery of the iron heel
>
> Arise ye peoples
> The clarion is calling
> For freedom's struggle is now
>
> Wound for wound
> Hell for hell
> Bullet for bullet
> To struggle we shall go

In this atmosphere we heard the news of the 1905 Revolution in St. Petersburg, Moscow and other large cities. And, gradually, of the disasters that ended it. The intelligentsia had drummed for an uprising for over ten years. Some of the Czar's advisors had fought back, but the Ministers of State had never conceded the reforms that would have robbed the radicals of issues. Instead, many argued that a quick victory over Japan would create a surge of popular feeling for the Czar and the opportunity to crush the radicals at home. If Russia had won the war in a series of victories as brilliant as those that favored the Japanese, this might have worked—in which case it is very probable that the world would not have heard of Lenin and Trotsky, and the Red Revolution of October, 1917, would never have taken place. Instead, the uprising of 1905 became a rehearsal for the successful revolt of 1917.

The Bolsheviks were only one of the elements involved, and they played a very minor role. Their leader, Lenin, took no part at all. Trotsky, who didn't join the Bolsheviks until 1917, after many years of independent action floating between them and the Mensheviks, was prominent among those who saw the revolt collapse around their ears. He was one of the lucky ones who was able to flee the country. Thousands of others, among the rank and file, were shot or shipped to Siberia.

The future of the Marxist movement in Russia had been decided by a split that occurred at the Second Party Congress in Brussels, Belgium in 1903. The issue was whether to have a large party, modeled after the German Social Democrats, or a small one. Lenin, leader of the forces that controlled the Congress, the *Bolsheviks* (majority), called for a small, disciplined party, maneuverable and reliable, that would be ready to seize power at any time. The *Mensheviks* (minority) wanted a larger representation, and it was they, assisted strongly by Trotsky, who were the leaders—and the losers— in 1905. The Bolsheviks, perceiving early that the odds were against any success, ducked for cover and continued their organizing work for the next twelve years.

Accordingly, word had come down for the Petrikov unit to lie low and wait for the storm to pass. No uprising was attempted and activities were curtailed. But that summer, as the excitement subsided and the police assumed a more somnolent attitude, special meetings were held in the woods. Romantic socialists (utopians, not affiliated

23

with the Marxian movement), anarchists and nihilists were invited. The Bolsheviks were willing to work with these people, to stir them up in order to create a climate of revolution; but none were acceptable as members of the tight little Bolshevik cell because they were not considered reliable. They were given directions to the locale of the meetings only a few hours before they were held. Lookouts would be posted along the route and around the assembly area. On one occasion a policeman, learning where a meeting was to be held, tried to sneak in. He was detected by one of the Bolshevik guards, who sent him on his way with a warning that if he ever tried again he would be shot.

The original Bolsheviks, today's Communists, had an origin that is typically Russian. It was deeply conspiratorial and distrust was a basic ingredient. Wherever the Communists operate today they have retained these characteristics. Then, as now, they were very successful in penetrating the most confidential circles of their enemy—at that time the Czarist Government. One agent, named Malinovsky, was revealed after the 1917 revolution to have been a trusted official of the Czar's secret police for years—while he was actually a member of the Bolshevik Central Committee.

As the 1905 rebellion was being stamped out, the Bolsheviks worked quietly. They infiltrated trade unions and created front organizations. Their underground printing presses spewed forth a stream of revolutionary literature.

Resorting to brigandage and robbery, they levied tribute against peddlers and small merchants. The money obtained went to feed the printing presses, to support organizing efforts and to hire legal talent to defend comrades who had been arrested.

In Petrikov I saw synagogues invaded while religious services were being held. The Bolsheviks, hooded and masked, like the Ku Klux Klansmen of the South after the American Civil War, would distribute literature and depart with a warning that if a word were whispered to the police, the informer would die.

These sudden appearances were most effective. The Bolsheviks desired to create an impression of strength and they strived for an effect of mysterious power. An enemy would find his store wrecked at night, or his business boycotted. The Bolsheviks were a largely silent but sometimes visible force in Petrikov as winter closed over the frozen marshes.

24

CHAPTER III

It was March, 1906 and the raw winds swept back and forth across the half frozen but thawing plain. Word had reached the Bolsheviks —through a member who worked at the Post Office in Petrikov— that the Postmaster was expected to return from the railroad station at Kapetkevitch with a valuable Easter payroll.

Orders came from above: "Capture the payroll!"

Plans were worked out at secret meetings in our house. Instructions had come by coded telegram from district headquarters in Minsk, with information on what day the Postmaster would pick up the payroll at the Kapetkevitch station. The Petrikov Bolsheviks were ordered to intercept him on his journey through the lonely marshes and take the money. It was needed badly to repair damaged Party equipment and to pay for new printing presses.

The Bolsheviks did not call their operation a hold-up or robbery— it was *Expropriatsia*, a word with special meaning for Communists. It was considered a legitimate means of financing revolution. (See Appendix I, p. 229.)

I was only six, but I sensed something urgent in the air when Party members began to assemble. It was a blustery, bitter afternoon and, as usual, they arrived separately to avoid suspicion. Father, as always, was away looking for work. We younger children had been trained never to tell him of the meetings that took place while he was gone. I don't know what Father would have done had he known. He strongly disapproved of the Bolsheviks, but I think he may have guessed, with secret sorrow, that Nathan and Joseph were involved in the movement.

I sat on the floor, playing with a brown and white puppy that someone had given me; a mongrel I named *Geroi* (hero). My eyes kept straying to the far end of the room, to the Bolsheviks huddled around my brothers, whispering in earnest conversation. Occasionally someone would laugh. Then the whispering continued as before.

My brother Joseph was the leader of the group and Nathan was second in command of the Petrikov Bolsheviks. Eventually I knew them all. They often played and laughed with me. One was Stepnyak Vasill, a blond, blue-eyed young Russian giant of six foot six. I called him "Ox" because he could lift me with one hand and, with a mighty shout, toss me high above his head. There were Chaibenzion Warenik, Nicholas Volski and the Semochki brothers, Alexander and Stepan, all neighbors and close friends. They were experts with arms—the rifles, revolvers and home-made bombs hidden in the hole beneath the sub-flooring of our house. I would sit and watch, fascinated, when they lifted the boards and took out the arms to clean them.

And there was Hillel. Decades later, I met him on the boardwalk at Coney Island. He, too, had left the Marxist movement, and we stood and talked on a pleasant summer day in 1943 about the old times in Petrikov. And of the raw spring afternoon in which the robbery of the Postmaster was plotted in my house. It was reliving a nightmare; something remembered from a bad dream. I recalled the way I had watched his eager young face as he spoke with the determined group. One side of his face was drawn and twisted from a terrible scar near his mouth—left by the butt of a Cossack's rifle when he was a young boy.

Vasill, Warenik, the Semochki brothers and Volski were chosen to stage the hold-up. Others were assigned to find out the exact route the Postmaster would take from Kapetkevitch and the number of armed guards who would accompany him. The robbery was to take place in a wild region of marsh and scrub bush, about eight miles east of Petrikov. Finally, the floor boards were carefully lifted and the necessary revolvers and rifles removed from their hiding place, and distributed.

When the last of the visitors had gone, Joseph, looking grave and mature despite his eighteen years, told us that something important had just been planned. Success depended on utmost secrecy. He looked from Mother to the children. If questioned by the police, we were to tell them that we knew nothing. And we were not to tell Father—which was not unusual. For a long time we had understood that nothing was ever to be said to him about the meetings in the house.

Mother was seriously bothered by this deceit; but she went with it. She was devoted to Father, but was also sympathetic to her sons. She shared Father's religious belief that somehow God would provide and that a terrible fate awaited men who turned their backs on Him. Men should have a code of honor—should live by the Ten Commandments and the Golden Rule. The mysteries of the Universe, the great unfathomable meaning of life and death, was something that wise men left to God.

For this philosophy, my brothers had a shrug and a condescending smile. What had religion done for us? This miserable log cabin? An empty larder? Starving, half naked children? Religion was the instrument of the Czar—a weapon to keep the working class down-trodden!

There was only one solution: "Marxism." Only "scientific socialism," as they called it, could relieve the human race of brutality, discrimination and injustice—of hunger, poverty and the drudgery that filled the days of ordinary working people everywhere.

So ran the controversy that divided our house.

Mother was caught in the middle. On the one hand was faith in her husband, and her own belief in the religion of her parents. But it was awful to see her children go to bed hungry—to see her husband return, tired and dejected, after a day of fruitless search for work.

The only outside kindness she knew came from the Bolsheviks. It was they who helped protect us from the dreaded *pogromshchiki* (the activists who carried out pogroms)—especially at Christmas and Easter times. The Bolsheviks were our friends, and perhaps Father was too dogmatic and harsh. Perhaps the Bolsheviks, if they did succeed in overthrowing the Czar and his Cossacks, would make life less difficult for all of us.

The discussion over what we were to tell Father ended happily, I remember, when he returned at dusk carrying a jar of crab apple jelly, a large loaf of bread and a big sack of potatoes. He had found a job doing some carpentry work for a peasant, and the food was an advance payment. We were so overjoyed that we forgot about the Bolshevik meeting. We had a banquet of boiled potatoes, herring, bread and crab apple jelly. Busy eating and talking, Father never thought to ask if there had been visitors during the day.

He told of his good fortune in finding a job that would require the making of doors and windows for a Muzhik (a peasant). The job would take a long time, and he would earn between fifty to seventy rubles. Fifty rubles were then worth $25.00 in American money and we could live well on that for at least three weeks. Growing lavish in his talk, while waving a half slice of bread in his hand, Father turned to me with a happy smile. "When I get paid we will buy you a pair of warm leather boots." I had never had boots, and the thought of owning a pair thrilled me to my naked toes. Boots cost one and a half rubles. (In Communist Russia today, many items of food, such as a loaf of bread like the one Father brought home that night, are far more expensive. The same type of boots would cost many times as much.)

After the meal, my brothers grew restless. Presently, they went out to be seen in the town. But somewhere in the night, on a country road, other young Bolsheviks moved stealthily toward their dark assignment.

The next day was quiet and life went on as usual in Petrikov. But 24 hours later rumors of an armed robbery circulated through the town. The Postmaster, his assistant and two police guards were said to have been killed. Nervously, people gathered in small groups. Then came a report that a wagon was approaching the village with the bodies of the victims. Fear dominated the Jews. In Czarist Russia it was nearly certain that they would become scapegoats.

I went with two neighbor boys to see the wagon. We found people queuing up on the square in front of the firehouse. We fell in line, and the gossip I heard, as the line inched forward, disturbed me greatly. A peasant had witnessed the robbery and had recognized three of the bandits! They were the Semochki Brothers and Volski, and the police were already looking for them. I shuddered and nearly froze with fright for my brothers. The saliva went dry in my mouth. Then I reached the improvised morgue where the bodies were on a wooden slab. Dried blood streaked their faces and the smell of death was terrible. I turned quickly and got out of there.

At home, police were swarming around our house. Inside, they had ripped up the floor boards. My anxiety eased a bit when I remembered that Joseph and Nathan, the night before, had removed the weapons to a safer place. I was taken aside and questioned. They were kind to me: they laughed and acted very friendly. But I had been carefully schooled: I knew nothing! I had heard nothing and I had seen nothing.

Joseph and Nathan were taken into custody, however, and we

stood and watched them being led away. I never expected to see them again. Mother, who had borne up magnificently—shouting at the police, ridiculing their suspicions—suddenly ran into the house. She sank in a corner, behind the stove, and sat rocking herself in helpless misery.

Two weeks later, Joseph and Nathan were released for lack of evidence, but the hunt for the Semochkis and Volski went on. Eventually, they were caught. After a speedy military court trial they were hanged.

This incident was personally significant in another way because, a short time later, I began my education in the meaning of Marxism and the class struggle. Joseph was my dedicated and very patient teacher. I was a rather lonely child. Because I belonged to an outlawed family, few parents were willing to allow their children to play with me. Often I would sit alone and wonder about things. Why were we so unfortunate and so poor? Was it because we were Jews? "No," Joseph said, "it is because we are workers." As Jews, he explained, we were the convenient scapegoats of the ruling capitalist class. But the basic problem was much deeper. The real reason for our lack of food, clothing and a decent house, he explained, was because the capitalists took from all workers what was rightfully theirs. Joseph named the few well-dressed, well-fed children in the village. Why did they have plenty while I had nothing? It was because I was the son of a worker and they were the sons and daughters of an owner. "There are two classes of society in the world. One class owns everything and does nothing. The other class does all the work but owns nothing." He called the owning class "capitalists," or "bourgeois." The others, the vast majority, were workers, or the "proletariat." The mission of the working class, he said, was to take, through violence, what rightfully belonged to them.

This was heady stuff. I was unable to read or write and I had never been to school. But, when explained in such simple terms, I began to grasp the meaning of the class struggle. Joseph would illustrate his lectures in ways that I could understand. Each spring Petrikov became alert to the menace of mad dogs in the streets. These slobbering animals, infected with rabies, would run wild, and were hunted down and shot because anyone bitten by them died a terrible death.

"The capitalists are like mad dogs," Joseph said. "They are mad n power. They must be hunted down and shot."* This was the reason for the murder of the Postmaster and his assistant, he explained. They were victims of the class war that must go on with increasing violence until the workers rule the world under one government, "the dictatorship of the Proletariat."

I was told that the money taken in the Post Office robbery, some 23,000 rubles, had been sent to the Bolshevik headquarters in Minsk. Although it vanished into the Party underground, there was soon evidence that some of it had been returned to Petrikov—literally "in our own back yard."

As summer came, and the robbery receded in my young mind, a small shack began to take shape behind our house. It was the sort of shack that Boy Scouts in the United States might build for their club pow-wows. It had a barren dirt floor—but under the dirt were some boards, and under the boards was a hole in which my brothers had concealed a small hand press. It was used for printing handbills and propaganda leaflets. The press was sometimes operated at night, or during the day while Father was at work in the country.

The leaflets, in screaming words, called attention to government blunders, abuses, and instances of police brutality and undercover work. Policemen were warned, often by name, and told what to expect if their actions were continued. I remember one such case in particular. It concerned two police informers—one was a man named Michaelko—who were given the Czar's medal for excellency in ferreting out the leaders of the 1905 revolution. They were the subject of one of the leaflets printed in our back yard and were given 48 hours to flee the province of Minsk. When they ignored the warning, both were found shot to death in their homes three days later. This sort of action breathed fear into government agents and brought a kind of respect to the Bolshevik movement.

Father found a succession of jobs during the summer and was able to bring home a little money. Then one night, as September drew near, he announced that he had engaged the services of a tutor for me. I was going to school at last! The tutor, a regularly employed Jewish school teacher, had agreed to give me lessons in his home at night. A hunchbacked scholar, he lived in a two-story house near the Orthodox Jewish cemetery, three miles from our home. I had to

*See Appendix I, p. 230.

climb the stairs to the tutor's living quarters—he maintained his school in the rooms below. I would leave for home carrying a lantern with a candle in it. About midnight the candle would burn out and I had to grope my way, in the dim light, past the mud holes and swill ponds that filled the streets.

My tutor gave me a start in reading and writing, and taught me the rudiments of mathematics. From there I carried on under Joseph, who taught me from Marxist literature.

One of the first sentences I learned to read was the last paragraph of the *Communist Manifesto:* "Workers of the world unite; you have nothing to lose but your chains and a world to gain."

But one lesson I never learned from Marxist and Leninist teaching —it had not been written in any of the literature Joseph showed me —is that zealots in power with messianic illusions are the world's worst tyrants. There is nothing they will not do to put across their plans for a "better world." They will pour medicine down the throats of their flock, though they strangle and perish while being "helped."

CHAPTER IV

In 1909 Russia was still in turmoil. The 1905 revolution had been crushed and order restored, after a fashion, but anti-Semitism was worse than ever. Much of it was incited by the Black Hundred, with the secret backing of Czar Nicholas II himself. Many members of the organization were sincere monarchists, but there were others, ordinary hoodlums and vicious members of the Orthodox clergy, who incited pogroms and brutal atrocities against "enemies of the Emperor." Although most victims were Jews, the terror was also frequently directed against Germans, Poles and Armenians.

Many intellectuals, including a great number of Jews, refused to be pacified by the concessions in the Manifesto of October 30, 1905, which gave a little more freedom to the peasantry and the population. Infuriated, the Black Hundred and police turned with new vigor against "radicals." The result was a series of atrocities against Jews that were the most ghastly in the history of pogroms. Most of the victims were innocent, since the actual Jewish revolutionaries had managed to escape.

Authorities have estimated that after 1905, political prisoners of all classes, including Jews, rose from 85,000 to 200,000 annually.

Better news came from the United States. Our infrequent letters from Harry and Abraham in New York were cheerful and hopeful, even though they wrote of their loneliness and longing to see us. They had steady work and managed to send a little money to us, which considerable enriched the drabness of our normal bare existence level.

Father found work ever more difficult to obtain. Many who had given him jobs in the past, now refused to do so because they were afraid. It was general knowledge that we were under continous police surveillance. We were a "dangerous family," and people wished to live with as little trouble to themselves as possible. It was wise to steer clear of us, and "respectable" Jews, as well as Russians, did so.

Joseph managed to earn a little from occasional jobs of tutoring. Nathan returned to his theatrical career, with a traveling troupe of actors, but the company was soon stranded in a distant village, and he was forced to make his way back home.

Father began to talk seriously about going to America. He had mentioned this for years, but it had been idle talk. Now he meant it and wrote to Harry and Abe, asking for a steamship ticket. A short time later, in March, a letter came to one of our relatives—we never received mail directly—enclosing a ticket and a little money.

Father was excited. Age seemed to lift from his drooping shoulders. He immediately got busy and sold our house, along with a few pieces of silver and some odds and ends that he and Mother had received at their wedding. He left most of the money with us and departed for America on forged travel papers and a passport supplied by Joseph's Bolshevik organization.

We received our first word from Father a few weeks later: he had reached Hamburg! In another month, we had a letter from New York. He was living with Harry and Abe in Brooklyn, and had gone to work as a carpenter. "Everything is so unbelievably wonderful in America," he wrote. But he missed his family, and longed for us every day.

Father had left us quartered temporarily in one room of a Russian peasant's log house at the edge of the village. His name was Yatsko, a Bolshevik of sorts and a friend of Joseph. The log house had three large rooms. Yatsko, his wife and their two sons, one 14 and the other 17, shared the front room. Mother, my sisters Elsie and Bertha, my younger brother Solomon and I—plus Joseph and Nathan when they were home—occupied the rear room. It looked out on a vegetable garden and the barn. The third room was the kitchen, which we all shared.

Yatsko's wife was a large, cheerful, blonde woman—typically Russian and always busy. He was also blond, a big man, six feet two, with a broad pleasant face. I remember him vividly. He had the strength of an ox. He laughed most of the time—and was nearly always drunk. I can't recall a single day when he was not intoxicated, but he was a happy drunk, who would sleep it off peacefully in the barn with the cows. During a police raid and routine search of the house, they went into the barn and found Yatsko hiding under a big bull. When they dragged him out he fainted from fright!

About two months after Father left—it was late in June—we had a routine visit from the police. It would have been unimportant except that Joseph had carelessly left his shirt hanging behind the door, and in the pocket of the shirt was a letter. It was from Minia Varenick, a member of the Petrikov Bolshevik unit who had been sent by the Party to Minsk for special training. She wrote about a recent bombing there—which she and other Bolsheviks had planned!

Both Joseph and Nathan were arrested, and after five days in the Petrikov jail they were taken aboard one of the riverboats, under heavy police guard, and conveyed down river to Mozir. Here they were lodged in a grim, grey military prison. Fortunately, Nathan was released a few days later, for lack of evidence, and came home.

Mother was almost insane with worry about Joseph. Most of her time that summer was consumed in journeying back and forth between our home and the prison to see him. She wrote regularly to Father, keeping him advised, and visited all of our friends to enlist their aid in securing legal counsel for Joseph. Eventually three lawyers were supplied by the Bolsheviks. They came all the way from Kiev, capital of the Ukraine.

Then the dreadful moment of truth. Joseph was tried, found guilty, and sentenced to ten years in Siberia!

Adding to our woes, I came down in late summer with croup, and soon passed it on to my sisters and Solomon. In our weakened condition, for we were half starved, the disease became a most serious malady. Finally, my sisters and I recovered, but Solomon seemed to get no better.

As soon as Father heard the news of Joseph's arrest he made preparations to return to Russia. He arrived home in November, the first day of Succoth, the week-long Jewish holiday. On the seventh day, a Friday, he set out for Mozir to visit Joseph, and took me with him. Among the gifts he had brought back with him were a pair of buttoned American shoes for me—the first time in my life I had owned a pair. I wore them on this trip. We boarded the riverboat *Litvinka* at night, and arrived the next morning.

Visitors were only permitted in the prison between the hours of 11:00 A.M. and 1:00 P.M., and it was early when we arrived outside the great, foreboding stone walls. We waited on a hard wooden bench until the doors were finally opened. Inside the courtyard we mingled among a hundred solemn-faced prisoners, looking in vain

34

for Joseph. Finally, Father stopped at a little group and aske\ knew him. One of the men smiled; he knew Joseph and wen\ him. When he appeared, Joseph embraced us gravely. His\ face looked tense and drawn. His long blond hair had not bee\ Whenever he spoke he looked nervously toward the guard slou\ against the prison wall.

Father assured Joseph that every effort would be made to secure his release—or, at the very least, get the sentence reduced.

He was my favorite brother; I almost worshipped him. He told me to keep up my school work, and continue my study of Marxism. "You will find the answers in those books," he said. "Read them; remember what they say. There is no hope for Jews—no hope for working men anywhere—until we have a world-wide Socialist Republic. One government, one people—regardless of race, creed or color! No Czar! No capitalists! But you must work for it, Mishka. You must work for freedom in the world!"

He believed this—he believed it with all his soul! And he made me believe it.

"Whatever happens to me," he said, "you must continue the struggle. You must never give up."

It was a melancholy journey back home.

Father devoted full time to the search for a good attorney, and the Bolsheviks came to his aid. They put up some money, and this, added to what my father had gathered, enabled him to secure the services of a well known lawyer in Kiev. This skillful man eventually got a new hearing for Joseph. After an appeal to the highest state court at Minsk and to the State Governor, the sentence was reduced to three years' solitary confinement. Given credit for the time already spent in jail, and with time off for good behavior, Joseph had to spend only a little more than a year in Siberia.

Even during the most brutal Czarist regime, the worst enemies of the State could appeal and get some form of justice. Today, under Soviet law, there is little chance for any meaningful appeal.

During late November, my baby brother, Solomon, died, mainly of malnutrition. He was only five; a thin, sad-faced little boy. During his few dark years on earth he had known nothing but disaster and misery.

With the new year, 1910, times finally improved. Father had brought saws, planes and several other marvelous new carpenter's tools from America. He had also acquired skills that were unknown in Russia, and was the best craftsman in town. He was able to find work, and we began eating a little better.

Then more good fortune. The government announced it was going to build a school and a hospital in Petrikov and Father persuaded a contractor, with whom he was friendly, to bid on both jobs. When the man got the contracts, Father was assigned to make all the doors and windows for both buildings. Steady employment at last, and Father began looking around for a new home. With his first earnings, he bought a house on the edge of town—a one-story, thatch-roofed log structure like our previous homes, except that the interior was panelled with boards. And to the delight of Mother, there was a plot of ground in the rear for a vegetable garden. It was a great day when we moved out of the crowded discomfort of the one room we shared in the peasant's house.

We were living happily in the new home when Joseph, looking much more mature, came back from Siberia. Grimly, he plunged once more into the revolutionary underground activities of the Bolsheviks.

Joseph had been home about three months, in the fall of 1911, when one night the house was surrounded by police. He and Nathan were arrested, taken directly to Mozir and turned over to the nearby military reception center for induction into the army. Here they were separated; Nathan was assigned to an artillery unit at the fort in Babroisk and Joseph to the cavalry in Gomel.

When we heard that they were at the Mozir reception center, plans were discussed for getting the two boys out of Russia immediately. Until they joined their assigned units, draftees did not take the oath of allegiance. If they deserted after that they could be put before a firing squad and shot. The Bolshevik underground offered to help, and for the second time Father, a religious man with no sympathy at all for their atheism, found himself working with these revolutionaries to save his sons. To him, the Czar's army was a fate almost as bad as death itself.

Harry and Abe, who had been alerted as soon as Joseph and Nathan were arrested, sent word from New York that two steamship tickets were being held by Harry's father-in-law at Mozir. Meanwhile, the Bolsheviks secured forged travel papers, passports and other credentials needed to get Joseph and Nathan across the border.

Joseph deserted the army two days before he was to take the oath of allegiance and made his way to Mozir, where he went into hiding. With Nathan, things were not so simple. He was in a solitary cell at the prison post hospital, under guard and awaiting court-martial for striking a superior officer. The officer had called him a "Jew bastard," and Nathan had leaped at him.

Two grim soldiers in the uniform of military police called one night at the hospital for Private Nathan Malkin and marched him away. Through the dark streets of the military post they silently walked to the edge of the compound and entered a dense wood. Here the guards halted, turned to Nathan and smiled. They were members of the Bolshevik underground!

Nathan quickly changed to civilian clothing. He was given travel papers and escorted to the railroad station, where he caught a train for Mozir. Two days later, he and Joseph left for America.

In a month, we received word that they had arrived in Hamburg and boarded a steamer for New York. A short time later letters from the United States brought the good news that they were with Harry and Abe.

After the escape of Joseph and Nathan, Father was arrested as an accomplice. He was freed, after being ordered to pay a fine of 100,-000 rubles,* so that he might continue at his job. As an outlaw, he was not supposed to work, but the government permitted him to go on making doors and windows for the school and hospital—and collected half of everything he earned, as an installment on his fine. This meant that we were back to near starvation.

Father began talking about America again, but remembering the disasters that had befallen us the last time we had been alone, he was reluctant to go. Finally he made the decision, and in January, 1913 he sold our home. Mother, my two sisters and I moved in with a cousin who lived in a large one-room house at the edge of town.

Before he left, Father took me to visit his close friend, Rabbi Moses Myer. I was to continue my religious education under the Rabbi, who also promised to look after me.

No wonder Father respected him so much and left me in his charge. I found the rabbi a warm human being who would explain

*The fine covered all four sons who escaped serving in the army of the Czar—25,000 rubles for each one.

37

things to me so quietly, and with such patient understanding, that I had complete trust and faith in him. He knew five languages—Russian, Yiddish, Hebrew, Polish and Aramaic. He prepared me for my Bar Mitzvah (Confirmation) and officiated at the ceremony on my 13th birthday. After the First World War, our Petrikov synagogue brought him to the United States where he soon became a frequent visitor to our home.

Today Rabbi Myer is buried within five feet of Father in the United Hebrew Cemetery on Staten Island.

When he reached New York the second time, Father resumed his trade as a carpenter and sent us a little money each month. With this, we paid a nominal rent to our cousin and there was a little left over for my schooling and the bare necessities of our meager existence. Most of Father's savings, and those of my brothers, was put aside for our passage to America.

Almost the entire town resented us. My four brothers had escaped from the army and were in America, making good money. As "enemies of Russia" we were openly insulted on the streets. Since all the men of the Malkin family were in America, Mother and my sisters, now teenage girls of 14 and 16, became constant targets for vile names. Elsie worked in a clothing store that belonged to a friend of our family. Mother found part-time employment selling fruit in the public market, while Bertha stayed home and attended to the household duties.

I also received my share of abuse, much of it from Ivan Schtub, a policeman and friend of the bullying Chief of Police. He was mentally ill, but since nobody in Petrikov understood anything about psychology, he was hated by Jews and laughed at by his fellow Russians. Schtub had marched off to the Russo-Japanese War, full of starch and vinegar, but the realities of battle had taken it out of him. He returned, wearing a large medal which, according to rumor, he had not deserved, and settled into the lazy job of a policeman. Schtub's greatest interest seemed to be in punishing helpless, innocent scapegoats for the defeat that he and Russia had suffered at the hands of the Japanese. As a boy of 13, with no one to protect me, I was an ideal victim.

Schtub would abuse me and try to provoke me into some act of physical retaliation, such as throwing rocks at him. But I knew that if I did this, he would, with impunity, shoot me down on the spot. Any time I caught sight of him, I immediately took to my heels. This terrible man was said to be a member of the Black Hundred, and he had spread the rumor that this dreaded organization, which had recently incited attacks on Jews in Odessa and Gomel, was out to murder the entire Malkin family.

During the late summer a group of ruffians, boys in their late teens, seized me as I was walking near the river. They dragged me, screaming and kicking, to the bank and filled my pockets with sand and rocks. Then they pulled me into the river and pushed me toward the swift current where the water was over my head. Fortunately, my screams attracted the attention of a group of people downstream and they came running to my rescue. The first person to reach me, strangely enough, was my sister, Bertha, who happened to be visiting some friends in the area. My tormentors took to their heels as she and three men plunged into the river, where I had already been swept off my feet by the swiftly-flowing water. Weighted down with rocks and sand, I was thrashing about helplessly when she got to me and was herself knocked down. She was swimming and holding me up when we were reached by the three male rescuers and pulled to safety.

This event brought a quick decision from my family in America. They somehow gathered enough money and we received a message that steamship tickets were on the way. We were to get ready to go to the United States! Within a few days came the word that we would be contacted by the Bolshevik underground.

CHAPTER V

When we received the news that steamship tickets were coming, our joy was without bounds. Soon we were alerted by the Bolsheviks that forged papers were being prepared and that we should be ready for immediate departure.

Then came bad news from an unexpected quarter. To get into the United States we would need health certificates and Dr. Shapiro, a close family friend, agreed to examine us. Mother and my two sisters were in good health, but I was found to be suffering from an acute eye infection. The treatment would take months and we settled down to the unavoidable delay, while I visited the doctor daily.

When Joseph and Nathan left, they had asked the Bolsheviks to look out for the Malkins left behind. They were particularly requested to look after my schooling, especially my Marxist education. I became their ward, and we received frequent calls from members of the Petrikov section.

Our impatience became almost unbearable after the Bolsheviks delivered the forged passports, birth certificates and travel papers which would get us to Hamburg and aboard a Hamburg-American liner. But my medical treatment had to be continued until the first of the year. Then, in late January, 1914, we were finally ready to go.

On the eve of our departure, we received a secret warning that the Black Hundred would raid our house in two days. We were to be the victims of a massacre that would eradicate our family and serve as a warning to all radicals in Petrikov! With this dreadful news ringing in our ears, we departed in the night and drove through the raw February cold to the small railway depot in Kapetkevitch, 15 miles to the northeast. We reached the station just before the train pulled out, and barely had time to throw in our belongings and climb aboard.

The only person who demanded our identification papers was an obvious agent of the police. He wore civilian clothes, while all railway employees, and anyone else engaged in public service in Russia, wore uniforms.

This man examined our papers in a cursory manner and was glad to let us go so that he could return to the warmth of the station.

Aboard the train we were met by a Bolshevik agent, bundled to his ears in a greatcoat. He accompanied us to Warsaw, where he left us with instructions to go to the station and wait for a man using the code name "Spark." This was the name of the newspaper Lenin had edited.

We went to the waiting room and huddled in a corner while hundreds of travelers moved about, squatted on the floor or slept on benches. In about two hours, a man came over and asked us if we had seen "Spark." Mother said that we were looking for him, and his eyes twinkled. He began laughing and talking, as he threw his arms around each of us with lavish hugs and kisses. He could have been a close and dear relative, which was obviously the impression he meant to convey to anyone who might be watching.

Our new guide was young—he looked about 25—clean-shaven and dressed in the uniform of a student. We followed him, carrying our scant belongings, to another train. As we walked, he loudly chatted nonsense while quietly passing on instructions: we were to assume completely new identities. He slipped us papers with the family name Rappaport on them. We were to memorize our new names, and practiced calling each other by them as the train slowly lurched toward the Austrian border.

We arrived at Illova, a border town, on a Saturday morning. At the station we were met by another "student" who had already engaged a droshky, a covered horse-drawn vehicle. Our luggage was tossed in and we were driven to a small old building. Before he left, our guide warned us not to venture out until someone came for us.

The house was occupied by an aged Orthodox Jewish couple who spent most of the day at the synagogue. While we ate bread and salami, which we had brought from home, our guide reappeared with a bag of oranges. They were the first such fruit I had ever seen and I began trying to eat an orange like an apple. Our Bolshevik friend laughed and showed me how to remove the rind. He then told us that arrangements had been made for an easy trip across the border Sunday morning. We were to remain where we were until he came back.

The "student" returned at 1:30 A.M., and said the time had come for our escape from Russia. We quickly gathered our belongings and followed him into the cold darkness. A short distance down the street we came to a wagon loaded with hay, and were told to climb aboard. Hidden under the hay, we arrived at a farmhouse on the Russian side of the border. We silently crawled from the wagon and concealed ourselves in a haystack in the barnyard. We were so close to the border that we could hear the soldiers calling to each other on patrol. 25 yards from us, a voice would sing out every ten minutes: "Post Number 3. All is well."

We dared not utter a sound. As I lay close to Mother, I could hear the beating of her heart and the chattering of her teeth. About 4:00 A.M., just before the changing of the guard, a peasant came to the haystack and whispered instructions to come out. But we did not move until he finally gave the password, "Spark."

As we crawled out and took hay out of our hair and off our clothes, he warned us to keep quiet. Then, each of us carrying a bundle or bag, we followed him cautiously a hundred yards to the border. A soldier, the Sergeant-of-the-Guard in this area, had been previously contacted by the Bolsheviks. When we reached him, he and the peasant held a brief, whispered conversation. The peasant left after assuring us that the sergeant would see that we got safely across the border. Our new guide growled for us to remain quiet and to follow him. He led us, single file, across a board over a narrow ditch. On the other side we were in Austria—free of Czarist Russia!

Bertha was the last to cross over. Mother stood waiting and greeted her with a triumphant cry. Safely across the ditch, we burst into sudden song, but were quickly hushed by the startled sergeant. He warned us to "pipe down," that we would arouse the entire border patrol and bring about his arrest by our "idiotic demonstration."

We went a few yards further into Austria, and discovered that we were not the only ones who had crossed the border that night. As our guide left us, we were joined by a group who had also just escaped and were fully as excited as we. As the sergeant scurried back through the darkness, we burst spontaneously into a song popular in Russia, but sung only behind the backs of the police: "Russia! Russia! How sorry I am for you! Freedom for the dead and jail for the Jews! And the Czar rides on a horse like a crow on a pig." The words of this song echoed in the darkness, and soon we were joined by others dressed like us and carrying bundles and awkward, bulging bags.

We were at a place called Malava. It was in Austria, and nothing ahead of us could be as bad as what we had left behind.

An Austrian guard met us and conducted the joyful group to the Malava immigration station. Here was gathered a nondescript army of refugees—men, women and children. More than 100 had come over the border during the night. A few others had been here for a day or more. Most were waiting for transportation, but some tensely awaited relatives or friends who were scheduled to join them after fleeing Russia.

Eventual destinations were the four points of the compass, but most of us were going to America. From their talk and the songs they sang, nearly all were Bolsheviks or Social Democrats—dedicated left-wing radicals, driven to desperation by conditions in Russia, in search of more fertile fields in which to cultivate the seed of Marxism.

In Hamburg we went to the waterfront immigration depot operated by the Hamburg–American Line, which did a thriving business carrying emigrants from Central European countries. The building was a great barracks-like structure with long rows of double-decker bunks. Men and women were provided with separate quarters, the children left with their mothers. There were between 400 and 500 emigrants, most of them Russian Jews.

On a foggy Friday in February, 1914, we boarded the S.S. *President Lincoln,* a combination freight-passenger ship which sailed non-stop between Hamburg and New York. Our cramped quarters were in the steerage compartment—double-decker bunks that were smaller and less comfortable than those in the emigrant center. I still remember the foul smell, the sound of babies crying and the terrible coughing of old people. As we came on board, each of us was handed an aluminum cup, a plate, a fork and spoon, and were warned to hold on to them until we reached New York.

Despite our cramped quarters and the medley of smells and sounds, we felt that we were living in the lap of luxury in comparison to our life in Russia. I was a spindly-legged, undernourished boy of 13, and found the voyage one continous round of exciting adventure. The steerage section had a community kitchen, and, since most of the passengers were Jewish, the food was kosher. But the meals were still strange to us—different foods, prepared in unfamiliar ways, by the ship's mess crew. We had rice cooked with raisins, beef stew, coffee and occasionally an apple for dessert. We had eaten both rice and raisins but never the two cooked together. While many others complained, I took to the food like a cat to milk. The beef stew was delicious. I found everything delightful.

Able to speak Yiddish, Russian and Hebrew fluently, I quickly made friends throughout the ship. But my wandering aroused angry complaints from many passengers—and the fears of my family. This resulted from my friendship with three young Americans whom I met on deck, where steerage passengers were permitted for exercise and air. The complaining passengers, with their suspicious Russian backgrounds, immediately pegged these strangers—from their "foreign" dress and manners—as American Secret Police. To them, the three young men were obviously agents of the American government, sent to spy out the radicals who would be turned back at New York! Did not the Marxist literature teach that all capitalist countries employed such spies? In Russia, we never trusted a stranger—a rule that should apply here too.

They spoke Russian, though they were born in America, and delighted me with stories about the country I intended to call my home. They fed me chocolates, cakes and fruits from the ship's canteen. These gifts only confirmed the suspicions of my critics: police everywhere used candy to get information from children. But I continued to associate with the Americans, eating food that I had never tasted before. I picked up such phrases as, "How are you?" "Good morning," "Good night" and "Thank you."

The weather that February was raw and windy—despite a beautiful blue sky. The sea was very rough, and the *President Lincoln* pitched like a floating match box. Many passengers, land-lubbers and in mortal fear for their lives, began to wish they had never left shore. During a run of unusually rough weather, the elderly Orthodox Jews would give us no peace until we had assembled in the dining room for prayers.

The last day at sea the weather became calm. Mother and my sisters ventured on deck for the first time and met my American friends. But Mother's fears remained. She was sure I had fallen into the hands of slick police agents and that we would be arrested and sent back to Russia the moment immigration officials came on board.

As we neared New York, a tense atmosphere settled over the passengers. Would loved ones be on hand to meet the ship? What of the others who were still in Russia? What was ahead in a strange world?

In the late evening we passed a ship, a great floating palace of light and wealth, outward bound for Europe. A short time later, about 9:00 P.M., I caught sight of a light on the starboard side. It glimmered, far off, vanished and came on again. It slowly became more distinct, and then there were others, hundreds of them—glimmering lights, a necklace of sparkling jewels that stretched along the northern horizon. I remained on deck all night, crowded with others at the rail, for a first glimpse of New York.

The ship reduced speed and plowed slowly forward through the darkness. Then, with the first thin dawning of day, thudding sounds came over the water. We were in the Narrows, the lights of Coney Island and Sea Gate on the right and the shores of Staten Island and New Jersey twinkling to the left.

The ship stopped at quarantine, and a doctor came on board with immigration and customs officials.

At about 6:30 A.M., in the murky dawn, we began moving again, as the ship's engines hummed and vibrated under our feet. Voices could be heard shouting orders. We were told to go to the dining room on the starboard side and line up as our names were called.

At the head of the line sat two men at a desk, our papers in front of them. When they called a name, the immigrant designated would move forward and a colored card was attached to his chest. He was to wear this card until he left the ship. There were cards of different colors, and they designated, at a glance, the status under which the bearer was to be admitted to the United States. Some were to go free the moment we docked; some were to remain on board; others were to go to Ellis Island.

Mother, my sisters and I went to Ellis Island.

As the day began, filled with unspoken fears and anxieties, we were marched aboard a ferry and taken across the bay. We headed toward the greenish Statue of Liberty, then turned toward the Jersey Shore. We approached an island of great brown stone buildings with castle-like turret roofs. Finally, the ferry slowed and slid smoothly to a stop.

CHAPTER VI

—————————————————————————————

At Ellis Island men and women were conducted to separate quarters and given medical examinations. When the doctors finished with me, I put on my clothes and found myself in an immense and lonely hall. I remained there, waiting for my family, until after 2:00 P.M. without breakfast or lunch. Since I had eaten nothing since the previous evening, hunger finally drove me to look for Mother and my sisters.

I found them in a crowded hallway, waiting anxiously for me. I began to cry, and Mother tried to tell a guard that I was hungry. He looked at our papers and conducted us to another large room. Behind a low fence, a crowd waited—eagerly peering at the incoming passengers. Among them was Father! Beside him, waving at us, stood a man I couldn't recognize. Finally I realized that it was my brother Abraham.

The guard led us through a gate, and we fell into one another's arms. Immediately, all loneliness vanished and the hunger pangs were no longer noticeable. Joyful crying quickly changed to laughing and talking. It was about four o'clock on a chilly February afternoon when we boarded a ferry for the Battery. We had been accepted! We were free! We were in America!

On the ferry, Abraham opened a brown paper bag and handed me a banana. I had never seen one before and, as I bit into the bitter, yellow peel, Abraham and Father doubled up with laughter. I looked at them out of a wry face. To be so hungry and to be laughed at made me angry. Tears had come to my eyes when Abraham showed me how to peel the fruit. I made the journey across the harbor eating bananas one after the other.

Waiting with a crowd at the Battery was Nathan, and there was another round of kisses and hugs.

Everything on shore seemed wonderful. We went to the old South

Ferry elevated station and boarded a Second Avenue "El" to Delancey Street. There we changed to a trolley that took us across the Williamsburg Bridge to Brooklyn. During the entire journey I peered at the tops of the lofty buildings. The trolley was amazing and the elevated seemed a miracle. I had no time for words; every turn presented a new and wonderful sight. The towers of the financial district, and the roofs, so many of them, as far as the eye could see, left me shaking my head.

We reached the red brick tenement where Abraham lived at 17 Scholes Street, between Union Avenue and Lorimer Street, next to a firehouse. Abraham lived in the rear of the ground floor, behind his carpentry shop. In this three-room apartment, my parents, sisters and I made our home for the next two months with Abraham, his wife, Hanna, and their six-months-old boy, Carl. Abraham had met my sister-in-law in America, and it was the first time I saw her. Later in the day, Joseph, who had been unable to find us at the Battery, came to the house. Again, we fell into one another's arms with tears, and then there was laughter and no end of talking.

Joseph lived on the Lower East Side of Manhattan, where he shared a single room with a young book salesman and union organizer—David Dubinsky. Years later, as president of the International Ladies Garment Workers Union, he became one of the most powerful men in the United States. Dubinsky came from a town in Russia not far from our own, and he and Joseph had become fast friends.

Nathan made his home with Harry at 1599 East New York Avenue in Brooklyn. Harry was out of the city when we arrived and we didn't see him for several months.

On the first night in America our reunited family sat and talked, weary as we were, until after midnight. Finally, with the grown-ups still talking, I began to nod and fell asleep.

Next morning I ventured into the street and at once met the taunts of neighborhood boys. They made fun of my strange-looking clothes and uncut hair. Unable to speak English, I stood and gaped. Later I came to understand what they said, and the refrain of their taunt is still vivid: "Greenhorn, popcorn, five cents apiece; July, July, go to hell and die!" But when they tried to gang up on me a few days later, I knocked two of them down and the rest took to their heels. After that, they gathered on the corner to goad me—but always from a safe distance. My ready

47

fists had earned their respect and it was not long until I was welcomed, and we became friends.

Abraham took me to Public School Number One, on South Fourth Street, where I registered and was enrolled. It was the first time in my life that I had dared enter a school with other children.

Saturdays and Sundays were wonderful. Joseph came for me and we would journey about the city. After a trolley ride across the Williamsburg Bridge, we would transfer to the subway. A favorite walk was through the financial district, along Wall Street and lower Broadway, down to the Battery, where we would look at the ships. It was fine along Fifth Avenue, too, above 59th Street, with Central Park on one side and white stone mansions on the other.

Here were the homes of the rich—the Frick mansion and other near-palaces. Joseph would point them out, and each was an object lesson in Marxism. These were the cold, stone symbols of capitalism! He would contrast the splendor of the Frick house with the squalor of the tenements. When I pointed out that even the tenements were palaces compared with what we had known in Russia, and that some of those living in the mansions had once been poor—some even immigrants—Joseph offered me a quick simple explanation. Things were the same in America as in Russia, but the appearance was deceiving.

The capitalist class in the U.S., he said, were just as brutal, but more clever than their Russian counterparts. Here the capitalists pretended to give the workers freedoms and better working conditions; but while giving these things, they managed to grind out more production and more profits in sweat-shop factories. Free speech, free elections and free schools, he said, were the sugar coating on the pill of bitter reality.

To a boy of 13, who worshipped his older brother, this was explanation enough.

I was determined, as I listened to him, to devote my life to the working class struggle, to the revolution that would free the peoples of the world from their slums, poverty, sickness and injustice. All peoples everywhere would be united in one community. All men would be brothers, regardless of race, creed or color!

We lived with Abraham in his crowded apartment until about May. Then we moved to a place of our own on Manhattan's Lower East Side. It was a three-room, cold-water, walkup apartment on the sixth floor of 610 East 13th Street, between Avenues B and C. There was a big coal-burning stove in the middle of the kitchen and the only hot water we had came from a kettle on the stove. But compared with the hovels we had known in Russia, it was a mansion. It was wonderful!

Nathan moved in with us, while he pursued his theatrical career. Although he frequently had parts in Yiddish stage productions, Nathan earned his living in a raincoat factory. And he remained active in the Socialist Party.

Joseph signed me up with the Young People's Socialist League a few days after I arrived in the country. Y.P.S.L. headquarters was at Seventh Street and Avenue C, not far from our Manhattan apartment. After school I would rush to the third-floor club rooms—an auditorium with adjoining small rooms for class instruction. Public lectures were given twice a week, where Morris Hillquit, an attorney and national Socialist leader, was a frequent speaker. Among many others I heard there were Abraham Shiplakoff, noted Socialist labor leader, Abraham Cahan, editor of the Jewish Socialist newspaper, the *Daily Forward*, and Charley Vladeck, later to become a member of the City Council.

That summer, when school let out, the young Socialists journeyed frequently in groups by subway to Van Cortlandt Park, in the Bronx. We would carry our lunches and sit on the grass singing revolutionary songs. *Red Flag*, sung to the tune of *Maryland*, was a favorite. It went something like this:

> The Worker's flag is deepest red,
>   It shrouded oft our martyred dead;
> And ere their limbs grew stiff and cold,
>   Their hearts' blood dyed its every fold.
> CHORUS: Then raise the scarlet standard high,
> Beneath its folds we'll live and die;
> Though coward flinch and traitor sneer,
> We'll keep the red flag flying here!

The Socialists have kept the red flag flying ever since. In 1957, I heard members of the Socialist Party and Social Democratic Federation sing this song at their unity meeting in the Grand Ballroom of the Biltmore Hotel in New York City.

Among our instructors and counselors on these Elysian outings were Jacob Pankin, who later became a judge of the New York City Domestic Relations Court, and August Classens and Algernon Lee, both leading lights in the Socialist Party.

Nathan belonged to the Sixth Assembly District Socialist Club, and Joseph was a member of the one in the Eighth A.D. Joseph also belonged to the Number One branch of the Russian Federation. Socialist membership was largely composed of foreign-born, who were also members of the various language federations in the city and the nation. Of these, the Lettish group, with headquarters in Boston, was possibly the most powerful.

Joseph had become a leading member of the Russian Federation where he became friendly with Lev Davidovich Bronstein, better known to history as Leon Trotsky. A left-wing Russian socialist refugee, Trotsky used his sanctuary in the United States to carry on a propaganda battle for world revolution. By 1917, he had become a frequent visitor in our apartment.

I distinctly remember a little man with thick, bushy black hair, a high forehead, thick-lensed pince-nez glasses, a thick drooping mustache and gold teeth; 38 years old, he had a sensual mouth, and an almost daintily pointed chin. In our home, Trotsky was always a picture of dignity. He would sometimes sit with me to discuss the faults of capitalism, pointing to what he called its inherent vices and quietly explaining the necessity for violence in the revolution. Trotsky insisted on blood-letting. Capitalism, he said, would never be defeated by the so-called constitutional or parliamentary process. "Bullets, not ballots," would liberate the workers.

Trotsky spoke from first-hand experience in revolution—he had been president of the ill-fated First Soviet of 1905. He was a gifted writer and impressive speaker. I first began reading his articles in *Novy Mir*, the official Russian Federation organ which he helped edit. Other of his writings appeared in the Jewish Socialist newspaper, the *Daily Forward*.

This relaxed and reflective man became a pyrotechnic orator when he mounted a platform before an audience. His hands would shoot into the air. He would pivot from foot to foot. His voice, at one moment soothing, would suddenly shriek with indignation and his whole body would tremble. Then, suddenly composed, he would be soulful and lugubrious.

I heard Trotsky many times at the Rand School and at the Labor Temple, which still stands at 14th Street and Second Avenue. His theme was Marxism and the proper interpretation of the *Communist Manifesto*. In all his speeches he sneered at "bourgeois reforms," while preaching force and violence in the overthrow of capitalism. He scorned Morris Hillquit, Victor Berger, Algernon Lee and other leaders of American socialism. He called the leaders of the Second International in Europe "capitalist agents"—traitors to the revolution—planted in the working class movement. In the most vituperative language—quoting Marx and Engels, and inventing dogma of his own—he would rip into those who disagreed with him. A trenchant phrasemaker, he was the first to use "class struggle," "mass struggle," "worker solidarity," "bullets, not ballots" and other such terms to promote militant socialism. Trotsky did more to educate me in the few months that I knew him, listened to his speeches and read his works, then all the years I spent later in the communist movement. Joseph planted the Marxian seeds in me, but Trotsky brought these seeds to full fruition. Lenin was the dogmatist—a theoretician—but Trotsky was the doer, the organizer and the builder.

In 1916, shortly before meeting Trotsky, I became a full-fledged member of the Socialist Party. I joined Joseph's club in the Eighth A.D., at Second Avenue and Eighth Street, and also became a member of Branch Number One of the Russian Federation. The Eighth A.D. leader was Jacob Pankin, and second-in-command was an up-and-coming young labor lawyer, Louis Waldman. He later became chief counsel of the International Longshoremen's Association—the stevedore union that in later years became one of the most anti-communist labor organizations in the United States.

The Socialists had purchased a Y.W.C.A. building at Seven East 15th Street, and established the Rand School of Social Science—still there today—as a national training school for leaders in the Socialist movement. I was enrolled in 1916 and attended classes at night. During the day I was a student at P.S. 64, at Tenth Street and Avenue B.

One of the most popular Rand lecturers was Karl Steinmetz, one of the outstanding electronics engineers in the world. I remember him as a frail-bodied man with a too-large head; a hunchback, who stood about five feet, eight inches tall and peered through thick eye glasses as he talked with a heavy German accent. He was a kindly

51

man of simple tastes, who spoke in the tolerant, easy tones of a parent talking to his children. During the question-and-answer period, which always followed his lectures, he would stand at ease and talk to us in conversational tones while chain smoking one cigarette after another. His brand, I remember, was *Mecca*, an American-made cigarette that has long vanished from the market.

Among other lecturers were August Classens, Morris Hillquit, Algernon Lee, Victor Berger, the Socialist Congressman from Milwaukee, labor leader Eugene V. Debs and Leon Trotsky.

The outbreak of World War I had brought confusion to socialists. The Party, already split into Left and Right factions, was further divided by the war. Patriotism was the big issue that confronted each socialist—first in Europe and later in America. What was the individual to do? The radical Left and the Bolsheviks had a ready answer: Patriotism was the weapon of Wall Street and other capitalist scoundrels. Nationalism must make way for membership in a one-world Socialist State. But in Europe, patriotism and nationalism prevailed, and most socialists went with their respective countries in the world conflict.

In America, however, the story was different. Socialist majorities went on record time and again as being opposed to *both* the Central and the Allied powers. The war in Europe was branded an imperialist, capitalist war. Workers on both sides were called on to strike and all soldiers were urged to turn their guns against their officers.

During a New York City meeting at the old Lenox Casino in Harlem, on March 4, 1917, a rousing crescendo of shouts greeted a series of resolutions that placed American Socilaists in active opposition to the war effort.

Trotsky, one of the leading speakers, exercised his powerful oratory to secure the adoption of these resolutions. He quoted from Marx and Engels, from the *Communist Manifesto* and, most effectively, from Section Six of the Socialist Constitution. This provided that any Socialist who opposed sabotage and other direct means of overthrowing capitalism should be expelled from the Party.

This was intended as a warning to America that the Socialists would not support the Government if it entered the European War. These same resolutions were adopted at the National Socialist Convention in St. Louis in April, although the country had already declared war. The convention called on workers to refuse to support the war in any form, and to refuse to serve if they were drafted for the Armed Forces. American workers were urged to unite with German workers and convert the capitalist war into a proletariat revolution. For preaching these sentiments, while the country was at war, Eugene Debs, Kate Richards O'Hara and other Socialist leaders were arrested and given prison terms.

Under the personal tutelage of Trotsky, I was thoroughly convinced by 1917 that the Party was not revolutionary enough. I had previously joined the Industrial Workers of the World, who, under the leadership of William D. (Big Bill) Haywood, openly preached and practiced violence, and in consequence had been expelled from the Socialist movement. The I.W.W. was especially virile on the West Coast, and the "Wobblies" spoke the simple language of rugged working men. The Socialists, in comparison, were pretentious; they were Marxist theoreticians and intellectuals, whose speech came from books and not from personal experience. The Wobblies had worked and sweated. They were tough, two-fisted men, who had earned a living at hard labor. Their language, in speeches and literature, carried a solid appeal to real working men.

As a Marxist, I knew enough to realize that the I.W.W., for all its hairy-chested shouts for world revolution, was politically naive. It believed in trade unions as the only power source, and called on workers to seize industry. As a Marxist, I knew that political power came first—it would be necessary to seize the government before we could take over industry. Political power, gained through force and violence, was the immediate objective.

My revolutionary zeal was aroused, however, by the short, blunt editorials in the I.W.W. organ, *New Solidarity*, and the Wobbly handbills I sometimes helped to distribute. I felt out of the swim of things when passively listening to the Socialist theoreticians such as Morris Hillquit and Karl Steinmetz at the Rand School. Though he was a brilliant, active man—including chief of the General Electric research laboratory at Schenectady, New York—Steinmetz, like other Socialists, was a bookish, monkish personality who only found true expression when he undertook, with cigarette in hand, to explain the perplexities of the Marxist dogma.

In early 1917, news reached us that the Imperial Russian government was floundering. Then came the revolution of March 2, which saw the overthrow of Czar Nicholas II. Conservative and radical elements united under Prince G. E. Lvov and moderate Socialist Alexander F. Kerensky to form a provisional government.

Trotsky heard this news, and was almost frantic. He had to get back to Russia immediately, and plunged into feverish activity. And among those who proposed to return with him was Joseph. Despite the pleadings of my family, he was firm in his resolve to go. World history was being made in Russia and there he was needed!

Concrete plans for the departure rapidly materialized. Trotsky bid farewell to American Socialists at a mass meeting in Harlem. Between 800 and 1,000 people jammed the meeting hall, while others stood on the sidewalk.

I was seated—or rather standing and cheering most of the time—inspired and enthused by his oratory and plain talk, with none of the Morris Hillquit dogma. I shouted *"Da! Da!"* ("Yes! Yes!") and "Down with the Capitalist War!" Joseph was on the platform and Nathan sat next to me, giving me encouragement.

"We are going home," Trotsky shouted, "to dig the grave of capitalism!"

He said that the war, thus far, had been a capitalist war, where millions of workers had died for a criminal cause. But now it would all change. The war would now become a "people's war!" "We are returning to Russia," he thundered, "to rip apart the very foundations of capitalism! We shall raise aloft the red banner of the workers' revolution! We shall establish the first republic of the Socialist world society!"

Seated on the rostrum were left-wing Socialists Nicholas Hourwich and Gregory Weinstein, a Russian engineer who had been in the United States since about 1908 and edited the Russian Socialist newspaper *Novy Mir*, Louis C. Fraina, the best-known radical Socialist writer of the day, and Santeri Nuorteva, who in 1919 would become the first Soviet Consul General in the United States.

Trotsky finished speaking, but it was half an hour before the crowd would let him leave. He was cheered to the rafters by socialists of all stripes. Trotsky was a powerful force at work for communism, and I believe that his ability as a speaker alone—his other great assets aside—earned him a far more important place in the Bolshevik victory than has been conceded. He was the greatest rabble rouser I ever heard.

54

CHAPTER VII

On the day the ship sailed, Papa remained at home on Tenth Street. He blessed Joseph and predicted mournfully that we would never see him again. It was about 8:30 A.M. when the rest of the family left the house to accompany Joseph to the Hoboken pier. It was a pleasant spring morning, with a slight fog rising above the river.

At Hoboken, a crowd had assembled to bid farewell to loved ones and "comrades" leaving aboard the S.S. *Christiansfjord*. Between 150 and 175 radicals were making the trip back to Russia with Trotsky. We Malkins felt that we were part of the "In" group—and rightfully so. Comrade Trotsky, who lived on Vyse Avenue in the Bronx, had made a special trip to our house the previous day to say goodbye to our family.

Joseph took the bag I carried for him, and, with the small typewriter he had carried himself, went below deck to stow his luggage. I looked curiously at the crowd around us. Small groups stood chatting and laughing. Others sang revolutionary songs. Some carried red banners that read: "Long Live Socialism!" and "Long Live Revolutionary Russia!" Amid the turmoil Mother stood and sobbed. Joseph joined us a few minutes later and put an arm around her shoulders, and with comforting words assured her that we would all meet again in Russia—"a new Russia where conditions would be truly wonderful." But Mother was skeptical and, between sobs, said over and over: "I'll never see you again."

The ship's whistle sounded a warning blast for passengers to assemble on board and for visitors to go ashore.

Joseph hugged us all and squeezed Mother's shoulders tightly. With an arm still around her, he turned to me. "Now don't forget what I taught you," he said. "Let the revolutionary movement be the first and last thought of your life. We are relying on you. With fellows like you, the revolution will succeed because you are not afraid and your courage will inspire others."

As the ship moved off, backing into the river, we saw him standing at the rail waving at us, his blond hair blowing in the wind. We watched until the ship became a mere dot trailing a smudge of smoke across the sky.

In a few days, on April 3, we learned that the vessel was being detained by British authorities at Halifax, Canada, and some passengers, including Trotsky, his wife and Joseph, were taken off. About ten days later, London received a strongly-worded protest from the Kerensky government, and the travelers were set free. They proceeded to Copenhagen, and in early May reached Petrograd.

From Copenhagen we received a brief letter from Joseph. "We are on our way to make world history," he wrote. And he ordered me to do the corresponding for the family. "Actually, you are the family's brave, strong leader. I expect to hear great things from you during the coming world revolution because you know Marxism, both in theory and in practice. Keep up the struggle!"

We didn't hear directly from him again until 1923, six long years later, when he came to New York City to help establish Amtorg, the Russian American Trading Corporation, on lower Broadway. The revolution had swallowed him completely. Problems of communication and an enormous work load took him from us.

Meanwhile, the United States had gone to war. While Father and my brother Abraham worked as carpenters at Camp Yaphank, later Camp Upton, on Long Island, I was busy attending Socialist meetings and distributing literature against the war. American socialists had lined up solidly behind the program of international left-wing socialism adopted in September, 1915, at Zimmerwald, Switzerland. This program was highly critical of the majority of European socialists. It called on workers to refuse to support the capitalist war, and to turn the struggle into a civil conflict. Accordingly, in the summer of 1917 at the St. Louis convention, American Socialists called on our people to openly defy their government. Workers were urged to call a general strike—to go to jail rather than be drafted into the Armed Forces. Sabotage was openly promoted.

The Socialist objective was a paralysis behind the lines that would break down authority and pave the way for a proletarian revolution. Soldiers were urged to turn their guns against their officers and to fraternize with the enemy.

I had become educational director in the Eighth A.D. Socialist Club and had joined in the feverish activity to line up a solid slate of left-wing delegates to the St. Louis convention. This became an easy task in our Russian, Jewish and other foreign language federations in New York, and our organizers in other cities met with equal success. As a result, we were able to control the St. Louis convention and jam through the anti-war, anti-capitalist platform which defied Washington and brought the arrest of Eugene Debs, Kate Richards O'Hara and others.

Behind this success was an organization that had taken years to build. The Socialists held a peculiar position among American political parties. *They, alone, maintained a system of organized and politically oriented schools.* Here, new members were recruited, and old and young alike were instructed in the intricacies of Marxist "scientific" Socialism. The new recruits received their indoctrination through the Young People's Socialist League or the district Socialist clubs. For the most advanced on the educational level, was the Rand School of Social Science.

The Intercollegiate Socialist Society, organized by Upton Sinclair, John Dewey and others in 1905, was a sort of intellectual flanking movement, which, by 1917, boasted a chapter on the campus of most large universities. Walter Lippmann, the columnist, was one of the "bright young men" of this group.

The backbone of the Socialist numerical strength lay in the foreign language federations, which held semi-autonomous status within the Party. In 1915, there were 14 such groups, and of a total membership of 80,126, forty per cent—32,894—belonged to these federations.

In the 1912 Presidential election Debs polled 897,011 Socialist votes, nearly six per cent of the electorate. But the Socialist strength was broader than even this sizable vote would indicate because, in the foreign language federations, whole families—including non-voting minors and aliens—were enrolled as Party members. The Federations were alien to everything American. Their objective was a world Marxist society.

Every Socialist, whether of the "Right" or the "Left," was dedicated to the class struggle, and all were united in the burning desire to destroy capitalism. But there was a great inner-movement argument over how this was to be done. The radical Left would have nothing to do with the "gradualism" and the "bourgeois" legislative reforms favored by the Right. Although the proletariat was the hero to all factions, the middle class was a potential ally to some, but the main villain to others.

Dedicated left-wing Socialists, the "true" believers in the doctrine of Marx, hated the middle class—especially the American Federation of Labor, which was branded a petty bourgeois organization headed by "the labor lieutenants of capitalism," Samuel Gompers and William Green.

The militant Socialist Party that emerged from the St. Louis Convention was a party divided over method, but united in the struggle to overthrow capitalism and establish a universal Socialist state. It was the party of Eugene V. Debs, Victor Berger, Algernon Lee, Morris Hillquit, Norman Thomas (though he was little known at the time), Louis C. Fraina, Ludwig Lore, Santeri Nuorteva, Louis B. Boudin, Gregory Weinstein, James Joseph Larkin, founder of the Irish Transport and General Workers Union, Ludwig C. A. K. Martens, John Reed and others who have left their mark on history.

The life of the Malkin family centered around the radical movement. Even my sisters became active members of the Party. Bertha, employed as a dressmaker, joined Local 25 of the International Ladies Garment Workers Union, and Elsie was active in the Furriers' Union. Although she never joined the movement, Mother was somewhat sympathetic to our activities. Only Father remained totally immune from the radical fever that ran in our family. He remained a devout, religious man all his life, and believed we had found a wonderful home in America, a country worthy of his full allegiance.

Daily, after public school classes, I turned eagerly to Party work, which was intensified after the Red revolution in Russia. I became intimate with most of the figures who were to play leading roles in founding the Communist movement in America.

Though unrecognized by our Government, the first Communist consulate in the United States was established by Santeri Nuorteva to represent the short-lived Red government of Finland, which came into existence January 27, 1918. Nuorteva was a leader in the Finnish Socialist Federation, and the publisher of its official organ, *Raivaaja*. He opened a Finnish Information Bureau at 299 Broadway, after receiving a cable on February 18, 1918, from Yrjo Sirolo, the Finnish Red Foreign Minister. The Finnish Communist Government was quickly snuffed out by the spectacular advance of the German armies on the Eastern Front, which led to the Brest-Litovsk Treaty and the wresting of large areas of the Russian Empire from the Reds.

The first Soviet Russian office in the United States was opened the first week of April by Ludwig Christian Alexander Karl Martens, who billed himself as the Ambassador of the U.S.S.R. and who almost always used all of his middle initials. The office occupied two floors of the World Tower Building at 110 West 40th Street in New York City, between Broadway and Sixth Avenue. Nuorteva moved in to help Martens launch a massive propaganda campaign.

Gregory Weinstein called me aside one day at the Eighth A.D. Socialist Club and asked me to go downstairs with him. On the sidewalk at Eighth Street and Second Avenue, he told me to report to Marten's office at 9:30 the next morning for a very important secret meeting. I was instructed to bring along a tried-and-true Bolshevik, Alexander Frignow, a man in his mid-twenties who lived on the Lower East Side at Fourth Street and Second Avenue.

I contacted him later that evening at the club and told him to meet me at 8:30 the next morning at a restaurant on the southwest corner of Second Avenue at Twelfth Street. I warned him to tell no one about the meeting.

At the office, we were met by Nuorteva and Weinstein, who took us to Martens, whom I had seen many times at Socialist meetings. He was a lithe, thin man, with sallow cheeks. He wore pince-nez glasses and had a neat, dark mustache—the appearance of a professor.

After motioning us to sit down, his first words, without preamble, were that we had been selected for a post of the highest importance in the revolutionary movement. We were selected, he said, because of our working-class backgrounds and our thorough schooling in Marxism. Our jobs were secret—very secret! As he talked, I gradually began to realize that we were to become members of the American arm of the *Cheka*—Moscow's dreaded secret police.

After 30 minutes, Martens got to his feet. The interview was over. We all stood with him, and he instructed Nuorteva to give us detailed instructions about our work. Behind his mahogany desk, Nuorteva leaned back in a leather swivel chair and looked at Frignow and me. "You have been chosen as security officers for the Embassy." We were to take turns standing guard outside Martens' private office. Under no circumstances was a visitor to be allowed inside without Martens' express approval. In addition to screening outsiders, we were to keep special watch over the employees—who already numbered 60 or 70.

Finally, Nuorteva turned to his desk and opened a drawer. Dramatically, he took out two .38 caliber revolvers. "You will be armed," he said crisply.

He put one of the guns in my hand. As I stood looking at it, the full meaning of my job began to sink in.

Nuorteva said that we would be trained as experts with the weapons, and should carry them at all times when in the building. But while not on duty, we were to leave the guns locked in an office safe. Under no conditions would we carry them into the street. "The last thing we want is to have one of you picked up by the police."

The next day we reported for target practice at a house on Main Street in Yonkers, a New York suburb. Two instructors, experts in arms and marksmanship, worked with us in the basement, where there was a large supply of ammunition. After two weeks, I qualified as a crack shot, and had learned to strip and assemble a gun in total darkness.

At the "Embassy," as we called it, my tour of duty was from 4:00 P.M. until midnight—or whatever hour Martens left his office for the day. He held many secret conferences late at night, usually with Soviet couriers who had just arrived, disguised as seamen, aboard some ships.

One of these agents was a big Slavic sailor, a large man, weighing well over 200 pounds, who appeared at the office on Washington's birthday in 1919. There was coal dust ground into his overalls and his manner was brusque and surly. He demanded to see Martens at once and started to push past me. Even though I had been alerted to expect such a visitor, I took the gun from my pocket. I pointed to a chair and, in Russian, told him to sit. He saw I meant business and obeyed. While Frignow stayed with him, I went to Martens and told him about the visitor. I was ordered to bring him in but to stand by while the sailor was in the office.

The yellow-haired giant took off a sweater that had been tucked into his trousers. He started disrobing, removing a shirt, two pairs of pants, and finally, two suits of underwear. He stood naked in the middle of Martens' office, except for two bulging canvas money belts, around his waist.

In one of the belts were English gold guineas and a thick pad of banknotes—altogether about $100,000. The long bills made a thick pile on Martens' desk.

From the other belt came diamonds, rubies and other precious stones of assorted colors, shapes and sizes.

The sailor dressed and left the office. He had hardly spoken a word. After he had gone, Martens warned me never to reveal what I had seen.

The jewelry, I later learned, was valued at more than $1,000,000. Part of this hoard of jewels went to the Irish Free State as collateral for a loan, which was later redeemed by Moscow.* The rest was converted into cash through fences in New York, some of whom were Party members. One of them, M. Brainin, had a jewelry establishment on Bryant Avenue, in the Bronx.

Most of the money was spent for propaganda in the United States and Canada. But some of it went to Dr. Jose Bravo, President of the first Pan-American Socialist and Labor Congress, who was in charge of Latin American activities. Prime targets were Guatemala, Costa Rica, El Salvador and Colombia.

A short time before the jewelry had arrived, we had been shocked to learn that the poet, Carl Sandburg, had been detained by U. S. Customs officials in New York. He was one of our mainstays among American intellectuals, and had gone to the Scandinavian countries and Finland as a correspondent—and as a Soviet courier. We had eagerly awaited his return with an important message from Lenin and a large quantity of money and literature. News that he had been detained on his arrival caused great concern. "I hope they didn't get those papers," Nuorteva said.

After a while, we received a call from the Customs House. A $10,000 check to Nuorteva, drawn on a New York bank, had been taken away from Sandburg, and he was being held for questioning.

A week later the poet appeared at our office, accompanied by Charles Recht, legal representative of the Soviet government from 1917 until his death nearly a half-century later. Sandburg had been permitted to retain the messages from Lenin, which were later translated as *A Letter to American Working Men,* and published in *The Revolutionary Age* and *The Liberator.*

Carl Sandburg remained a loyal friend to the Soviet Union—a

*See Appendix I, p. 230.

61

friendship that continued for decades, as evidenced by his membership in such fronts as the National Council of American-Soviet Friendship and the American Committee for the Protection of the Foreign Born.

With smuggled funds we quickly established a weekly magazine, *Soviet Russia,* to proclaim the beauties of the happy life under the intellectual dictatorship of the proletariat. Martens tossed tow lines to every Socialist and syndicate organization in the country. From most we received comradely greetings and felicitations—and a few sent some money.

Martens was born in Russia of German parents. He had studied at the Technological Institute at St. Petersburg where he was associated with the revolutionary Union for the Liberation of the Russian Working Class. Here he was befriended by the organization's leader, Nikolai Lenin. He was arrested in 1896 and sentenced to three years in prison. Later, he was deported to Germany, where he continued his revolutionary activities with exiled Russians, as a member of the Russian Socialist Central Revolutionary Committee. Active in international revolutionary circles, and in close touch with Lenin and Trotsky, Martens was living in London when the war broke out in 1914. He registered as an enemy alien, and in 1916 was permitted to travel to the United States as a German national.

With the outbreak of the revolution in Russia in 1917, he immediately applied to the Provisional Government for Russian citizenship. When this country entered the war, he claimed to be a Russian, but the only evidence he was able to offer was a letter from a sister in Petrograd (previously St. Petersburg, and later Leningrad) stating that his request for citizenship had been honored by the government. Strangely, it was accepted as sufficient proof and he was permitted to register as a Russian citizen—remaining free in this country throughout World War I to carry on his revolutionary activities.

With Prussian thoroughness, Martens set about to capture the machinery of the Socialist Party. Members of his staff—and even Martens himself, when he could spare the time—toured the country, addressing radical meetings and proclaiming the greatness of Soviet Russia. Those engaged in this work included Kenneth Durant, Dorothy Keen, Mary Modell, Alexander Coleman, Blanche Abushevitz, Nestor Kuntzevich, Lieutenant Colonel Boris Leonidovitch, Tagueeff Roustam Beck, Ella Tuch, Rose Holland, Henrietta Meero-

wich, Rose Byers, Vladimir Olchovsky, Evans Clark, Nora G. Smithe-
man, Etta Fox, Wilfred B. Humphries, Arthur Adams, William Malis-
soff, Leo A. Huebsch, D. H. Dubrowsky, Isaac A. Hourwich, Eva Joffe,
Elizabeth Goldstein, Jacob M. W. Hartmann, Ray Trotsky, Theodore
Breslauer, Vasily Ivanoff and David Oldfield. John Reed, who had just
returned from Russia, became the apostle of the Red Revolution. He
traveled the country with his wife, Louise Bryant, telling of the
"wonders" he had seen.

Martens' campaign to capture the Socialist Party met with opposition from an unexpected quarter, the leaders of the Russian Language Federation. Until the October Revolution, they had held only
minor positions among the foreign language Socialist groups, but
with a newly found self-confidence, these left-wing Russians suddenly refused to mingle in a movement that contained so many
"bourgeois" Socialists.

One morning we received a visit from Alexander Stoklitsky, Oscar
Tywerowsky, Michael Mislig and a half dozen other Russian Language Federation leaders. They claimed that they were in close
touch with the leading Bolsheviks in Moscow, and were singularly
qualified to define the trend of the revolution. They were adamantly
opposed to a broadened membership. They wanted a small party, a
maneuverable nucleus of tried and trusted Marxists. They wished to
follow the example of Lenin's Bolsheviks, who had seized power
through discipline and unity—while the majority haggled and argued over parliamentary procedures. They demanded a simon-pure
party, uncontaminated by "bourgeois reform tendencies."

Martens argued that under his plan a hard core of revolutionaries
would own and control the larger Socialist movement, but the Russians were unconvinced. All radicals of the day believed that the
revolution was just around the corner, but there was great disagree-
ment over nearly every important detail. Actually, this meeting was
the first of a long series of disputes over who was to control the
Marxian Socialist movement in the United States. The other foreign
language federations quickly united with the Russians. The leaders,
few of whom spoke English, had no intention of sharing power in the
international movement with Americans whom they despised and
regarded as their intellectual inferiors.

CHAPTER VIII

_____

As the unrecognized ambassador of the Soviet Union to the United States, Martens played a key role in the battle for control of the American Socialist movement. And he was devious. On one hand, he secretly encouraged the militant left; on the other, he openly called for a united Socialist Party, with room in it for all, to fight the show-down battle against capitalism. Privately, he attempted to pacify the dissident leaders of the foreign language federations who wanted a small, hard-core Bolshevik apparatus, instantly ready to act on orders from Lenin. While counseling caution, Martens assured them that once the Socialist Party machinery was in his hands, a program of militant revolution would follow. But the federations would have none of it.

Although I was one of the militant, impatient left-wingers, I was able to appreciate Martens' sagacity. After all, I watched him plot his program.

Propaganda, financed largely by funds received from abroad, prodded the Socialists to line up solidly behind the Bolsheviks. The money was funneled through Martens, but much of it went to those who disagreed with him. The Soviet leaders called the shots and they ordered cooperation with the foreign language groups. The tone of the propaganda was set in the leading voice of left-wing socialism _The Revolutionary Age_, which received most of its financial support from the Lettish Federation in Boston and was edited by a brilliant Italian immigrant, Louis C. Fraina. Echoing its lead in New York were _Novy Mir_, voice of the Russian Federation and _Der Kampf_, organ of the Jewish Federation. The Socialist Publication Society added its influence with pamphlets and the magazine, _Class Struggle_.

In late 1918, _The Revolutionary Age_ published Lenin's _Letter to American Working Men_, which poet Carl Sandburg had brought

64

back from Sweden. The purpose of this hurriedly penned epistle was to harden the Socialist movement in America and mobilize aid for the "beleaguered fortress of socialism," Russia.

Lenin's letter spat venom on "bourgeois Socialists" who had aided their own countries in World War I—and left the Bolsheviks to the mercy of the "robber barons of German imperialism," who dictated the hated Brest-Litovsk Treaty. Lenin dismissed, with contempt, the liberals and Social Democrats, who criticized the brutality of the Bolshevik regime, the lack of free elections and the absence of freedom of press and assembly in the "new" Russia.

"To accuse us of 'destruction' of industries and 'terror,'" he wrote,* "is hypocrisy or clumsy pedantry." He added that it "shows an incapability of understanding the most elemental fundamentals of the raging, climactic force of the class struggle called revolution.

"In words, our accusers 'recognize' this kind of class struggle; in deeds, they revert again and again to the middle class Utopia of 'class' harmony and mutual 'interdependence' of classes upon one another. In reality, the class struggle in revolutionary times had always inevitably taken the form of civil war, and civil war is unthinkable without the worst kind of destruction, without terror and limitations of forms of democracy in the interest of the war. One must be a sickly sentimentalist not to be able to see, to understand and accept this necessity."

Lenin predicted that the "American working class," unlike the Social Democrats of Europe, "will not follow the lead of the bourgeoisie. It will go with us against the bourgeoisie."

"Let incurable pedants, crammed full of bourgeois democracy and parliamentary prejudices, shake their heads gravely over our Soviets," he added. "Let them deplore the fact that we have no direct elections—only fools or traitors will insist on the formal equality of the bourgeoisie. The right of free assemblage is not worth an iota to the workman and the peasant when all better meeting places are in the hands of the bourgeoisie."

Something new had happened in Russia. Under militant left-wing leadership, he said, "There arises before us a new world, the world of socialism. Such a world cannot be materialized as if by magic, complete in every detail as Minerva sprang from Jupiter's head."

*Liberator, September, 1918.

Familiar with Trotsky's thesis that "bullets, not ballots" would win the future, and fired with the rising tide of revolution, American Socialists ate it up.

Lenin completed a second letter on January 21, 1919, which was published in this country. Again addressed to American workmen, it claimed great improvement in the revolutionary struggle. Indeed, there was ground for optimism: the letter cited rising Communist Parties in Latvia, Poland, the Ukraine, Switzerland, Holland, Norway, Austria and Germany. Everywhere, Lenin boasted, workers were turning to communism and following the leadership of the Bolsheviks. He recalled that on the date of his last letter, August 20, 1918, "Our Bolshevik Party was the only one which determinedly fought the old Second International, which lasted from 1889 to 1914, and which was shamefully bankrupted during the imperialist war of 1914–18. Our Party was the only one which unqualifiedly took the new road, which leads away from socialism and Social Democracy contaminated by an alliance with the brigand bourgeoisie, and toward communism—the road which leads away from petty bourgeois reformism and opportunism which had completely permeated, and still permeates, the official Social Democracy and Socialist Parties, and toward real proletarian and revolutionary tactics."

What Lenin was after was a new left-wing party in America that would accept the lead of Russia. He wanted a break with the Social Democrats and with all "moderate" socialists who rejected the Bolsheviks and sought their objectives through "gradualism"—a personal income tax, state control of the basic industries, etc.

Action along the lines laid out by Lenin came on February 15, 1919, when a handful of left-wing delegates—I was one of them—bolted a meeting of the Socialist Central Committee of Greater New York. We adjourned to a separate room in the Rand School, where we were joined by additional leftists, and selected a committee of 14 to prepare resolutions and a manifesto for a "dynamic new party."

Maximilian Cohen was named Executive Secretary, Bertram D. Wolfe, Recording Secretary, Rose Pastor Stokes, Treasurer, and Rose Spanier, Financial Secretary. (Wolfe was later succeeded by Fanny Horowitz and Rose Spanier by Milton Goodman.)

The Executive Committee, with instructions to push the organization of the left-wing, was composed of the following:

Benjamin Gitlow, Nicholas I. Hourwich, George Lehman, James

Larkin, L. Himmelfarb, George C. Vaughn, Benjamin Corsor, Edward I. Lindgren and Maximilian Cohen.

The adopted manifesto proclaimed:

> "It is the task of the revolutionary Socialist Party to direct the struggle of the proletariat and provide a program for the culminating crisis. Its propaganda must be so directed that when this crisis comes, the workers will be prepared to accept a program of the following character . . ."

The provisions included workmens' councils, control of industry by the workers, repudiation of all national debts, expropriation of the banks, railways and "the large trust organizations of capital."

The resolution stated:

> "We stand for a uniform declaration of principles in all Party platforms, both local and national, and the abolition of all social reform planks now contained in them.
>
> "The Party must teach, propagate and agitate exclusively for the overthrow of capitalism, and the establishment of socialism through a proletarian dictatorship.
>
> "Socialist candidates elected to office shall adhere strictly to the above provisions."

The left-wing interim committee established headquarters at 43 West 29th Street, and a vigorous campaign was launched to capture the rank and file of the Socialist Party. *The Revolutionary Age* in Boston echoed our propaganda, as did *Novy Mir* and *Der Kampf* in New York.

An effort to move *The Revolutionary Age* to New York was rejected by the Boston local of the Socialist Party. A spokesman, Amy Collier, stated in a letter dated April 1, 1919, that the Boston Socialists would keep the publication "until a national convention of the left-wing organizations shall be held."

Shortly thereafter, a new publication, *The New York Communist*, was established in New York City with financial help from Martens. John Reed was the editor, Eadmonn MacAlpine associate editor, and Maximilian Cohen business manager. The first issue appeared April 19, 1919.

In Moscow, meanwhile, the Third International had been

launched, signaling a final break with the "reformist socialists" of the old Second International. The action was taken at a meeting held March 2–6 and attended by 32 delegates from Communist and radical socialist groups from twelve countries. Represented were Russia, Germany, Hungary, Austria, Sweden, Norway, Bulgaria, Roumania, Finland, the Ukraine, Estonia and Armenia. Present, but not voting, were observers from Holland, Yugoslavia, Switzerland, France, Great Britain, Turkey, Turkestan, Persia, Korea and the United States.

The lone American was Boris Reinstein, a native Russian who had immigrated to the United States but returned to Russia in 1917, after attending a Stockholm socialist conference as the representative of the U.S. Socialist Labor Party. Enthralled with the Soviet regime, he had remained in Moscow.

News of the organization of the Third International galvanized the left-wing socialists in America. The Boston group immediately called for a national conference to unite left-wing elements across the country. It opened in New York on June 21, 1919.

The big question was whether immediately to organize a Communist Party or to continue to fight for control of the Socialist Party. The conference, after long wrangling over this question, voted to continue the fight to capture the Socialist Party machinery "in order to rally all revolutionary elements for a Communist Party, meanwhile organizing temporarily as the left-wing section of the Socialist Party."

Keynoter and moving spirit was Louis C. Fraina. He declared that "the proletarian revolution in actions has modified the old tactical conception of socialism; and the inspiration of the Bolshevik conquest, joining with the original minority socialism in the (U.S.) Socialist Party, has produced the left-wing."

It was voted to combine the *New York Communist* with the *Revolutionary Age* and issue a combined new organ as the voice of the left-wing section of the Socialist Party. The publication took the older name, and was published at 43 West 29th Street in New York City.

But there was still a major problem among American revolutionary circles—how far left? An insurgent separatist movement was initiated by the Russian Federation and was joined by other foreign language groups. They voted to take no further part in the courtship of "bourgeois" socialists and withdrew from the left-wing section, issuing a call for immediately setting up a Communist Party. As a member of the Russian Federation, I approved the action—while maintaining a precarious balance with one foot in Martens' office.

What had set in was a power struggle between the right, the left and the far-left for control of socialism. The old line socialists, goaded by vitriolic language and other abuses, were eventually moved to retaliate. They still controlled the Party, and in July they voted to expel the foreign federations and those groups and individuals who had joined the left-wing movement. They called for an emergency convention—the first since 1917—to be held in Chicago on September 1.

The far-left faction of those ousted announced a convention of their own, also to be held in Chicago, beginning the last week in August.

The more moderate left-wingers, led by Ben Gitlow and William Bross Lloyd, still had hopes of uniting the socialist movement, and presented themselves at the regular Socialist Party convention in Mechanics Hall. But when they tried to gain recognition, they were repudiated and ordered expelled. In the rumpus that followed, they were ousted by the police and retired to a nearby poolroom where they proceeded to organize the Communist Labor Party.

Meanwhile, the "simon-pure socialists" of the foreign language groups were meeting at 1221 Blue Island Avenue, headquarters of the Chicago Russian Federation, where they founded the Communist Party of America.

This left three socialist groups on stage in Chicago: the Socialist Party, comprising a much-reduced membership of "moderate" socialists; the Communist Party of America, led by the foreign language federations and boasting the largest membership of all; and the Communist Labor Party, which insisted that the only way that Marxism could be sold to the American people was through a broad missionary movement.

CHAPTER IX

While these developments were taking place, I was busy at Martens' office with a dozen facets of his subversive program, including one of the first Communist fronts tailored especially for American liberals. This was the People's Council of America, with such slogans as: "Be a true American citizen and an internationalist and join this great new world movement for democracy!" Charter members were Charles Recht and Joseph Brodsky, both Communist attorneys who were destined to serve the Party for a half century. A flock of "liberals" were netted, some of them still active in the cause. One of our earliest friends was Roger N. Baldwin, just out of prison as a conscientious objector. Intellectually, he remains today about where he started out.

The People's Council fired off a cable to Lenin in the name of the American Soviet People's Council, offering to raise money and an American Red army to fight for Moscow. This was eventually "vetoed" by the crackdown on communism of Attorney General A. Mitchell Palmer.

I was the Assistant Secretary of the New York Central Committee of the newly formed Communist Party of America. Orders came to me to print thousands of leaflets, and to stimulate a campaign through foreign language newspapers, calling for the withdrawal of American and Allied troops from Russia.

I was also ordered to create a department of secret investigation from among Russian Federation members, which would be under the direct command of Martens and Nuorteva. The chain of command of this unit was connected directly with Felix Dzerzhinsky, chief of the *Cheka* (Extraordinary Commission Against Counter Revolution), the dreaded Soviet Secret Police. One of the first members was a *1903 Bolshevik,** Rose Barron, who later managed the

---

*All those who agreed with Lenin in the 1903 split between the Bolsheviks and the

Workers Book Shop in New York City. Among other early agents were Gregory Weinstein, Nicholas I. Hourwich and Alexander Stoklitsky, leader of the Russian Federation. We called ourselves the Control and Investigative Department, our main job being to keep a close watch for anyone suspected of feeding information to the United States government, or of being in any way disloyal to left-wing socialism. Character assassination was agreed upon as the most effective means of dealing with the guilty.

Rose Barron and Gregory Weinstein were also assigned to gather industrial and military information which was channeled, through Nuorteva, to Trotsky in Moscow. Stoklitsky was in charge of moral agitation—the destruction of the morale of the American people by undermining their faith in their moral laws and social patterns. This was a major work the Communists have continued with increased effectiveness in the United States and the entire non-communist world. Nicholas Hourwich, in this same general field, was placed in charge of anti-religious activities.

On still another front, I was the assistant to Stoklitsky in the creation of a strong-arm squad. We called it the Direct Action Committee. We enrolled all the toughs we could find, many of them underworld characters with long criminal records, and were told to stand by for action.

There was a boldness about all this that disappeared for nearly half a century, until revived in the late 1960's when youthful anarchists became a force in American society. Socialists and communists held their conventions and meetings with total disregard of the police and the public. But when the war ended, and American soldiers started coming back from foreign battlefields, things began to change. A resentment started to develop toward radicals, slackers and professional pacifists who had preached treason while the shooting was on. The newly-formed American Legion became very vociferous and has remained so.

Martens was keenly aware of the trend and scented danger in the air. He frequently warned me to have my strong-arm squad on the alert. I had rounded up 50 or more rough characters, dressed them

Mensheviks had organized a group known as the Society of Old Bolsheviks. It is still in existence to the present day for those lucky enough to have survived the passage of time, especially the Stalin purges.

71

in the partial uniforms of discharged American servicemen and armed them with switchblade knives, bayonets, lead pipes rolled in newspapers, etc. They were trained in Bolshevik hit-and-run tactics and received military close order drill in a rented hall on 23rd Street.

The first call to action came on May 1, 1919, at a meeting in the Old Madison Square Garden at 26th Street and Madison Avenue. A big May Day meeting was planned and we had received word that groups of veterans were going to break it up. I formed a battle group and placed it under the command of Abe Levine who had been in the Army. They marched down the stairs and filed across 23rd Street into Madison Square Park, carrying an American flag and two Springfield rifles at the head of the column. A band from the Amalgamated Clothing Workers Union (the Sidney Hillman union) was in the street, and as it struck up the "Marseillaise," I ordered the men forward in a column of twos.

A swarm of ex-service men, some wearing American Legion caps, but most in civilian clothes, had converged outside the hall. Our advancing column, displaying banners that called for an end to capitalism and the immediate withdrawal of American troops from Siberia, attracted their attention. They shouted insults and displayed their own banners and placards. The objective of my squad was to clear an entrance into the Garden for the arriving socialists and communists—but we never reached the arcade. We were met halfway by a charge of angry veterans, and were overwhelmed. In the swinging and slugging that followed, my "Army" took to its heels or melted into the crowd. I finally joined in what I'd prefer to call a "tactical withdrawal."

This was the end of the "Soldiers, Sailors and Marines Protective Association," as I had named my muscle men. I could never get them together again for a drill session.

CHAPTER X

To understand the Palmer raids of 1920, it is necessary to understand the feeling that swept the United States in 1919—a year of defiant, militant, clamorous and arrogant radicalism. Strikes, bloodshed and general disorder were commonplace.

It was the year of the Boston Police Strike, the Coal Miners' Strike, the Seattle General Strike, the Lawrence Textile Mill Strike. Railroads were shut down and goods piled up on sidings across the country. At the very time that the two Communist Parties were born and the Socialists were meeting in Chicago, William Z. Foster, a former I.W.W. organizer and agitator who had wormed his way into the American Federation of Labor, triggered a steel strike that paralyzed Gary, Indiana. It took Federal troops to restore order.

More than 365,000 workers were involved in strikes that year, and not until the depression years of the 1930's would the country see anything like it.

Half of Europe lay in the shadow of revolution, while at home a Republican Congress remained at odds with a Democratic President who suffered a stroke during a headstrong attempt to carry the country with him, and lay prostrate through the last nervous months of his administration.

There was nothing modest or timid about the two Communist Parties launched in Chicago. Both saluted Moscow, gave the Bolsheviks their total allegiance and marched into the battle for a one-world Socialist government.

To obtain this objective, they were against "bourgeois nationalism," and promised to destroy the government in Washington by whatever means necessary.

They were intensely hostile to the American Federation of Labor and the craft labor movement, charging that they betrayed the workers by making them docile in the struggle for higher wages and better working conditions. Communists of all shades were for revolution and violence—not reform.

"Trade unionism is the arch enemy of the militant proletariat," declared *The Communist,* newly created organ of the Communist Party of America. "This is one of the tasks of the Communist Party —the destruction of the existing trade union organization."

These were the avowed feelings of the two communist parties, split not in basic aims, but only by rivalry for control. But how about the "moderate" Socialists who had been abandoned by the left-wingers? They took the position that Lenin and the Bolsheviks had not criticized them but only the European Socialists who had abandoned the principles of the Second International when they supported their respective countries in World War I. The American Socialists pointed to their 1917 St. Louis convention, which had proclaimed internationalism while openly calling for sabotage of the war effort. They proudly recalled these words:

"The Socialist Party of the United States, in the present grave crisis, solemnly reaffirms its allegiance to the principles of internationalism and working class solidarity the world over, and proclaims its unalterable opposition to the war just declared by the government of the United States."

And this militant appeal addressed to the American people:

"Let us proclaim in tones of unmistakable determination: 'not a worker's arm shall be lifted for the slaying of a fellow worker of another country, not a wheel turned for the production of man-killing implements or war supplies! Down with war! Forward to international peace and the world-wide solidarity of all workers!' "

The socialists boasted that they had pledged themselves at St. Louis to resist "compulsory training and the conscription of life and labor" and had called for "repudiation of war debts."

This was the record to which Morris Hillquit, Norman Thomas and other "moderates" pointed during the fierce struggle for power inside the Marxist movement. Hillquit, in an article in the *New York Call* of May 21, 1919, reviled Lenin in his contempt of European socialists. He charged that German Social Democrats, "far from prov-

—the American arm of the Cheka—to begin collecting arms. In addition, he began to gather intelligence files. We were ordered to learn the location of every National Guard arsenal and cache of arms in the New York area and to compile a list of communication centers on the East Coast. Other subjects of our interest included power stations and railway terminals.

We had begun this work when we received an urgent telephone call in the late afternoon of June 12. Nuorteva's secretary answered, then spun around excitedly and spoke to Isidor Blankstein,* "The Lusk Committee has just obtained a warrant to search our offices!" Our informant was a socialist who was an obscure clerk in a city Magistrate's office where the order was issued.

Martens and Nuorteva sprang into action, and ordered us to begin burning their most incriminating documents and making bundles of others, tied and wrapped inside of newspapers. Frignow took them to my mother at our apartment on Third Street, near Avenue C.

I remained at the office where Nuorteva had me carefully wipe our revolvers clean of fingerprints. He then took the weapons, holding them with a handkerchief, and hid them on top of the water box in the men's toilet.

Shortly after I left the building, at about 6:30, members of the Lusk Committee drove up in three automobiles. From down the street, I watched them carry cartons of papers out of the building and into their cars, then hurried to a room on the Lower East Side where Gregory Weinstein had called an emergency meeting of the Control and Investigative Committee.

We decided to stir up public protest, primarily through the Civil Liberties Bureau and the People's Freedom Union, against the search and seizure. Among those who rushed to our support were Rabbis Dr. Judah L. Magnes and Stephen S. Wise, but they failed to stop the Lusk Committee. On June 21, there was a raid on the headquarters of the left-wing section of the Socialist Party, at 43 East 29th Street, and some 2,000 membership cards were seized. At the same time, raids were carried out against the Rand School and the New York City office of the I.W.W. at 27 East 4th Street.

These harassments came at a time when we were struggling to take over the Socialist Party or to organize a Communist Party. As the delegates were preparing to depart for Chicago, Martens—who

* See Appendix I, p. 231.

77

continued operations despite the raids—became very interested in the labor trouble brewing on the West Coast. The I.W.W., with a national membership of some 350,000 had called a general strike that paralyzed the City of Seattle. The communists wanted it to spread so as to blockade all Pacific Coast ports and force the withdrawal of U.S. troops from Siberia. I was called in for a special assignment—recruiting a force of gangsters and Communist toughs to be dispatched to the scene. Money was supplied by Nuorteva, who served as paymaster for this kind of work.

I made the trip to Seattle myself, stopping off in Chicago for the convention, my first time west of New Jersey. I made some good contacts and a few personal friendships among the Wobblies, but the strike fizzled out and I returned to New York after the first of the New Year.

On New Year's Day, 1920, I read some startling news in a Seattle newspaper: The Cook County District Attorney had ordered a round-up of radicals in Chicago. Hundreds were netted—mostly Communists and Wobblies—but the worst was yet to come. On January 2 there were raids across the country by Attorney General Palmer. The sweep was carefully planned and coordinated to begin at night and, despite the gun-jumping by the District Attorney in Chicago (a Republican), the raids were startlingly successful. In Chicago alone, there were 650 arrests and the national total exceeded 3,000. The action had a paralyzing effect on the two Communist Parties and was a death blow to the I.W.W.

Of those rounded up, only some 400 were actually deported— perfectly legal—a small number considering the furor that has continued over the affair for a half century. The radicals, nearly all of them communists and anarchists, were put aboard two ships—the S. S. *Buford*, dubbed "the Soviet Ark," and the S. S. *Savannah*—and sent back to their native countries, most of them to Russia. Among the passengers were two celebrated anarchists, Emma Goldman and Alexander Berkman.

With scores of ranking Communists deported, Party membership dwindled rapidly. The Communist Party of America had numbered 87,000 dues-paying members, 35,000 in the Russian Language Federation in Chicago and New York. By April, 1921, the total membership was down to less than 3,500 members.

It would seem that the American people owe a debt of gratitude to the memory of U. S. Attorney General A. Mitchell Palmer. Instead of the willful act of an irresponsible government official, as Marxian historians have made them appear, the Palmer Raids simply met the challenge of radicalism. Continuing through 1920, they were an answer to a deadly menace and a clearly spoken popular demand. Before World War I, only two states, New York and Tennessee, had sedition laws, and no one had ever been prosecuted under them. But by the end of 1919, outraged by radical excesses, 35 states had enacted such laws.

During my absence, things had been happening in New York. On the evening of November 8, police and staff members of the Lusk Committee staged simultaneous raids on the 71 local headquarters of the Communist Party of America in the five boroughs. Over 1,000 persons were rounded up, but most were released after questioning.

Among those held for grand jury action was Ben Gitlow, a former Socialist Assemblyman and a founder of the Communist Labor Party. He was tried and convicted of criminal anarchy and sentenced to five to ten years in Sing Sing. Although his career as a Red leader continued for some time after his release from prison, he eventually quit the movement and became one of the country's leading fighters against communism.

Another arrested was James Larkin, an Irishman who had helped found the radical Irish Transport Workers Union and was later deported from the United States after serving a prison term in Sing Sing.

Martens was arrested on November 14, after he had ignored a summons to appear before the committee as a witness. Compelled later to testify, he acknowledged he had received $90,000 from Soviet Russia but refused to tell what he had done with the money or to name the couriers who had brought it to him. Pressed for answers, Martens, through his attorney Dudley Field Malone, claimed diplomatic immunity. But the claim was brushed aside by State Supreme Court Justice Samuel Greenbaum, and Martens was held in contempt. Free in $1,000 bail, he fled to Washington, D. C.

Martens* and Nuorteva** were both deported in early 1920. Martens turned up later as the Soviet Ambassador to Turkey and Nuorteva became a Party functionary in Moscow.

* See Appendix I, p. 231.
** See Appendix I, p. 232.

CHAPTER XI

To me, on my return home from Seattle, New York was a cold and lonely city. Martens' bureau was closed. The communists and socialists with whom I had associated were in hiding or had been deported. But the "revolution" was not totally dead. Gregory Weinstein and a few others were still operating, mainly from an isolated farmhouse near Peekskill, New York, and they immediately put me to work. I was ordered to round up used typewriters and mimeograph machines to produce handbills in a Lower East Side tenement basement.

I was a kid of 20, full of life and fired by a rabid belief that Marxism was the salvation of the human race. Better educated than most people of the era, I had graduated from Erasmus Hall High School in Brooklyn in 1919. More than 2,000 students attended this highly rated institution, famed for its Latin studies, and every one of them studied the classic language. When I visit the place today, not far from my home, its Gothic entrance under the lofty, castle-like tower looks old instead of impressive.

My sister Elsie was employed in the fur trade, and helped me to get a job in the industry. I became an apprentice, and went to work for Hausman & Berlin, who had a loft at 30 West 26th Street, After three months, I became a full-fledged machine operator, sewing skins for fur coats.

The Furriers' Union was headed by Morris Kaufman, president of the International Fur Workers' Union of the United States and Canada, with headquarters at Nine Jackson Avenue in Long Island City, Queens. Its leaders were socialists and radicals and their political thought was reflected in an article by Dr. Judah L. Magnes which appeared in the union's publication, *The Fur Worker,* in March, 1920. It began:

"Soviet Russia stands as a beacon on the hilltop, cheering on the agonizing people with a light in the darkness, with new hopes and philosophies, with wondrous longing . . ."

But the leaders of the union were not disciplined Marxists, and it was gangster controlled. I was one of those assigned the task of delivering the fur workers to the Communists.

No one suspected, apparently, that a kid of my age could hold a position of importance in the Party, and I made progress in the Furriers' Union. I joined Operators' Local Five and became acquainted with Ben Gold and other young radicals. Gold had just returned from Mexico, where he had fled to evade the draft during the war. He came under the eye of Fanny Warshafsky, who paraded as a vociferous socialist who had a mania for young, good-looking men, but was actually a secret Communist Party member. She took Gold under her wing, developed him into a good Hebrew-Yiddish speaker and used her influence to push him into a prominent position in the Furriers' Union.

Gold was then about 25, good looking, with long black hair, combed back, and rosy cheeks; he had strong appeal to women like Fanny. The Communists found him a good asset—he was willing to take orders and was a perfect front man.

I worked hard, and sometimes not too secretly, to help take over the union from the Kaufman crowd. First, we set up a branch of the Trade Union Educational League for younger members, and gradually won over a number of them to communist views. The come-on was that all decent people should unite to kick out the racketeers, a truly worthwhile cause.

The League held meetings at the old Manhattan Lyceum at 66 East 45th Street, and it was here one night that we undertook a premature test of our rival's strength. Between 800 and 900 fur workers had gathered for a monthly union meeting. The leaders had stationed goons about the hall, a usual precaution, where they could pounce on any member who dared open his mouth to criticize union policy. We had taken steps to have two of our men flanking each union bouncer. The goons were armed with knives and blackjacks, while our men carried lead pipes wrapped in newspapers.

At a signal—I lifted my handkerchief from my jacket pocket—Ben Gold rose and started toward the speaker's platform, demanding to be heard. When one of the goons standing near the platform made for Gold, a free-for-all broke out immediately in every part of the hall. Suddenly the lights went out, and for the next few minutes the near total darkness resounded with shouting, curses and the sounds of combat. When the lights came on again, there were 15 casualties.

As the police arrived, my men stood about innocently, having tossed away their weapons. The casualties were loaded aboard ambulances and carted away. I was in good shape, except for a swollen fist which I kept carefully concealed in a jacket pocket. I had injured my hand on the jaw of "Big English," one of the leaders of the strong-arm squad. In the light, he stormed around, cursing and holding his jaw. I'm sure he doesn't know yet who hit him.

Another casualty was Harry Yurman, a goon who was picked off the floor near where I had been standing when the lights went out. He never knew what hit him, but an educated guess would be that it was a fist wrapped inside brass knuckles.

Nearly every one of our men managed to get back to his job next day, where the fur market hummed with gossip. At noon, groups stood on the sidewalks talking about the "riot." Who had dared to start trouble in the union? It was unheard of! The consensus was that there had been a rank and file uprising which the goons had put down.

That evening, immediately after work, I quickly composed a leaflet which was distributed next day throughout the fur district. It was in the name of the Fur Section of the Trade Union Educational League and began:

"Kaufman Gangsters Stab and Wound Furriers at Union Meeting!
Drive the Gangsters Out! Kaufman Must Go!"

A tag line defended Soviet Russia.

The following night I was called to a meeting of the Central Executive Committee of the Communist Party. We were introduced to a visitor, who had just arrived from Russia—"John Pepper." Also known as "Joseph Schwartz" and "Joseph Goldberg," his real name was Joseph Pogany.* He had been sent as the official representative of the Third International and held the posi-

*See Appendix I, p. 232.

82

tion of Lenin's personal emissary to the American branch of the Party.

When he rose to speak, talking in German, Pepper was received with awe. One of the first things he did was to congratulate me on the methods I had employed among the fur workers. I had displayed the right kind of initiative, he said, in getting out leaflets immediately after the fight at the union meeting. My tactics had assured us of a moral victory. We had fought for what was honest and decent and had taken the part of the underdog. We had won sympathy among the fur workers that would reward us greatly, Pepper predicted, in the days to come.

He then plunged into an outline of the strategy we were to use in winning over the union. I was placed in command of the action committee, and was to have a free hand in the propaganda campaign. The *Freiheit*, official Communist Jewish organ, was to be placed at my disposal, and I was to receive funds from the Profintern Section of the Third International through the T.U.E.L., which Foster had brought to the Party.

I found myself working almost every waking hour. In addition to holding a full-time job with Hausman & Berlin, I was busy far into the night with Communist duties. I had taken on two new jobs—as a member of the national committee of the T.U.E.L. and in the Friends of Soviet Russia, which had been created as a "liberal" buffer in the early days of the movement. Sidney Hillman, head of the Amalgamated Clothing Workers Union (and a Communist) was the financial angel of this early front. For this, and other services to the Party, he received the personal blessings of Lenin during a visit to Russia in 1921. On his return, Hillman tried to establish the Russian-American Textile Syndicate to promote a business partnership between American textile manufacturers and Moscow. But Americans of that day would have nothing to do with the scheme and it died a quick death.

The presidential election of 1920, ushering in a Republican administration, had put an end to the Palmer raids, but the police—and Federal authorities—remained alert and active. A raid on Communist Party headquarters at 799 Broadway, near Eleventh Street, almost netted me. I just managed to escape from the building, but at 14th Street, I was suddenly confronted by Jake Spolansky and Tony Taplovsky, agents of the Department of Justice. Taplovsky pointed to me and shouted: "There goes that little communist bastard!" Spolansky grabbed me by the collar and, with a shake, told me to "Beat it!" He gave me a parting kick in the pants and a warning: "If I ever see you around here again, I'll break your neck!"

Although my pride was hurt, I smiled when the two agents disappeared. Had Spolansky searched my pockets, he would have found the membership list of the entire Party in New York State!

At age 20, I was assistant to Harry Winitzky, the State Secretary of the Party, and in charge of the City Central Committee. My headquarters were at Delancey and Rivington Streets on the Lower East Side, in a place called the Minsk Relief Society. But when we held a meeting of the full City Committee—generally to hear some speaker who had just arrived from Moscow—I would rent a hall near the Bowery, at 11 East Third Street. The members would gather in darkness, and not until we had taken the precaution of stationing look-outs at the windows and in the street, would the lights be turned on and the meeting opened.

At one such gathering in 1920, I read a letter handed to me by a courier, just arrived from Russia. The message was from Lenin and had been dispatched by Nikolai Bukharin. It saluted American Communists for their "heroic" stand against the Palmer raids and applauded the "revolutionary bravery, zeal and integrity" which enabled them to withstand "persecution and police terror." It ended with the words: "Long live the American Communist Party! Long live the American revolutionary movement! On for a Soviet America!"

Lenin's message was in sharp contrast to other Red reactions to us. We were bombarded by criticism from Communists abroad—demands to know why the American Party had lost its influence and dwindled to almost nothing. It was easier to ask questions from Moscow or Guatemala than to face the American people in 1920. I firmly believe that had the country remained on the alert, with city, state and federal officials maintaining the same high vigilance against subversion, Communist influence would have remained insignificant. This is to suppose that the "intelligentsia" would have found other obsessions than the doctrines of Karl Marx. The fact is that Ivy League socialists and "liberals" popularized a theory few of them understood and played the decisive role in halting the prosecution of Communists after convincing themselves and the country that these revolutionaries were only idealists struggling to make a better world in a backward region of the earth. The surprising thing is that they go on preaching this line, even after communism, time and again for a half century, is proven to be a brutal tyranny. What does it take to awaken some people to reality?

Throughout this period, the Communists were bitterly fighting among themselves and confusion reigned. But in the winter of 1920 word came from Lenin himself that the warring factions were to unite, or they would both be expelled. The "unity" convention, after buck-passing and in-fighting, was held in May, 1921, at an isolated farm near Woodstock, New York. The house, I recall, was owned or leased by Alfred Wagenknecht, Executive Secretary of the Communist Labor Party. Placed in charge of security, I recruited 125 trusted Party workers, most of them Russians and Finns. They were arranged in a guard line that stretched from the railroad station at Beacon to Woodstock, and from Woodstock to the farm. Each was armed with a flashlight and had instructions to flash a signal to the man ahead of him should police or any suspicious person appear on the road.

After five days of bickering, but ever mindful of the order from Lenin, we agreed to merge and form the United Communist Party. Within six months, however, the title was changed to the Communist Party of America.

A small dissident communist labor group remained outside the new alliance.

Lenin again gave the Party inspiration with a cablegram which I received and read at a meeting of the Central Executive Committee. It was the famous message that stated: "If the American Party remains underground it will stifle to death. Propose immediate setup of legal apparatus."

This was taken under consideration by Joseph Brodsky and other top Party attorneys. They advised us to set up a legal party, which was to function as an open political organization, but with the controlling agency kept underground. We called the two organizations *number one* and *number two;* the first was the underground apparatus and the second a legal sham.

We received another message from Lenin: "You talk so much about workers—aren't there any farmers in America?"

Overnight, the Party became interested in agriculture. Most of us hadn't been to a farm since leaving the old country—many had never seen one. Since we knew almost nothing about American agriculture we sent a delegation to Moscow to learn "first-hand" about the U.S. farm problem from Lenin. This quest was led by Harold Ware, son of Ella Reeve Bloor, famous in the Movement as "Mother Bloor." Lemuel Harris, who later worked on farm research in Washington while linked with Max Bedacht, J. Peters and William Weiner in industrial and military intelligence, went with Ware to Russia, Ware remained in Moscow until late 1922 or early 1923. He later organized the notorious "Ware" cell in Henry Wallace's Department of Agriculture during the early New Deal days.

CHAPTER XII

In 1921 the Communist International adopted the first of its many tortuous tactical maneuvers. "Pure" communism was abandoned in favor of something more opportunistic. It called for two "united fronts," one from above and the other from below. From above, a pact would be made between Communists and leaders of non-Communist organizations, with the understanding between both that the Communists would take over. From below, Communists would undertake, through stealth, to capture a group through the cooperation of "liberals" and "intellectuals" who were willing to do business with them.

This theory developed after Lenin witnessed the agonizing, stunning defeat of the Red Army by the Poles at the Battle of Warsaw. Part of my information on this historical battle came to me first-hand from my brother Joseph who was a Red Army intelligence Commissar directly under Trotsky on the Polish front. The Soviet troops had swept across Poland to the very gates of the city, when suddenly the Poles opened a counter-attack on August 17, 1920. By the 21st, the Russians were in headlong retreat, ending with the armistice of October 10. By the Treaty of Riga, the Polish boundary was set far to the east, where it remained until 1939.

This was bitter dregs indeed to the Communists. Once again the workers had "failed." The confident boasts that the proletariat of Poland had deserted the bourgeois mocked them in the empty silence of their defeat. Trotsky had warned against over-confidence that the Poles would revolt: "The Polish workers haven't the organization to lead them and neither have they the means or readiness to revolt." Lenin disagreed: "As soon as the Red Army reaches the gates of Warsaw the Polish workers will revolt and, together with our Red Army, will establish a Polish Soviet Government." Later, he acknowledged his mistake and paid tribute to Trotsky's wisdom. A year before he died, he stated at the Central Committee meeting of the Russian Communist Party: "On the Polish 1920 campaign against Poland, Trotsky was right and I was wrong."*

Lenin was quick to rally with orders that the Communists were now to become a stalking tiger, winning by stealth what frontal attack had failed to obtain.

In the United States this brought a maneuver toward labor that ushered William Z. Foster and Earl Browder into the Party. Lenin first startled, then dumbfounded, his American followers by demanding that they join craft labor unions and work from within. It was a complete reversal of the historical dogma that permitted no temporizing with a craft union. But by adhering to this principle, the Communists had automatically placed themselves outside the labor movement in America. When Lenin issued his demand for a more vigorous labor policy, the Communists had to go outside their fold and take in Foster and Browder.

Foster founded the Trade Union Educational League in Chicago in 1920, after the failure of the steel strike he had led in nearby Gary, Indiana. The T.U.E.L. became the main hope of the Communists in the labor field after Foster, Browder and "Mother" Bloor visited the Soviet Union in 1921—a historic trip financed largely by Sidney Hillman's Amalgamated Clothing Workers. Moscow accepted Browder and Foster, and adopted the Trade Union Educational League. The Kremlin hoped to influence American workers through organization, rather than ideology, by banding the workers together to be captured en masse by the Communists and converted into a political force for the creation of a Soviet America.

The abandonment of "pure" ideology in favor of this expedient theory called for profound new thinking. It touched off turmoil inside Marxist circles that has continued to this day. Lenin, in his *Letter to American Working Men,* had called for a death struggle against "bourgeois reforms" and "bourgeois institutions," especially the American Federation of Labor. The *Communist,* in 1919, had echoed the line: "Trade unionism is the arch enemy of the militant proletariat." Charles Ruthenberg, as leader of the Communist Party of America, is on record: "The Communist Party of 1919 stood out-

*Statement to Christian Rakorsky, an old-time Bolshevik who was a member of the Central Executive Committee.

side the labor movement, endeavoring to draw the workers into its ranks through agitation and propaganda which pointed to the necessity of a revolutionary party fighting for the overthrow of capitalism."

The defeat before Warsaw called for an "agonizing" re-appraisal —new conditions demanded new tactics. Lenin hastened to draw up a blueprint that has guided Communist strategy until this day.

But even before Warsaw, in the spring of 1920, Lenin had written *Left-Wing Communism: An Infantile Disorder.* He was already faulting the "ultra-left," and saw the necessity of Communists participating in "bourgeois parliaments," even as the Bolsheviks had taken part, after faction fights within, in the hagglings of the provisional government in Russia in the summer of 1917. Lenin came to scorn communists who could not see the need for "compromise* and maneuver," even compromise with opportunism—which he had been among the first to abhor.

Overnight, every Communist in the world was ordered to change his mind. Most did—but some refused.

Old-line Communists, like Reed and Hourwich, could not change. To them, the abandonment of a faith that seemed so simple and direct in favor of something devious and complex was madness. The old Bolsheviks were perplexed and angry. The 1919 vintage communist became a political anachronism.

At first they tried to pretend that they had not heard correctly. But Lenin demanded that they join the hated craft unions and other "reactionary" bourgeois organizations.

Reed and Fraina, leaders of the two opposing factions of the Party, had gone to Moscow in 1920 to settle their differences and were there caught in this new twist of the Party line. Fraina, always an opportunist, quickly gave in; but Reed refused to surrender, and managed publicly to get away with his defiance. It was the *last time* any American Communist openly opposed the Moscow leadership and survived in the Party. But beyond a personal victory, Reed's opposition was meaningless.

When orders were received in New York to enter the labor movement and take it over, union by union, I was one of those chosen to pioneer this effort. Our first objective was the International Fur

---

*Not to be confused with *compromise,* as non-Communists would use the word. Lenin's *compromise* is merely a tactical move.

Workers Union and Eneo Sormenti was assigned to help me do the job.*

He claimed to have fled Trieste, where he was a top Communist agent, and had recently arrived here as a stowaway. He boasted that he had manned the barricades against Mussolini's Black Shirts, and had organized the general strike that gripped Trieste in June, 1921. He said that his top associate in Italy was "M. Ercoli"—better known to the world later by his real name, Palmiro Togliatti, chief of Italy's sprawling Communist Party—who was then in Moscow hiding from the Fascists.

With a wink and a look that suggested he knew far more than he was willing to tell, Sormenti boasted that he had established contact with the Mafia in Sicily and had worked out an agreement whereby international gangsters worked for international communism in return for narcotics supplied by Moscow. If the Communists wanted someone murdered, the Mafia was obligated to do the job.

Mussolini's top agent in New York, Count Revel, was trying to organize fascist action squads among the Italians. He had met with some success, which both angered and embarrassed the Communists. Although Mussolini and the fascists were socialists, they were *national*, not *international* socialists, and this the Communists could not tolerate. Sormenti wanted a head-on collision with the Count's forces—to create a challenge that would echo in the newspapers. I stalled him by insisting he first have a talk with John Pepper and Charles E. Ruthenberg, who was General Secretary of the Communist Party. Sormenti was a stranger to me, and I had no intention of saddling myself with one of his schemes without the backing of Party leaders.

I finally arranged for a meeting with Ruthenberg and Pepper, who knew each other from Moscow, to put Sormenti's plan before them. Pepper was enthusiastic as Sormenti outlined a plan to recruit tough, Marxist-trained Italian youths for a strong-arm squad that we could use to break up fascist meetings. The go-ahead signal was given, and I began recruiting personnel. Joseph Brodsky gave me the necessary legal advice and also put me in touch with underworld figures he had defended in criminal court.

*Nearly 40 years later, Sormenti would be loaned to Castro by Moscow to help him organize Cuba.

Pepper and Sormenti, I later discovered, had been associates in Moscow and were tough taskmasters. Pepper was cautious and Sormenti daring, but both believed in thorough planning. It was not until almost a year later, on Columbus Day, 1924, that we made our first move in public.

The fascists had planned a mass demonstration at the statue of Giuseppe Garibaldi on Staten Island, and a crowd of several thousand gathered for the occasion—most of them sincere in paying tribute to the great Italian leader of unification. Early that day a strong-arm squad of over 50 men was assembled in a tenement on 13th Street, between First Avenue and Avenue A, where we had a cache of arms. Sormenti, with a sureness in his quick commands, armed his men before leading them to the Third Avenue "El." We rode to the South Ferry and took the first boat to Staten Island.

Among Sormenti's chief aides were Pete Benccich, "Bambino" Milano, Frank Minela and Francesco Coco. We approached the celebration singing *Bandiera Rosa* (Red Flag) and *Noi Bolsheviki* (Hail Bolsheviks) in Italian. Although I spoke little Italian. I'd learned the words while Sormenti was teaching them to the squad. We broke off singing as we neared the crowd and began to run. We shouted *"A la morte Mussolini!"* ("Death to Mussolini!") and *"Ell Vivo Communismo!"* ("Long live communism!").

Our opponents were caught flat-footed as we tore into them, shooting, slashing and swinging lead pipes wrapped in newspapers. It was a quick, cowardly and brutal attack. We took to our heels before they could recover, leaving 20 wounded fascists on the ground.

Although we had a few casualties ourselves, we managed to take them with us back to the ferry. In Manhattan, we had our wounded treated in secret by Communist doctors.

The attack made headlines in all the newspapers and was discussed in radical circles for weeks. Many believed that the Communists were tightly and mysteriously organized, able to strike a lightening blow and slip below the pavement. It was the kind of impression we wanted. We had surprised and defeated the fascists, and we were clever—too clever to be caught by the police.

"This is what we have been waiting for," Ruthenberg said. "Now we are getting somewhere! Things are going to start happening!"

One night, while sitting with Sormenti in his apartment on 13th Street, near First Avenue, we discussed the Mafia, one of his favorite subjects. He assured me that if it became necessary to resort to violence he need only say the word in the right quarter to bring the criminal empire to our aid. Included among those who did strong-arm work for the Communist Party were such famous gangsters as Anthony Cafano, known as "Little Augie Pisano," and Jack "Legs" Diamond. Sormenti and I even succeeded in later winning over some hoods to Marxism, among them Pietro Lucchi, who became Secretary-Treasurer in the Communist-controlled fur union. I also managed to contact about 600 Greek longshoremen and underworld characters who, for a price, pledged their support.

At a conference one afternoon at Party headquarters, with P. Gus-sev, Communist International Representative in the United States, we decided to hire two of the most prominent lawyers in New York City, Goodman & Snitkin. They had made a specialty of defending professional criminals, and had no ideology other than making a dollar. Brodsky met them next day and outlined our "problem"—the capture of the fur union. Goodman & Snitkin gave their legal advice: talk to Arnold Rothstein, underworld banker and king of the gam-blers.

I was present at the meeting. Rothstein promised to loan the Com-munist Party $1,775,000 at a rate of interest exceeding 25 percent. Repayment of the loan was guaranteed by Amtorg, the Russian-American Trading Corporation, which had recently opened offices on lower Broadway.

Rothstein also agreed to put us in touch with police officials and Magistrates who were on his regular payroll. As the Communist organizer of the strike we planned, I became the paymaster for these corrupt cops and judges who were to look the other way when the rough stuff started.

We were particularly eager to secure the aid, or at least the neu-trality, of police in the areas where the fur industry was located—the Mercer Street, Fifth, West 30th and 47th Street stations. We received the assurance of many police that they would not take action against our gang. In cases where newspaper publicity might make booking a necessity, we had the assurance of the Magistrates that charges would be quietly disposed of.

I sometimes meet people today who accepted those bribes. We are in the same boat, in a way—sincerely sorry for what we did. In their defense it should be noted that it was during an era of "liberalism," when it was no longer prudent to prosecute radicals. Indeed, in many "intellectual" circles it had again become the fashion to have a Communist in for tea.

In the midst of these preparations to capture the fur union from the Kaufman gang in October, 1923, we suddenly received word from Joseph in Moscow. He was about to depart for New York.

He and his wife, Maria Davidovma, whom we had never seen, arrived first-class aboard the White Star liner *Olympic,* one of the finest passenger ships of the day. Joseph, a representative of the unrecognized Bolshevik government, and his fair, blonde-haired wife, were ushered off to Ellis Island.

I had escorted Mother and my sisters to the pier, but when I learned what had happened, I hailed a cab and took them home. Next day, presenting myself as a member of Brodsky's law firm, I obtained a pass and took the ferry to Ellis Island. I had not been there since 1914 and the journey brought memories which were not entirely pleasant. Joseph was angry and impatient. I told him to relax and we would have him free within a day.

Acting on Brodsky's advice, I had been in touch with Representative Nathan D. Perlman, of the 14th Congressional District in Manhattan, who agreed to lodge a protest with the government in Washington. Working through Edward Corsi, who was then a commissioner of immigration, Perlman got an order for the release of Joseph and Maria, in $10,000 bond each.

The Congressman telephoned from Washington with the good news and I hurried back to Ellis Island to post bond. In little more than an hour, Joseph and Maria were on a ferry headed for New York and our apartment on the Lower East Side.

Joseph, as a top official of the Soviet government, was plentifully supplied with money and could easily have stayed at the swankiest hotel in the city. Instead, he and Maria chose to share our tenement at 284 East Third Street, between Avenues C and D. Besides wanting to be with the family, there was, of course, a matter of appearance involved. For propaganda purposes it looked better to have a representative of the "only Socialist Government on earth" living among the proletariat in a tenement than among the bourgeois in capitalist luxury.

It was wonderful to have Joseph with us, and there were seven days of celebrating—with the house open to friends, relatives and hundreds of Party workers and fellow travelers.

Three days after his arrival, while we were alone one night, Joseph opened his luggage and took out two leather bags. Hidden inside were handfuls of diamonds, emeralds and other precious stones. I recalled the glittering pile of gems the naked sailor had dumped on Martens' desk five years before.

I went with Joseph next day to the Amtorg office on lower Broadway, near, ironically, Wall Street. The Soviet central trade unit included agricultural and industrial representatives and a motion picture department, *Prolet-Kino*. Actually, the main interest was industrial and military espionage.

Joseph held a brief conference with the Russian officials after showing them his credentials, signed by Lenin, which identified him as a member of the all-powerful Central Executive Committee of the Russian Communist Party.

In a cab on the way home, Joseph asked me for the address of his old roommate, David Dubinsky, who had risen to eminence in the International Ladies' Garment Workers' Union. He also asked me to pick up tickets for the Moscow Art Theater production of *The Brothers Karamazov*, which was playing at the Al Jolson Theater, 59th Street and Seventh Avenue. He handed me a wad of bills to buy tickets for Maria, him and me. He was anxious to compare the performances as presented in the U.S.S.R. and in the U.S.A.

Joseph and I settled easily into our old habit of discussing Marxism, the revolution, and the future of the Party in America. Joseph explained in detail the meaning of Lenin's new doctrine of compromise and maneuver. He said that the people, left to themselves, might reject socialism and that we Communists must be skilled enough to present it to them in disguise, until they learned to accept it. This was counter to the Marxist theory of inevitability, but I stilled my doubts, listened to Joseph and was convinced. An important concept, he stressed, was secrecy—the necessity of guarding against premature exposure.

It was sufficient that a few trustworthy leaders knew what the plan was—"It is not necessary to shout our plans from the house tops." The role of the Communist rank and file was to see that the plan was put into operation. Discipline was the key. "Discipline," he repeated. "Absolute, unquestioning discipline!"

In this light, he analyzed our plans for the fur strike. We had started well—our plans were a deep secret. When the order came we should act ruthlessly to carry out our mission. This was where discipline would come in. I went over with him in detail the preparations we had made for a general strike in the fur industry and he offered some suggestions—which I quickly adopted and put into operation.

One day I went with Joseph to the Bronx to visit several jewelers to whom he had been referred to dispose of the precious stones he had brought from Russia. We visited a wholesale jewelry outlet on Bryant Avenue and another on Webster Avenue. The owners of both places were trusted members of the Communist Party, and the establishments were frequently used by Soviet agents as mail drops. Joseph left quantities of jewelry at both places.

Late in the evening of January 21, 1924, Joseph received news that Lenin was dead.

There was no sleep at our house that night. Visitors came and left. A cablegram was received from Moscow.

Joseph and Maria expressed their fears of what might happen in Russia and one name was mentioned with dreaded foreboding, that of "the mad Georgian." I had never heard the nickname before and was told that they meant Stalin. They described him as an ambitious, scheming, ruthless opportunist, who was already locked with Trotsky in a struggle for power. They predicted that in the event Stalin won, Felix Dzerzhinsky, head of the dreaded Cheka, would begin a bloody purge of Stalin's enemies. First on the list would be Trotsky.

Joseph knew intimately the leading figures of the Party because he had worked closely with them to promote the revolution. He worked under Trotsky in the diplomatic service, and in 1920, was the Red Army Commissar in charge of intelligence on the Polish front. The Soviet defeat had given Stalin and Dzerzhinsky ammunition for use against Trotsky and his friends.

CHAPTER XIII

Lenin's death had a profound effect on New York Communists and socialists, and also a great outpouring of "liberal" sympathy. The Communist Party organized a Lenin memorial demonstration at the old Madison Square Garden a few days after his death. Joseph, Maria and I occupied seats of honor reserved for us by the arrangements committee headed by Joseph and Carl Brodsky.

When we reached the Garden about 7:30 P.M., the great auditorium where the Democratic Party would shortly hold its longest and most futile convention was filled to the rafters. The street doors were closed against a great crowd unable to gain admission. We found David Dubinsky and his wife, Emma, sitting in the same row with us.

The meeting opened with an orchestra playing the "Internationale," as the audience stood at attention and joined in the singing. Then came the "Red Funeral March." Then in hushed silence, Moissaye J. Olgin, editor of the *Freiheit*, rose and began to speak. During the evening, speakers were interrupted by different groups yelling out carefully rehearsed slogans: "Lenin Is dead! Long live Leninism!" "Long live the Soviet Union!" "Down with American Capitalism!" "Long Live the Revolution!" "Long Live the Third International!"

The meeting ended by 11:30, but it was after midnight before we could get out of the Garden. Joseph, Maria, Carl Brodsky, the Dubinskys and I went to a restaurant on 57th Street, near Carnegie Hall, for a late supper.

George Lehman, from the Mohegan colony in Peekskill, an old-time socialist who had married one of Joseph's old sweethearts, came over and joined our party. Lehman had turned to bootlegging and profitably supplied liquor for the New York trade until his business disappeared with the repeal of the Volstead Act. He and Dubinsky were close friends.

When we reached home, Joseph discussed the necessity of his immediate return to Russia. He would need permission from Gregori Zinoviev, head of the Comintern, and he resolved next day to send him a cable. Because of the confusion in Moscow, Zinoviev's reply did not come until eary March. Joseph was ordered back to the Soviet Union. Once again, on a cold, damp day, I took Mother and my sisters to the docks to say goodbye to Joseph. He and Maria Davidovma sailed aboard the Cunard liner, *Aquitania* from Pier 54 on the Hudson River. Father, as we left the house, had kissed Joseph and then, sitting on a stool, began a *shiva,* or seven days of mourning for the dead, while repeating to himself that he would never see Joseph again. This time he was right; he never did.

As we stood with the crowd in the raw March cold, Joseph kept repeating words of comfort to my Mother and praise for the work I was doing. The ship's whistle sounded a hoarse warning. Joseph kissed Elsie and Bertha, and held Mother tightly for a long moment. Then he turned quickly, with a motion for me to follow him to the gangplank. Maria had gone on ahead. He put an arm across my shoulder and said that I was "a good son of the revolution." I had lived up to his hopes for me. Then he followed Maria, and I stood alone, saddened by the mist I had seen in his blue eyes.

At home, Father sat with bare feet, reciting psalms and prayers for the dead. Joseph had been his favorite son, and he had dearly hoped that Joseph might some day become a rabbi. As in the Bible, his was the story of Jacob and Joseph—of Jacob grieving for the son he had lost.

I plunged deeply into organizational work, getting ready for the capture of the fur union. Things moved smoothly until the union's annual convention in 1925, which was held in Boston at the America House. Charles E. Ruthenberg, the General Secretary of the Communist Party, very nearly wrecked a carefully laid plan by sending us orders via a Western Union telegram. Addressed to the Communist group at the hotel, it read "Utilize Straus-Schactman-Sorkin group to capture convention. Then rid union of the reactionaries." Intercepted by the Kaufman crowd, the telegram was read to the delegates at the convention, and created a furor. We had gone to a great deal of trouble and expense to secretly purchase the allegiance of the powerful Philadelphia delegation who did not approve of the gangster elements who were involved with Schactman. Delegates began asking questions, and to cover ourselves we "angrily" labeled the telegram a forgery. We denied we had made any pact with gangsters and claimed that our entire program was based on the desire to rid the union of the gangsters who supported the Kaufman regime.

By one such ruse and another, we succeeded in electing a national leadership that saw Oiser Schactman installed as president of the union. This was enough. We rushed back to New York and began final preparations for the general strike.

The loan from Arnold Rothstein had come through, and arrangements were made with the underworld to supply us with goon squads to force both workers and shop owners to fall into line. We were assured that key police and magistrates would be with us.

Long before this, we had carefully organized what we called the Committee of One Thousand to bear the brunt of picketing. Members of this committee were promised financial rewards and the best jobs in the industry once the strike was settled.

Everything prepared, we called a strike and issued our demands. For the first time in any industry, we demanded a 40-hour work week, a closed union shop and an average wage increase of 25 percent. The American Federation of Labor, branding us as Communists, refused to support our demands. But we knew that our program would appeal powerfully to the self-interest of the workers and would bring us the publicity we so badly needed as the "defenders of labor."

In charge of picketing were Samuel Mencher and Jack Schneider, both Communists. Schneider was ordered deported almost 30 years later by the federal government.

With Rothstein's money, we rented eight halls at strategic locations in which to house the pickets. A reserve strong-arm squad was housed at Astoria Hall, 60 East Fourth Street, where the headquarters of our general staff was also located. There was another terror gang in Beethoven Hall on Fifth Street and one on Eighth Street, between Second and Third Avenues, where I had my private headquarters. Here was also housed the "Out-Of Town Committee," which watched for any New York shops that tried to flee and set up outside the city. It was one of my responsibilities.

I had at my disposal a tactical detail of 56 picked union members and 22 professional gangsters. When a run-away shop opened at

Spring Valley, in Rockland County, New York, I used my squad to stage a lightning raid. We arrived on the scene in five automobiles, which included 13 members of the industrial, or gangster, squad of the New York Police Department, and kidnapped 22 workers and brought them back to Manhattan. To keep them silent, we assured them that if they cooperated they would receive full pay for the remainder of the strike and would have their jobs back once it was settled. But if they chose not to cooperate, they were warned to look out for their own safety and that of their families.

It should be added as a footnote that every one of these employees, despite the assurances, was driven from the industry. They were simply fined $9,999 each and, lacking the money to pay the union, were automatically barred from employment.

The kidnapping reached the attention of the *Jewish Daily Forward*, which had not supported us in the strike. Headlines told of Communists kidnapping fur workers in Rockland County. Although the paper had most of the facts, the authorities never did anything about it.

The strike started in February, 1926, and for 17 weeks I didn't once sleep in my own bed. I managed to get home sometimes for a change of clothing, but that was all.

In April we received word that two large shops had combined and opened new quarters at Rockville Centre, on Long Island's south shore. I immediately called a meeting of the action committee, the leading Communist Party members in the Union. It was decided that we should send an investigator to find out what actually was going on. Chosen was a man named Rosenbloom, who was a friend of two owners of the run-away shop, the Barnett brothers. He reported that the Company had incorporated under New York State law, and employed about 15 workers. He gave a general description of the building and its location.

The next day, Saturday, April 17, a meeting of the general strike committee was called. Ben Gold heatedly spoke. The Rockville Centre shop should be closed at once, he insisted. Behind his urgency was the fact that the strike had hit a low in morale and the workers were in a dangerous mood. A few more days, the way things were going, and they would go back to work. Action had to be taken to boost the sagging morale. But despite Gold's plea, no action was voted. Instead, I agreed to go out on Monday and look over the situation. To accompany me, I picked a young union member, Leon Franklin, and we rode out together on the Long Island Railroad.

We located the building at the corner of Observer Street and Central Avenue by noon, took out placards we had brought with us and began picketing in front of the main entrance. We intended to remain until the workers knocked off that afternoon, but about 2:30 cries of fear and pain, with shouts for help, suddenly came from the upper windows. The fur shop was on the third floor, and on the second floor was a Chinese restaurant—where a woman stood in a window screaming for the police.

"Let's get the hell out of here!" I said to Franklin. We dropped our placards in the hallway of the building and started walking toward the railroad station, but before we got there we were stopped by a police car. Rockville Centre was then only a small village where everybody knew everybody else who lived there. We were strangers.

We were taken to police headquarters, without explanation, and locked in separate cells. Soon, people were brought to see us, some of whom yelled angrily: "That's them, those two bastards! They are the killers! That's two of them! Kill the bastards!"

I was bewildered, and began fumbling for a cigarette—but the police had emptied my pockets. I began to make demands. I wanted a lawyer; I wanted to know what I was charged with.

The only replies were curses.

Franklin and I were handcuffed and taken out of our cells about 9:00 at night. Under heavy guard, we were put in an automobile, proceeded and followed by detectives armed with rifles and sawed-off shotguns. I asked a patrolman next to me what it was all about. He struck me across the mouth.

We were driven to Nassau County Police Headquarters at Mineola. Here, we were again searched and locked in separate cells. An hour later, about midnight, I was taken out and taken to an office where three men in shirt sleeves confronted me. They began to threaten me, demanding that I tell the truth and "give the names of the other members of the gang!"

"What gang?" I asked

I was knocked to my knees.

Utterly bewildered, I insisted I knew nothing. They worked me over with a rubber hose until I fell unconscious. I awoke in my cell, soaked, I thought, with sweat. I found it was water—the guard had sloshed a bucket of water over me. I sat up and shook my head, and I was taken out again for another session. This went on well into the following day, with the detectives demanding that I tell something I knew nothing about.

Finally, Franklin and I were taken down a corridor to Lt. Harold King, chief of detectives. I couldn't really understand what he said —something about a confession—but I was too weary to make a sound. Then we were taken to a room and told to stand in line with 12 other men, obviously detectives. They had spent a quiet night in bed, were shaved, had on clean shirts and freshly pressed suits. Standing among them, we looked like two shaggy bums. A group of people came in and, of course, picked us out right away as the ones who had committed whatever crime it was we were charged with. And that was still a mystery—I knew nothing.

Back in Lt. King's office, I was handed a statement and told to sign it. I demanded the privilege of reading it over and found that I was accused of being the leader of a Communist gang that had invaded Rockville Centre and brutally assaulted the employees of a fur shop.

I answered, "Not guilty," and refused to sign. So did Franklin. We were taken back to our cells. After the guard had gone, a prisoner in the cell next to Franklin offered to let us see a copy of the *New York Journal*. In red, inch-high headlines it told of Communist gangsters who had wrecked a Rockville Centre fur shop, assaulted the employees and fled in two automobiles. According to the story, police had captured two of the gang, who were left behind.

I began to realize what had happened. I remembered the speech Ben Gold had made, calling for action, for a demonstration that would serve as a warning to workers and employers alike. Behind my back, Gold had sent out a squad to wreck the shop!

Flames seemed to burn deep in me, rising gradually to my face. I sat in my cell, helpless and fuming. I was holding the bag. I was the sacrifice to the Red Revolution in America. I had been trapped by the Judas, Ben Gold.

CHAPTER XIV

I was an idealist. Or perhaps I was naive. I refused to believe that the Communist Party would frame one of its leaders, and pushed from my mind the thought that I was a patsy. No matter how it looked, I could not be convinced that the Party would use me as a scapegoat and promote the interests of a man like Ben Gold. But my morale was sagging.

The detectives gave me the impression that the owners of the fur shop were near death as a result of the beating they had received. One even said that a victim had died and I faced a murder charge.

After two hours of lonely, tormented thought, I was taken from my cell to the basement. Ordered to strip off my jacket and shirt, I was told: "Confess or we'll kill you!" When I refused, a husky detective worked me over with the rubber hose—taking care not to mark my face. He hit me about the back, on the legs and in the stomach until I was knocked unconscious. Later I was revived—I didn't know whether I'd been out for seconds or hours—and the beating resumed. Eventually I lost consciousness again and awoke in a cell, not knowing how I got there, my body one dull, consuming ache. About six hours later I was finally taken before a judge for arraignment. I kept asking my jailers for permission to use a phone, but this was denied me.

After two and a half days in the Nassau County Jail, Franklin and I were handcuffed together and taken to New York in the back of a limousine, flanked by two detectives. We made the trip with a police touring car in front and another behind, both loaded with detectives armed with shotguns and Thompson sub-machine guns.

At Police Headquarters on Centre Street, I recognized detectives and ranking brass who were on the Communist payroll and had accepted money from me. But that didn't stop them from cuffing me around and acting as though I were a stranger.

Afterwards, Franklin and I were taken to the 165th Regiment Armory on Lexington Avenue at 25th Street, where the furriers were assembling at noon, to listen to William Green, president of the A.F.L., who urged them to turn their backs on the communists and settle the strike. Our handcuffs removed, but flanked by detectives, we were ordered to stand just inside the entrance and pick out members of the mob who had gone to Rockville Centre.

My sister Elsie entered with her husband, Willie Wolliver, and came running over to me. She asked where I had been and what had happened, but before I could speak, she was turned away by the police. The was the first that my family knew of my arrest.

The picture of what had happened was beginning to focus, mainly through newspaper stories I'd seen. A gang had entered the shop by a side entrance, around the corner from Franklin and me. Some wore firemen's uniforms—a clever dodge that I had helped work out myself. Firemen were admitted without question to any building for the purpose of inspection. There was never any argument about that. A law requiring inspections had been put into effect, with much publicity, to prevent tragedies which had turned many a loft manufacturing establishment into an inferno of death. Once inside the fur shop, the gang seized Michael and Jack Barnett, the owners. They were beaten and knifed, and were in a hospital for days on the verge of death. Workers were roughed up, machinery smashed beyond repair and nearly a quarter of a million dollars worth of furs ruined. Some had iodine poured over them and many pelts were slashed with knives.

As we stood in the Armory, the detectives kept prodding us to identify members of the gang. I did see a few suspects, Otto Lenhart, Joseph Katz, a fellow who was known as "the knife man" and a couple of Italians from Sormenti's gang—men who were assigned to this kind of work. They were part of the Mafia faction the underworld had loaned us. Franklin and I remained until 2:00 P.M., long after the meeting was over, but we told the police we recognized no one.

The furriers had listened to Green's proposal of a compromise settlement for a 42-hour week, recognition of the union by the industry and a guarantee to raise wages. The Communist leadership turned him down cold and demanded the 40-hour week and a closed shop. This latter point was the real issue because it would guarantee Party control of the entire fur industry—which, of course, was our objective. The meeting resulted in no settlement, and the strike continued.

Franklin and I were taken back to the Mineola jail and kept there five or six days while the investigation continued. I had been arraigned on a charge of felonious assault and, with the victims near death, they could hold me without bail. Meanwhile, Barney Basoff* was placed in a nearby cell. A school chum of the Barnett brothers —they had all been reared in the Limehouse district of London—he was held on similar charges.

After nearly a week, we were called before a County judge on a writ of habeas corpus obtained by attorneys retained by the Communist Party and the union. We were released on $25,000 bail each, the union using some of the Rothstein money to make bond.

We left the Courthouse accompanied by Isidor Shapiro, one of the union's payoff men who later got into trouble over $45,000 of missing funds he couldn't account for, and the bail bondsman, Stitch McCarthy. We went across the street to a hotel, opened a bottle of prohibition-era Scotch and celebrated our release from jail. The union car then took us to the fur workers' headquarters at 22 East 22nd Street in Manhattan, where a tremendous crowd blocked the street in front of the dingy brownstone building between Fourth Avenue and Broadway. When I came into view they all began shouting at once and waving placards which proclaimed: "Welcome home, our martyr and leader! Welcome Comrade Malkin!"

We finally broke through, and I was carried on the shoulders of my admirers to the doorway. The crowd called for a speech, and with two husky strikers holding me aloft I spoke:

"The black forces of reaction, the American Federation of Labor, the bourgeois socialists and the *Jewish Daily Forward*—agents of the bosses—have united to break the strike! They have employed every method they can to smash our union! The brutality of the capitalist police could not break us, so now they are using the frame-up! My arrest and that of comrades Franklin and Basoff have not been a whim. They are intended to strike a serious blow—to weaken the ranks of the revolutionary workers! My arrest is just the beginning of the terror planned by the capitalist bosses. We must prepare and unite our ranks for the intensification of the struggle! Each of us must

---

*Barney Basoff, a furrier worker, was arrested by the police upon the identification of Michael Barnett as one of the gang that had assaulted him.

be prepared to pick up the banner the moment one of our leaders is taken from us.

"The terror will not stop us! No power on earth can stop the furriers in their just battle against the exploiting class and the fur manufacturers! Neither William Green, Matthew Woll, Abe Cohn or the New York Police are going to stop the progress of the struggle of the furriers for final victory! Not even if they frame us, send us to jail or to their torture chambers! In the end we shall triumph! Long Live the Revolutionary Fur Workers! Long live the Communist Party that leads them! On with the struggle!"

When I finally got inside the building and to the second floor, I met Ben Gold, Jack Schneider* and Irving Potash—they each grasped my hand clapping me on the shoulders. They had listened to my speech from the window and told me it was great. I was very proud.

After talking with them for half an hour I went to the offices of the Communist Party at 108 East 14th Street. Charles Krumbein, district organizer and a member of the executive committee, embraced me as I entered the door with him. We sat down to talk in his first-floor office. Margaret Cowl, his common-law wife, was there. Today, the widow of the one-time national treasurer of the Party, she operates a Communist book store, Imported Publications and Products Company, at 1 Union Square.

I demanded to know who had ordered me framed. Krumbein denied that he had anything to do with it; he suggested that it might be William Foster and the new representative of the Communist International, "P. Green."

Krumbein inquired about my injuries and said he had arranged to have a doctor look me over. The talk turned back to Green—"He wants to see you," Krumbein said. There was nothing unusual about this because I had always acted as liaison between the International representative (known as the "CI Rep") and the American Party. Green, who had recently replaced Pepper, was a major general in the fourth section of Soviet Intelligence.

I went over to the Algonquin Hotel on 32nd Street, near Sixth Avenue, and went to Room 406 after calling from the lobby on the house phone. I had to give my password, "Misha is here." Misha means Maurice in Russian.

Green was a brown-haired, blue-eyed man of about five feet five

*See Appendix I, p. 233.

whom I had met at the 1925 convention in Chicago. He stood for a moment with his hands in his trouser pockets, then he said in a deep, German voice: "Come in, come in!" He embraced me and kissed my cheeks.

The suite had two and a half rooms, and was richly furnished—far nicer than I had ever seen. Green was pleased to find that I spoke Russian and we talked in that language. With a bland smile, he told me why I had been framed: the strike had been deteriorating and the workers were trickling back to the shops. We needed a stimulant. At the same time, he explained, we had to put fear and discipline into the workers and owners alike—we needed to show them that we meant business.

"You know that during the class struggle—especially in a political struggle (and as Marx and Lenin stated, every struggle of the workers is a political struggle)—the workers must be ready to sacrifice everything for the dictatorship of the proletariat. During these struggles, our bravest men must be prepared to sacrifice for the Cause. You must not forget—not for a minute!—that you are a soldier and a leader of the proletariat. You must accept your fate as part of the struggle!"

As he went on talking, he poured me a whiskey and himself a brandy from a collection, in that Prohibition era, that would have brought hundreds of dollars. Green wore a dark robe of finest silk, and his shirt, also of silk, must have cost ten or fifteen dollars. In an open closet I could see an array of quality suits.

As I listened to this self-appointed representative of the workers speak, I felt the great pain of shattered illusion. He ordered me to reorganize my action and industrial espionage squads—then added a new responsibility. We faced a problem, he said, in regard to "certain people" in the Party. "These persons must be brought into line," he went on, by making them understand that things could happen to them physically, or through "other methods." One of these, he made clear, was blackmail.

Green paused, and sipped his drink reflectively. My duty at all times, was to report on the behavior of the Party leadership, either through my own investigations or those of my espionage and action squads. He told me to keep an eye on Jay Lovestone, William Z. Foster, Alexander Bittelman and Bertram D. Wolfe. He told me that Jay Lovestone "could not be relied on in a crisis"—he had failed the

Party on more than one occasion—and had given damaging testimony against Ben Gitlow and James Larkin when they were being tried for criminal anarchy.

"Bert Wolfe," he said, "had proven his cowardice twice when the Party was in danger." Green did not elaborate beyond saying that Wolfe had "run away to Mexico."

Foster, he recalled, had been "a national patriot" during World War I, and had worked with the A.F.L. of Bittelman, the Communist theoretician. Green said: "He was never a worker. He never did a day of work in his life. He has always lived off organizations and is generally ready to sell his services to the one that will pay him the most money."

Green ordered me to "watch them carefully" and report their activities directly to him. My normal transmission to Green, when he was in the Soviet Union, was to be routed through a man who lived on St. Lawrence Boulevard in Montreal, Canada. The name "Misha" would certify my signature. If all other communication broke down, I was to reach him through the International Control Commission in Moscow. He gave me an address: P. Gussev, No. 324 Tverskaya, Moscow. This was part of the office of the Fourth (foreign) Section of Soviet Military Intelligence. Green told me that from 1919 I had been carried as a member of the Soviet Secret Police in its Fourth Section, then known as the GPU.

I left him, with another embrace, after having enjoyed several drinks of the best Scotch I have ever tasted.

When I returned to the offices of the Party on 14th Street, I ran into Bittelman and Alexander Trachtenberg. The latter was the man the Communist International had selected to publish its educational and propaganda literature in the United States. Until his death in the 1960's, he headed the International Publishing Co. at 381 Fourth Avenue—which also engaged in espionage. On many occasions I was present in his office when Trachtenberg conferred with such agents as Anna Louise Strong.* Trachtenberg was also a director of World Tourist, Inc., which had offices in the Flatiron Building on Broadway at 23rd Street, another front for espionage activities. Associated with him in this enterprise were Jacob Golos, later involved in the Elizabeth Bentley case, and Abe Finkelberg, an old GPU agent and mem-

*See Appendix I, p. 233.

107

ber of the Central Control Commission of the American Branch of the Party.

When I reached home, Father and Mother were relieved to see me. But after we had embraced, Father began repeating once again the things he had warned me of when I was a boy. I should abandon my radical activities—if I didn't, I would wind up as Joseph had in Czarist Russia, in prison or worse. He told me that he was in the position of Jacob when Joseph demanded that his youngest son be sent into Egypt. "I have lost one son," he said, "and I don't want to lose my youngest!"

Father said that it was not too late to change my course—that the way of the Lord was the way of righteousness. The road of force and evil I was following, he warned, was bound to end in unhappiness and tragedy.

I was a Marxist, and had convinced myself that I didn't believe in God. To me, Father was an old man, filled with silly fears, superstitions and ignorance.

I reminded him of the conditions we had known in Russia—the poverty, misery and persecution. I pointed to the slums in New York. Without mentioning the beatings I had taken, I cited police brutality toward strikers, of which the foreign language newspapers were full. "I must fight against such conditions!" Father replied that he had seen little of such conditions in America, and much that was good. I told him that he was an old man who didn't get around enough.

It ended that way.

The next day I went back to the union and started reorganizing my top action squad. During visits to various picket lines and strike headquarters, I tried to infuse a new spirit into the strikers.

On my suggestion, we launched a new enterprise, a training—and refuge—center for men selected to be used in future strike work. This was at a summer camp near Beacon, New York—Camp Nitgedaiget, Yiddish for "Don't worry." Here young men and women were sent for training in leadership. And those who were injured or became the object of police attention used the camp to recover or hide or both.

This new camp was an auxiliary to Camp Unity, which had been founded earlier in the same region. We set up a rifle and pistol range against a hillside in back of the main camp building, and carried on target practice and close order drill as though we were operating a military training camp—which, of course, we were. We were training Red Army "soldiers" for use in the industrial war that was about to break out across the country. It was destined to culminate in the sit-down strikes of the depression years.

At a meeting with Foster and the entire Central Committee of the Party we discussed future policy. It was agreed that the organizing fronts should be emphasized in order to line up support, raise money and gain new recruits for the Party. Friends of Soviet Russia (later the National Council of American-Soviet Friendship) was the first to receive attention, and immediately launched a fund-raising and membership campaign.

A new organization, the International Labor Defense, had been launched in 1924. It succeeded the Workers Defense League* founded in 1920, which was originally part of the I.W.W. before being taken over by the communists.

The ILD, whose activities were to be stepped up sharply, was actually the American section of the International Red Air (MOPR), headed by Lenin's secretary, Stassova, with headquarters in Moscow. It was described as a "people's organization" for the defense of "political prisoners," and was to create a curious chapter in the antics of the literary set during the depression years—against the unlikely backdrop of the Kentucky coal fields. But that is a story for a later chapter. In the United States, the ILD was headed by James P. Cannon, destined to become a Trotskyite, and Rose Barron, an agent of the Cheka, or GPU as it came to be known, and a member of the Society of Old Bolsheviks.**

In the field of propaganda, a special effort to increase the circulation of the new English language magazine, *Soviet Russia Today*, was planned.

We decided at the same Central Committee meeting that the already expressed friendships of Senators William E. Borah and Burton K. Wheeler should be further solidified through friendly articles in the left-wing press. Senator Borah, our chief target, had advocated the recognition of Soviet Russia and, during the 1922 coal strike, had strongly proposed that the Federal Government take over the coal

*Not to be confused with a different Workers Defense League set up in the 1930's.
**The Society of Old Bolsheviks was organized by Lenin and was comprised of Party members who were active in 1905.

industry. Through these and other acts—he was a great pacifist—Borah had earned the praise of Marxist writers.

My activities were interrupted on June 8th by my approaching trial in Mineola. Franklin and I went out to Jamaica for a conference with our attorneys. We spent two days preparing our defense. The Furriers Union had engaged Edgar F. Hazelton, a Municipal Court Justice, and Dana Wallace, a Queens County District Attorney, who had retired from their offices in 1924 to form a law partnership. It was a formidable firm, and two years later they gained national prominence through their defense of Mrs. Ruth Snyder in the spectacular Snyder-Gray murder trial. Neither Judge Hazelton nor Mr. Wallace was a Communist or a Socialist; both were Republicans and staunch old-time Americans. The Communists had engaged them for this very reason.

In court Judge Hazelton presented a splendid figure in a cutaway coat, striped trousers and a white carnation in his lapel. He looked like the picture of Prince Albert on the tins of smoking tobacco bearing that name.

The trial before a jury took seven days. Franklin, Basoff and I were charged with second degree felonious assault. He put up a remarkably thorough defense, but the State had us trumped. They brought to the stand the detectives who had made the arrests, then paraded the witnesses who had identified us in the line-up. They all sounded very convincing.

The jury, after deliberating for a short time, brought in the verdict: Guilty. We were immediately sentenced to two-and-a-half to five years in prison.

Once more, I was in the Mineola jail, where I remained until the end of June, while our attorneys appealed to the Appellate Division of the State Supreme Court.

Pending the outcome of the appeal, we were released on bail.

Meanwhile, the 17-week strike had ended on June 17th. The union failed to get the closed shop—the main objective of the Communists —but the settlement provided for a 40-hour week, a ten percent wage increase and other concessions. Right-wingers insisted that the same terms were available nine weeks earlier. Indeed, on the debit side, as finally brought out by an investigation ordered by Green and the A.F.L., was an expenditure of $838,000. It left the union's treasury empty, and with a mortgage on its headquarters building. The labor investigators reported they were unable to audit more than $195,000 of the claimed expenditures. Gold and his Communist-controlled Joint Board replied that the money had been spent on defense and police bribes and could not be traced. This was partly true—but the A.F.L. committee knew nothing of the $1,750,000 Rothstein loan. Two years later, after Rothstein was murdered, investigators came across copies of receipts to the union for installments paid. Of course when the gambler died, with most of the loan still outstanding, no more payments were made.

The "victory" left Ben Gold a popular man with the fur workers in New York. But after the A.F.L. committee had disclosed what it called a "shocking state of affairs," the International Fur Workers' Union leadership asked for aid in ridding the union of the Communists. Green appointed a special committee headed by Edward F. McGrady, and he appointed a right-wing Furriers Joint Council to fight Gold's Joint Board. The result was a prolonged labor war, which the left eventually won.

The capture of the New York furriers gave the Communists their first strong beachhead in the labor movement and paved the way for other victories. That summer, we made plans to move in on John L. Lewis' United Mine Workers, the United Brotherhood of Carpenters and Joiners, and the International Ladies Garment Workers Union.

I was busy organizing gangsters for strong-arm squads while my conviction was being appealed to a higher court.

CHAPTER XV

A general strike in New York's garment industry was ordered on July 1, 1926, by the Communist-controlled Joint Board of the International Ladies Garment Workers Union. I was ordered into action with my strong-arm squads, employing virtually the same crew used in the furriers' strike.

The employers hired the "Legs" Diamond mob to counter the Brooklyn waterfront gangsters that "Little Augie" Pisano had dredged up for me. Ironically, both were controlled by Arnold Rothstein. My forces also included Sormenti's prize toughs from the Party and a rowdy crowd of Greek hoodlums controlled by John Popinas.

It was one of the most savage strikes in labor history—a rehearsal of Communist terror later employed around the world. People were intimidated, flogged and kidnapped.

Trouble had started after Morris Sigman was elected president of the ILGWU at its 1923 convention, in Baltimore. The 1920 depression was fading and good times were creeping back to an anemic industry. Shot through with inequities, the sweat shops were operated by sub-contractors who paid as little in wages as they could get by with.

Sigman, with the steam of a new leader, offered a "New Program" that promised to benefit workers and owners alike by providing greater efficiency and higher standards of competition for the employers, and a forty-hour week, with an annual minimum of 32 weeks employment, for the employees.

A commission appointed by Governor Alfred E. Smith, with Herbert H. Lehman as one of its members, recommended adoption of the "New Program," but the employers were less than luke-warm. Adoption was also blocked by the Communists and left-wing radicals who, under Charles ("Sasha") Zimmerman and Louis Hyman, had captured the Cloakmakers' Joint Board.

In the resulting stalemate, the national committee of the Communist Party, headed by Jay Lovestone, suddenly ordered the strike. Sigman, as head of the parent international union, opposed it. Zimmerman and Hyman were not too enthusiastic—the New York unions could ill afford a strike—but when the Party ordered, they obeyed.

Over 30,000 cloakmakers quit their jobs in a futile strike that was to last for 28 weeks. Dave Dubinsky, manager of Local 10, the cutters' local, went to the Communists with an appeal that he be permitted to play on their team. The Party didn't trust him, and soon he was ousted from any part of the strike settlement committee. We—I sat in on the discussions—turned him down because he wanted control of the treasury, for the treasury is the most important place in a union, because the Communists are able to syphon off funds for the Party, and with him as treasurer it would close the source of finances, and he was too close to the Lepke-Gurrah gang. We didn't need Dubinsky.

It is ironic that Jay Lovestone, the man who made the decision, eventually became Dubinsky's chief political advisor.

Communist strategy required that I keep in the shadows—especially in view of my precarious legal position. The man who ostensibly headed the picketing was Elias Marks who in 1919 was indicted on criminal anarchy in New York State. Ben Stolberg, a newspaper columnist and free-lance writer who wrote for the Hearst and other newspaper chains and author of a few books on labor problems, writing on the subject, called him a "nonentity."

We spent over a quarter of a million dollars of union money on picketing, only about half of which was ever accounted for.* The other committees did even worse. The Joint Board itself, in an act of free-handed piracy, used $800,000 in the manufacturers' security fund which was pledged with the union—and which the international later had to make good. Most of the money, of course, went into communist organizing activities and propaganda.

All through July and August the Joint Board kept making contracts with individual firms. Most of these, it so happened, were the worst employers in the garment industry from a labor standpoint. But as a result, about 12,000 workers trickled back to jobs and the strike began to lose steam.

*A big slice of this money went to bribe police and Court Clerks the same way it did in the fur strike, and much was pilfered by the strike leadership.

113

At this point, through Arnold Rothstein, a tentative agreement was reached with the Industrial Council, which represented about a third of the industry. It provided for an average wage increase of ten percent, a 40-hour week and a guarantee of 32 weeks of annual employment. There were also concessions to employers, one of which would permit them to discharge up to five percent of their employees in the reorganization of their businesses.

Zimmerman and Hyman were all for settling, but their Communist bosses said no. Lovestone, general secretary of the Party, and William Weinstone, New York State district organizer, ordered that the "revolutionary struggle" go on.

Two months later, on November 12, a second agreement was reached with the Industrial Council. This time small manufacturers insisted on a 42-hour week and the right to cut the number of employees by as much as 30 percent during the following two years. The union accepted these terms and won pay increases for only 800 key workmen. There was also a guarantee of 32 weeks of work.

This pitiful settlement left a great segment of the industry on strike —mostly the sub-contractors, who refused to sign even on these terms. Finally, on December 13, Sigman stepped in and got a renewal of the same contract that had been in operation when the strike started.

It cost the union about three and one-half million dollars and left the New York locals bankrupt. The workers lost a busy season and suffered great hardships.

While this went on, I also looked after other facets of my many-sided Communist activities.

Gussev, alias P. Green, had come up with an idea for a system of military and political training camps across the country. In his travels he had found summer camps a thriving business—where young people went to relax, frolic and enjoy sports. Using such camps for the Communist cause was not original with Gussev, but he was quick to see the advantages.

Our first military training camp was opened on a 30-acre farm near Wallkill, N.Y. Named for its owner, Fred Briehl, Briehl's Farm was in a sequestered region of wooded hills. In addition to a 15- or 20-room house, a large barn and several shacks were scattered over the acreage. Recruits were largely drawn from among the more intelligent and husky young members of Marxian study groups. Young women took their place in the ranks along side of men. Training began with the military fundamentals, including instruction in small arms and explosives, and target practice. Most of the instructors at the "Farm" were former U. S. Army personnel who had joined the Communist Party and received training at either the Lenin School or Frunze Military Academy in Moscow. Many had attended both.

Among the leaders there was a great interest in the National Guard and the Citizens Military Training program, the latter set up by Congress to train officers for a possible future emergency. Gussev told me, "We must give this our special attention, Comrade Malkin, it is absolutely essential that we penetrate the capitalist military organization."

As chairman of the Control Commission of the Party, I was present at two meetings of the New York district committee where this problem was discussed. It was decided that picked graduates of our summer training camps should be infiltrated into the National Guard and the Citizens Military Training camps.

One of the first to make the grade was a clerk in a branch office of the New York Post Office on 13th Street. He was Phillip Frankfeld, who, a quarter of a century later, was convicted under the Smith Act in a trial in Baltimore.

Another was Phillip Barell, alias "Phil Bart," who later became national manager of the *Daily Worker*. Another was Abe Harfield, who was a Party functionary for two decades, including a period in underground activity. All three, later in the 1930s, attended the Lenin School in Moscow. Still another was red-headed Pete Shapiro, a pocketbook maker by trade, who was active in the Ladies' Handbag and Leathergoods Union. These men, and scores like them, after finishing courses at Communist summer camps, entered the U.S. military reserve. Some fought with the Abraham Lincoln Brigade in the Spanish War. Nearly all were active couriers or espionage agents.

Out of the summer camps grew the idea for a central training school that was opened in 1927 in New York City's Union Square. Operated by the political bureau and the secretariat of the Party, it enrolled promising young Communists from all parts of the country. Instructors included Jay Lovestone, Bertram D. Wolfe, Ben Davidson*, alias "D. Benjamin", Ben Mandel, alias "Bert Miller," William Z. Foster, Benjamin Gitlow, Louis Weinstock, Alexander Bittelman, Alexander Trachtenberg, Robert W. Dunn, Frank Palmer, Forrest

*See Appendix I, p. 234.

115

Bailey, Sidney Hook, then and now a New York University professor, E. V. Calverton and others. Many, like Ben Gitlow, left the Party with full confessions of the roles they played in the Communist movement. But most continued their activities or remained silent if they did drop out of the Party.

The curriculum was drawn up for the school by Professor Robert Morss Lovett, from the University of Chicago. I came to know the professor very well in 1932 when I went to Chicago as chief of the Chicago district. I personally handled his Communist Party membership book and in April, 1933, assigned him to lead a picket line in a textile strike at Sorkins Dress Shop in South Chicago. Also active in that strike was Carl Haessler, manager of the Federated Press and a charter member of the Party.

Professor Lovett had a young girlfriend at the time, a coed at Chicago University, named Martha Dodd—later a Soviet agent who fled behind the Iron Curtain with her husband, David Stern, in 1954.

Lovett's 1927 curriculum for the Party training school offered a ten-week leadership course for young Communists. It included Marxian economics and political science, labor journalism, Party organization and a tour de force in American, German and Soviet military theory and tactics.

Lovett disguised his long service to the Communists as aid to the League for Industrial Democracy, a socialist organization that was set up on the advice of Upton Sinclair, as a successor to the Intercollegiate Socialist League. Sinclair boasted that dropping the name "socialist" had made the league more effective, and he was probably right.

The membership eventually included such names as "Madam Secretary" of Labor, Frances Perkins, Walter and Victor Reuther and many other labor leaders (surprisingly, among them George Meany). And even the wife of President Franklin D. Roosevelt.

As a historical footnote, it can be noted that my testimony before a congressional committee in 1939 helped to end Professor Lovett's political career as the Governor General of the Virgin Islands.

116

CHAPTER XVI

By 1926, American Communists had their own military uniform. It was adapted from Ernst Thaelmann's Red Front Fighters in Germany. It was a dull, crushed-grass green, a color the U.S. Army came to use in World War II, especially in the Pacific. Communists called it the uniform of the American Red Army, and wore it openly at Party functions and on May Day parades.

The American branch of the Red Front Fighters maintained its national office at Party district headquarters, 35 E. 12th Street. In command were Israel Amter, J. Peters and Brooks Johnson, a steeplejack who married a hostess at the Crusader Restaurant on 14th Street, and later owned a profitable flagpole business. A colorful feature of their "army" was a squadron of motorcyclists mounted on German-built machines and a brass band that marched in uniform.

In March, 1926, while awaiting trial at Mineola, I took part in a pageant that featured these units as a colorful backdrop at Madison Square Garden. It was a salute to the Paris Commune, which had established the first "Workers republic" from March 18 to May 29, 1871. It was put down by General Adolphe Thiers, of the National Guard, who at first supported the Paris mobs. I played the part of Leon Gambetta—Minister of Defense—a swashbuckling, villainous role, as I portrayed it. A dramatic moment came in a scene before the Central Committee of the Commune. I drew myself up. "Citizens!" I said, "I want you to accept my resignation! I can no longer command a force where everyone deliberates and no one obeys."

The words could have applied to the American branch of the Party at that time—and somewhat to the Moscow headquarters as well. The struggle between Stalin and Trotsky was nearing a climax and would end with Trotsky's expulsion from the Party in November.

The appeal of my conviction for second degree assault had been reserved by the Appellate Division of the State Supreme Court and

I was re-indicted in connection with the Rockville Centre affair. Franklin and Basoff were named, but also indicted were Ben Gold, Isidor Shapiro, Samuel Mencher, Jack Schneider, Joseph Katz, George "Turk" Weiss, Otto Lenhart, Oscar Meilief and Martin Rosenberg. The Communists quickly hired a battery of new attorneys and started a defense fund drive to save us from the "frame up." Frank P. Walsh and George Z. Medalie, among the country's foremost trial lawyers, were retained for Gold and Shapiro. Two others were George Morton Levy, prominent Nassau County attorney, and Harry Weeks. Least known was Henry Udehardt, who represented Franklin and me. The lawyers, of course, were all hired and assigned by the Party leadership but none of them were Communists.

The trial was held in April, 1927, at the Nassau County Court in Mineola, before the same judge, Lewis E. Smith.

I soon learned that Basoff, who had been convicted with me in the first trial, had tried to make a deal with the Furriers Union. He'd demanded $35,000 to swear that Gold had nothing to do with the attack, but was turned down. Basoff then went to the District Attorney, Elvin T. Edwards, who, eager for a conviction, accepted his offer to turn state's evidence, promising to see that he got a light sentence.

On the stand, Basoff identified each of us as having taken an active part in the raid—and named me as the leader. But the defense for Gold and Shapiro produced a surprise witness in Major General John J. Phelan of the New York National Guard. He swore that Gold and Shapiro were in his office making arrangements to rent an armory for a union meeting on the afternoon in question, and could not have been at Rockville Centre. I am positive the General had his dates mixed up, but his testimony freed Gold and Shapiro.

The rest of us were found guilty* and sentenced to two-and-a-half to five years in prison, the same as I received the first trial.

The case was appealed, and I was again released in $25,000 bail.

The Sixth Party Congress was about to meet in Moscow as I resumed activities, and Gussev ordered me to meet two important comrades. A few days later, George Mink and Paul Crouch arrived. Mink, of Philadelphia, was a taxi driver whose duty it was to roll drunks to get money for the Party. He told me he was the brother-in-law of Solomon Lozovsky, international secretary of the Profintern.

*See Appendix I, p. 234.

Crouch had recently served time in a military prison for activities he had carried on, while a soldier, at the Army's Schofield Barracks in Hawaii.

Their problem was to get jobs as seamen so they could get to Russia, and I called Charles Ruthenberg in Chicago for advice. He told me to get in touch with the Amtorg Soviet Trade Agency in New York, which had a contact at the Moore McCormack Lines, then operating ships between New York and the Soviet ports. Mink and Crouch were signed up as crew members on a freighter carrying sheep to Leningrad. I supplied them with "credentials," written in invisible ink on silk strips, which would introduce them to the Russians. They were to swallow the silk if apprehended by the Capitalist police.

As these preparations were started in the summer of 1927, Stalin was making steady headway against the "left opportunism" of Trotsky. Later that year he was expelled from the Communist Party. Having ousted Trotsky, Stalin now turned on a new rival in his march to power, the "right opportunism" of Nikolai Bukharin and the Bolshevik "old guard."

This latest phase of the power struggle meant that our policy of boring from within, of joining craft unions and other bourgeois organizations in order to take them over, was temporarily shelved. The Trojan horse method was out. It was replaced by the frontal attack. This new policy, put into operation by Solomon Lozovsky, head of the Profintern, was partly responsible for the expulsion of Lovestone and other top leaders of the American branch of the Party—Ben Gitlow, Bert Wolfe, Ben Mandel (alias "Bert Miller") and a score of lesser figures. Among them was Zimmerman, who in 1932 was readmitted to the executive board of Dressmakers Local 22 and is still a leader of the ILGWU today.

Among the delegates to the Sixth Congress was James P. Cannon, who refrained from voting. After returning to the United States, he eventually broke with the Stalinist faction and joined the Trotskyist opposition, which he continues to lead.

A Stalin edict brought to the front William Z. Foster and Earl Browder, neither of whom were profound Marxists. They had not come to the Party until 1920 and 1922, and were regarded as neophytes by the old timers. However, most of the dissatisfied were critics-in-silence and obediently went along with the Moscow order.

119

I was not among them, and came out immediately in open support of Trotsky and his line of thinking. My sympathies, naturally enough, had been with Trotsky since the days he visited our house on the East Side. To me, he was the greatest hero of the revolution. In my opinion, he was superior to Lenin as a theorist and politician—and I considered Stalin a nincompoop.

Soon, I was placed on charges by the new leadership of the Party.

In October and early November 1928, at the very time the courts were upholding my conviction and I was preparing to serve a prison sentence, my trial was held before the full body of the Central Committee and the Control Commission. It lasted for 11 days.

The trial was at National Party Headquarters, 43 East 125th Street. During the proceedings, I was called out into a hallway by Foster and John Pepper. They offered to make me a deal: if I would sign a statement disclaiming Trotsky, I would be permitted to jump bail and go to Russia.

"Nothing doing," I said.

I told them it had taken me too many years to get to America. I liked it here and had no desire to return to Russia. My work was here and if I fled, I would be marked a deserter and a coward. Besides, I would probably be arrested in Russia and carted off to a concentration camp. (Hitler got that idea from the Communists, not the Communists from Hitler.) I would rather go to prison in America than return to Russia.

These were rash statements for a communist on trial. But anger over my treatment in the Rockville Centre case boiled over. I was fed up—I'd had a belly full of deals. Bristling, I turned and walked away.

There was one ace I held; a copy of a cablegram that I insisted they read into the record. From the Executive Committee of the Communist International in Moscow to the Politburo of the American branch of the Party, it said: "The example and leadership of Comrade Malkin, in his revolutionary zeal and tactics during the furriers and cloakmakers strikes, is worthy of praise as being in the highest traditions of the revolutionary working class." It was signed by Grigori Zinoviev.

But it made no difference. The cablegram had been sent in April and this was November and I was out.

They stripped me of all my posts, and suspended me from the

Party until such time as I saw fit to return on their terms. They left the door open, however, by stating that my working class background, the revolutionary tradition of my family and my own militant record since childhood, made it entirely probable that I should return to full Party membership.

One of my last acts before surrendering to the authorities was to defy the new Foster leadership at a convention called by the Furriers' Union to form a new needle trades local. It was held at the Star Casino, 107th Street and Park Avenue, in late December, 1928.

The furriers had been expelled from the AFL and were leading a Communist effort to create a new union leadership that would rival the AFL. Some socialist writers have called it "dual unionism," but "rival unionism" is the correct term. This meeting was aimed at getting the needle trades workers out of the AFL into a new union.

It was the old question of the Communists isolating themselves from the American labor movement. I was opposed to it.

I wanted to speak, since I was a member of the furriers and was about to go to prison for the union. Foster refused to permit me, but I defied him and said I would speak from the floor. He demanded to see a copy of my speech. I told him "I'm a working man, not an office bureaucrat with a secretary." I said that I had no copy and told him to listen and he would hear what I had to say.

I spoke for about fifteen minutes and had the pleasure of listening to a seven-minute ovation. The meeting came to a halt as the crowd cheered. Ironically, Foster, Pepper and other Party brass came around to shake my hand and bask for a moment in the glory.

Two weeks later, Irving Potash drove Franklin and me to Mineola. On the way, he assured me that my family would be taken care of by the union. This was no hardship for the Party since it had collected over $487,000 in donations for my defense. But my family never got a dime.

After five days in the Mineola jail, Franklin and I were handcuffed and, under heavy guard, taken by automobile to Ossining, New York.

It was January 15, 1929. That night I slept in a cell behind the dull grey walls of Sing Sing—the "Castle on the Hudson."

CHAPTER XVII

As I sat looking at the walls of Sing Sing, for the first time I fully realized that it would be a long time before I saw the outside world again. Somehow, I never really accepted it until it was uncontestable. I could see guards at their stations in the towers, and others marching along the walls, rifles over their shoulders. I muttered to Franklin that this looked like the end for a while. My heart felt heavy, and I could see tears in Franklin's eyes as he whispered back: "They've used us as scapegoats. It's a double-cross."

I knew his words were true, and I swallowed the bitterness that rose in my throat.

When we first arrived at Sing Sing, we were ushered into the office of the Head Keeper, Bill Sheehy, a 250-pound Irishman who demanded in a booming voice: "Who is the leader of this gang?"

It sounded pompous, since there were only two of us. "There is no leader, and there is no gang," I said firmly.

He looked at me harshly and said menacingly in his brogue: "Keep it down. Button your lip or I'll teach you how to behave yourself."

He ordered us to empty our pockets, which was superfluous since we had just come from jail where we'd gone through the routine of surrendering our personal belongings. One of our guards carried the two packages which contained such things as billfolds and the little money we had. The packages were turned over to Sheehy, and we were ordered to an adjoining room and told to strip.

This was the prison tailor shop where supplies were issued to new arrivals, and civilian clothes turned in. Before donning prison garb, we were told to take a shower. The water was cold, and I quickly sloshed myself and dried off. I was handed rough, prison-made underwear, of grey cotton twill, then a jacket, trousers and a pair of heavy black shoes. There was a white cloth disk on the sleeve of the jacket. The whiteness in the disk showed that you entered the prison with a perfect record. If you violated prison rules, the disk would be blackened and you automatically lost good conduct privileges.

Sing Sing was a very old prison even then, and the prison block where new arrivals were quartered dated back nearly a century. There was no running water or toilet facilities in the cells. I was given a plain spring cot, without a mattress, one blanket and no pillow. The only light that reached me filtered through a 4" X 4" hole in the door. The cell was dark and musty, and there I remained for 30 days.

The prison grapevine is something to marvel at. Insiders know about nearly everything that goes on outside, and often it is impossible to figure out where the information comes from.

On my first night in Sing Sing, the moment the guard had walked to the far end of the corridor, jingling his keys, a voice outside hissed through the door: "Bolshevik." I couldn't believe what I'd heard until the word "Bolshevik" was repeated again—unmistakably this time.

A sack of Bull Durham tobacco, a Hershey bar, a pack of Lucky Strike cigarettes and matches were pushed through the opening.

"This is a compliment," the voice whispered, "from the boys of the Mutual Welfare League. You are okay with us."

Even though they all seemed to know, as I found out later, that I had been framed, they knew, too, of the beatings I had taken after my arrest. I was "okay," of course, because I had refused to squeal. I was considered one of them.

I couldn't sleep, and sat up and smoked Bull Durham most of the night. You made your own cigarettes, pouring loose tobacco into thin paper and rolling it into the proper size. There's an art to it, one that takes practice to master.

By midnight I was half frozen. Cold seeped in from outside— dampish and raw, coming off the Hudson. It brought to mind the time Father and I visited Joseph in prison in Russia. I thought about my past, and Father and Mother—and how much they had suffered. Their sons had endured imprisonment in Russia and now here I was in prison in America.

I was still a Communist at heart, but I had doubts. America had never done me any harm, but quickly I put such thoughts from my mind. A Communist does not exist beyond the Party, and seeks to lose himself in the cause. But it wasn't working for me as I felt personal feelings of loss, of loneliness, of compassion for my parents. And I would roll another Bull Durham cigarette.

Finally, I sprawled exhausted on the cot, the blanket wrapped around me, and fell asleep. It was still dark when one of the guards rattled my door and yelled to get dressed. He ordered me to get the heavy cast-iron bucket that served as my toilet, and stand with it at my feet just outside my cell door. All down the corridor prisoners were coming out with their pails. We all stood in line until the last man had been checked and accounted for. Then, each carrying his bucket, we were marched single file into a courtyard, where a blast of winter air whistled through the darkness.

I saw a clock as we were marching out: It was 6:15. We stopped at a long trough with a number of faucets above it, emptied our buckets and flushed them out. Then we were marched through a lavatory to the mess hall. Here, in a large red brick building not far from the famed Death House, the entire prison population was fed under the watchful eyes of the guards. We stood at long tables with benches attached, each man in front of a tin plate chained to the table, until the hall had filled. Then, at a word from the head guard, there was a great rustling of shoe leather on the bare concrete floor and we sat down. No talking was permitted, and the only sound was the mingled noise of forks and spoons on the tin plates. We had no knives.

Breakfast was beef hash on toast and black coffee. After eating, we new arrivals marched back to our cells while the regulars exercised in the courtyard before reporting to assigned jobs in the prison. The new prisoners were segregated and the only time we saw the others was in the mess hall. Our last meal was at 5:15 and we were locked up for the night.

The second day, I was taken to the infirmary for a routine examination. A convict assistant with rolled up sleeves ordered me to strip. I recognized him as a man who had turned state's evidence in a case involving two brothers who had been electrocuted for the killing of a cashier in a West End bank robbery. I told him to keep away from me. The incident was noted by other convicts and soon reported, as I knew it would be, through the prison. It helped my reputation as one of the "regular guys."

After leaving the medical examining room, I was taken to the prison psychiatrist, known as the "bugs doctor." Short, grey and partly bald, he invited me to have a seat. He peered at me silently for a moment, through thick-lensed glasses which made his eyes look strangely large and distorted when I looked back at him. On his desk were several small cardboard boxes. The doctor asked my name, and where I was born. Then he suddenly started asking me questions in rapidfire order, rattling off words as fast as he could. He suddenly jerked up some of the boxes off his desk and demanded "How many boxes?" I said, "Well, how many do you have?" That's what I'm asking you," he said. "Well, if you don't know," I told him, "how in the hell do you expect me to know?"

He turned, impatiently. With a quick look around the room, he said, "How many flies do you see in this room?"

It was winter and there were none. I told him so.

I asked him if he saw any pink elephants flying around. He started screaming for the guard to come take me out, that I was driving him crazy.

The guard came in, grinning, and motioned for me to follow him. Outside, he told me, "That guy should be in a nut house."

The next day, I was taken before Sheehy for a job assignment. I stood stiffly at attention as he glanced at a card on his desk. "Your name Maurice L. Malkin?"

"Yes," I said.

"How much money have you got?"

He gave me a knowing look and held up two fingers. It meant that if I had $200 I could get a soft job. I told him I had nothing, since I had left most of my possessions at home, but pointed out that a representative of the fur workers union would visit in a few days, and we would see what could be done.

I served my first 30 days without further incident, and was moved to a better part of the prison. Here I had a mattress on my bed and two blankets.

The first day there I was called to the Head Keeper's office for job assignment. Nobody had come up from the union, so I was put to work on the coal pile. I shoveled all morning, but after lunch I was summoned to the office of Father McCaffrey, the Catholic chaplain. I had learned that Father McCaffrey was regarded with the highest respect, and that Jewish as well as Catholic prisoners turned to him for help. (There was a Rabbi, S. Katz, but the Jewish prisoners avoided him because of reports of some unfortunate affairs in the past.) When I walked into Father McCaffrey's office, I had no idea what he wanted but felt confident and friendly toward him—

though I had no religious feelings during that period of my life.

After talking with me for half an hour, Father McCaffrey asked if I would care to become his secretary. Surprise left me speechless, and I sat looking at him. "If you object," he went on, "we'll say nothing more about it. It just happens that I need a man, and I thought perhaps you might accept the position."

I had received a few books through the mail, and since Father McCaffrey was also censor of the reading matter that entered the prison, he was aware of this. I did not know then that it was against the rules to receive such material unless it was sent by the publishers. All the books were Marxian works—one was Lenin's *Materialism and Empirical Criticism*—and Father McCaffrey asked if I minded letting him read them before passing the material on to me. I told him I had no objections, and would be honored to serve as his secretary.

I was assigned to work with him immediately. In this capacity, I also served as a translator and correspondent for prisoners who could not read or write. This was a good job for me since I had a full knowledge of Yiddish, Russian and Polish and also knew some Italian and German.

Soon I was asked by several prisoners to run for secretary of the Mutual Welfare League. The election of the secretary was an annual event in the prison, and there were opposing political parties, the Tammany and the Cheese. Part of the secretary's job was to look after the minor needs of the prisoners who were without funds— seeing that they received such items as free smoking tobacco and toilet articles. But more important, he maintained contact with the families of these same men. Those on the outside were often destitute and in greater need than the prisoners themselves.

There was no contest that year since both sides agreed to support me. I was elected without opposition, and became known as the "Bolshevik" secretary.

Privately, I called the society the "Ossining Soviet," myself the provisional secretary and the Board of Trustees of the League, all prisoners, the provisional government.

Shortly after the election, and my new importance in Sing Sing society, I was visited by Juliet Stuart Poyntz,* acting national secre-

*Born in Nevada, Juliet Stuart Poyntz was educated at Columbia, Barnard, Oxford and London School of Economics. She taught history at Columbia and joined the Communist Party in 1919. It is believed she was kidnapped and murdered in January, 1937.

tary of the International Labor Defense. (Her total disappearance ten years later, when she was about to leave the Party, remains one of the great mysteries.) Since we were normally only permitted to receive relatives, she had some difficulty getting through, but Father McCaffrey got her past the red tape. We talked for half an hour and she told me the Party had opened an intensified fund drive in my name; that money was pouring in from all across the country, Canada and even Europe. I asked her to visit my Mother and Father, and try to see that they were taken care of. She promised to do so. I also asked her to have Party literature sent to me directly from the publishers, since the prison did not permit the sending of such material from individuals.

The books began arriving in due time. But neither the Party nor the union ever did anything for my family. My salary was cut off and nobody ever contacted my parents.

Max Eastman came to the prison once with his kind wife, Mme. Krylenke, sister of the then chief Soviet prosecutor. They brought a box of cigars, several cartons of cigarettes and a dark grey sweater, which I appreciated greatly—especially in my cell at night. One day I received an unexpected visit from Robert W. Dunn, a charter member of the Party, a factotum in the American Civil Liberties Union and a close personal friend of the ACLU's Roger Baldwin. All I got from Dunn was a sales talk about how I should keep up my strength as a symbol of the revolutionary class struggle.

For our exercise period in the prison yard (a large yard separated by a small island-like section with a few benches) the prisoners walked around in a circle, usually in double file. One side of the yard was the old cell block that looked like a medieval fortress with large barred windows. On the other side was a small wall with armed guards' towers and the Hudson River and New York Central railroad tracks. On the fourth side was the baseball field surrounded by the main brick wall with armed guard sentry towers.

CHAPTER XVIII

One of the first things I did as secretary of the Mutual Welfare League was to launch a plan to bring professional entertainment to the prison. Jules ("Nicky") Arnstein, the swindler, was a prisoner in my cell block and I thought it would be a wonderful thing if I could induce his wife, the great Ziegfeld star, Fanny Brice, to perform at the prison. I sent her a letter and also contacted some Party members who were active on Broadway and asked them to line up others to help. Fanny Brice was most obliging. She was no Communist; she just had a man in prison and wanted to see him. On Washington's Birthday, 1929, she headed a group of ten that included Guy Kibbee and Charlie Chaplin. She managed to smuggle in half a pint of prohibition booze and, as secretary of the Fund, I was the only prisoner permitted backstage. In her dressing room, the girl who later created "Baby Snooks" took the bottle of ersatz Scotch from under her skirts and handed it to me. One drink was enough for me—it was terrible liquor, but I said it was fine. I took the bottle with me and gave it to two convicts who were serving as altar boys. Then I climbed the stage and opened the show.

"Fellow students of Ossining University. Tonight we have a special show and a special surprise for a senior member of the student body —Nicky Arnstein." After a few jokes, I turned to the young woman who was just emerging from the wings, and said: "I give you Fanny Brice, who will sing, 'My Man.' "

She sang as she never sang before, and brought down the house. Nicky Arnstein was the "My Man" of that song, and the prisoners knew she was singing it for him. Many sat with tears streaming down their cheeks. They were so taken by Fanny Brice that even Charlie Chaplin couldn't follow her without a noticeable letdown.

The success of the show lifted me to new popularity, and I was hailed as "the best commissar of welfare we ever had." Outside the walls my appeals began reaching responsive ears. Funds began coming in, together with donations of tobacco and other small items. Soon we had all we could use, with some left over for the needy families.

During my free periods in the yard I would have a group of the more intelligent prisoners around me asking me such questions as how Communism could be attained and after it has been attained what would they get out of it, or what is in it for us, and would they be allowed to loot, rob, etc. without punishment during the revolution and after. These little gatherings were not to the liking of Warden Lewis E. Lawes, especially since he realized that I was not going to be an information service for him against my fellow "students" of the university. So he was looking for ways to get rid of me as the representative of the prisoners as a bad influence on the prisoners because I also made numerous complaints to the Warden of overcharging in the Warden's grocery and general store where prisoners paid three and four times the outside prices for groceries and clothes such as shirts, underwear, socks and civilian shoes, which the prisoners were allowed to wear. For instance, for a four-cent can of evaporated milk, we paid 16 and 17 cents, which went into the Warden's pocket. The store took in about $300–$400 a day, making approximately $150,000 a year. Not bad for a respectable, liberal Warden, who was featured in the press and later his book, *20,000 Years in Sing Sing*, and also a movie of the same title.

I was awakened one morning about 3:00 A.M. by the Tier Guard and told to take my belongings in a small pillow case. I was led into the ice-cold yard where 40 other prisoners, including Franklin, were already lined up with leg chains and handcuffs, and I also had leg irons and chains leading to my handcuffed wrists put on me. After about a half-hour wait in the bitter cold, my legs and hands were frozen. We were ordered to march to the New York Central Railroad prison siding surrounded by guards with sawed off shot guns and rifles pointing at us where prison armored railroad cars were waiting for us. We finally marched into the cars and sat two together with no windows or light except the dim lights of the car. Rumor had it that we were going to Dannemora, the Siberia of the American prison system. For breakfast, we were handed dry cheese sandwiches and a paper cup of mud called coffee. The same menu was repeated at lunch. During our 14-hour trip, my thoughts were on the words my

Father used when I said goodbye to him and my mother on the morning of January 10, as I was leaving to surrender in Mineola to serve my prison term. He said "All my life I have seen no happiness. I have lived a life when my sons from the oldest to the youngest would be locked in prison cells for not believing in God's laws." My Mother sobbed quietly.

None of us knew where he was being taken. Some of the prisoners said we were going to Dannemora, others said we were on the way to Auburn and still others guessed that we were going to help finish the new prison at Attica. Others guessed right when they said that we were going to Great Meadows, also known as Comstock, a former honor prison without a wall. However, they had recently built a high wall with towers and guard boxes like Sing Sing because too many of the prisoners had no honorable intentions. I did not get a chance to talk to Leo Franklin throughout the period he was with me on the convoy.

When we reached our destination, we were too tired to even rejoice that it was not Dannemora, because we had sat with our leg irons fastened to our seats for fourteen hours.

The train stopped and the captain of the guards ordered all guards on alert with their guns pointing at us while other guards ordered us to line up in double file in the aisles of the car. While handcuffed, with one hand we picked up the leavy leg irons and with the other the pillow case with a few personal belongings. We were ordered to file out of the railroad car and onto the railroad station.

CHAPTER XIX

We were lined up again and counted by the guard captain to make sure that none of us was lost on the way. After the count, we were ordered to march in the February cold and that march reminded me of the prison convoys under the Czar I had seen as a child. This is also reminiscent of the pictures I have seen of forced marches to Siberia and other prisons throughout Russia. It was a two-mile march from the station to the Great Meadows Prison. We walked along a rutty, snowy road and to me it seemed like ten miles because of the heavy chains, leg irons and handcuffs.

We began to see the smoke stacks, the guard towers and walls of the prison and finally reached it. My hands and legs were numb and my face and body were burning from the freezing cold and a wind that was blowing in the open field. So, in spite of all this misery I was glad that at last we would be out of the cold. We reached the prison gate and it swung open and as we passed through we were counted again, and lined up in the yard, and our names and numbers were called out. The leg chains and cuffs were removed. We were also given new numbers. In Sing Sing I was number 81542 and now in Comstock I was given number 10061 and assigned to a reception cell, a 4 X 4 cubicle facing the open field of Comstock. It seems my notoriety and my nickname "Bolshevik" given to me by the convicts in Sing Sing had preceded me here and the second day I received a few notes from cons not to worry because they considered me O.K.

I received some cigarettes and Bull Durham tobacco, thrown into my cell by some of the cons working as messengers and cleaners. The Prison Welfare League was not in existence in Comstock and there were no prisoner organizations. In the afternoon, a guard passed my cell who seemed decent enough, because he did not ask me if I was a "new fish." This is a degrading prison expression. Instead, he asked me if I was a new arrival because that tier was for punishment and new arrivals. I answered that we came in last night. I also asked him to do me a favor and find out the real reason for my transfer. He told me that he would try. He returned in 15 minutes and told me that my card read "Chronic Agitator" in red ink. I was in this cell for three days and on the fourth day they ordered me moved into a different tier and cell. I was told to line up for a work gang under the supervision of guards. About 20 new arrivals were taken out of the prison walls and began to dig large trenches used in constructing reinforcements of the walls from the outside. The temperature was five below zero and we were given cloth work clothes—thin prison grey jackets made in the prison tailor shop, and half rubber boots.

I later found out the reason for my new assignment—from common laborer to checker—was con belief from the Sing Sing grapevine that I was "real people" (meaning that I was anti-administration and anti-state). At 11:40 A.M. we piled up the tools in one trench and were lined up, counted and marched into our cell block. This gave us 20 minutes to wash up and march into the large mess hall for our lunch. At 1:00, we lined up and marched back to our ground-breaking tasks. At 4:15 we were counted and marched back into our cells until 5:00 when our supper was served.

The prison had over 1,100 prisoners working in different prison shops such as tailor, shoe, laundry, hospital and general construction —building new cell blocks and a new prison chapel. Once a week those who worked on the construction jobs—brick layers, cement mixers, etc.—got a little extra ration called steak, which looked like the worn-out sole of a shoe and, I was told, was just as tough to eat.

After supper, we were allowed one hour in the yard until 6:30 to walk around, smoke and generally exercise. It was my first day in the yard that three cons approached me and introduced themselves. One said his name was Vincent Capuana and he was an anarchist and so were his friends. He told me that he knew all about me and that I should know that I had plenty of friends here. I found out that one of them, Charlie Lipani, was an anarchist converted to Communism by Ben Gitlow when he was in Sing Sing and Charles used to wash Gitlow's laundry for a small weekly stipend. He was serving a life sentence for extortion as a member of the Mafia and Black Hand Society. The other was Vincent Lapozi—also serving a life sentence —which is 14 years with good behavior. Capuana himself was serving a life sentence for being caught with a suitcase full of bombs in 1927 in an attempt to blow up the police headquarters and Italian Consulate during the Sacco-Vanzetti demonstrations prior to their execution. He was a member of the Galiano Group of anarchists which were believers in individual terror, etc.

Talking to Capuana and his friends on my second outing in the yard, Capuana pointed out to me a young boy of about 21 named Mario Gilleti. He told me the boy was in for two years because of his participation in a murder of two fascists in New York, and that he got mail from the International Labor Defense. He also told me that he was a degenerate (sodomite) and very few people bothered with him. A few months later he was taken to Ellis Island for deportation and the Communist Party and ILD got him to leave to the Soviet Union as a hero, knowing that he was the one who accused Greco and Corrello of shooting the Fascist* during a parade in New York. They were defended by Clarence Darrow through the Communist Party and the I.L.D. and were freed.

From 6:30 until I fell asleep I used to sit and think of what I did to deserve this punishment. What was wrong with the way I led my 29 years. The whole picture of my life flashed through my mind— my father in Russia struggling for a piece of bread in cold misery; my mother sitting and crying for her sons, some in America, others in jail —and us kids sitting starved and cold, picking out chicken feathers. The police searches of our home, our being despised for being Jews and radicals. I was trying to figure out the reasons for our behavior in Russia, and I got the answer: no freedom and plenty of oppression.

I also began to analyze the reasons of our behavior in the United States, where education is free and everyone has the right to an education, where there is free speech and everyone has a right to say what he thinks, where there is freedom to work and make a living at whatever you are able to do, where there is freedom to worship as one pleases, where there is no official discrimination because of religion, where one is free to believe in anything he sees fit. In other words, where people have the right to live as human beings. I decided to speak to the librarian and try to borrow books from the library. I began to reread American history and the struggles in the establishment of the United States. The more I read, the more inter-

*Count De Revel was Mussolini's leader of the Fascists in the U.S.—The Lega Fascio de North America.

133

ested I became in analyzing the struggle of our pioneers, their suffering, sacrifices, misery, sickness and deaths; their oppression first by the British and then by their suffering in the wilderness with Indian massacres. Wars such as the American Civil War, the Spanish American War, World War I. The millions of lives given for just one word: Freedom. Freedom to worship, freedom of education and most of all freedom from oppression by kings and dictators.

I began to compare the teachings of Marx, Trotsky and Stalin and came to the conclusion that Communism, socialism and other "isms" are nothing less than a jealous fantasy, a distorted dream by those who had a "have not," "could not," and "will not" philosophy, distorted by people who, under oppression like that of the Czars, Nazis or Fascists, will condemn the whole world to ruin just because one corner of it is being corrupted, or junk the whole cart because one wheel is broken.

Little by little I began to have mental reservations about Marxism. I also began to worry after reading the reports of the First Five-Year Plan and the deportation of millions to Siberia.

One day I was called into the office of Warden Wilson and in the presence of H. Siebert, principal keeper and Deputy Warden and was told to stop the discussions I was holding, and since it was time for me to appear for possible parole, I had better stop or he would recommend that no parole be given me.

I had spoken with Capuana, who was one of the most intelligent radicals I ever met, many times, and we always discussed Marx, Lenin, Kropotkin, Schopenhauer, Voltaire, anarchism, socialism, Communism, etc. Every week we would continue our little debates until I began to have quite a following among the inmates on Saturdays and Sundays, because on these days we were in the yard from 1:00 to 5:30 P.M. unless it rained or snowed. They showed an old movie in the mess hall for those who cared to see it, others remained in their cells. In the yard, we carried out debates between me and Capuana on how to capture state power; Dictatorship of the Proletariat and Transition to Communism, "From each according to his ability, to each according to his need," the anarchist system without any state versus the Communist system of the Soviet.

After every debate or discussion, we practiced real American democracy by throwing open the floor for questions and discussions. We would sit on the ground in the yard in groups of 8 to 10, watching out for the guards, because of the prison rules of no grouping. The prisoners would agree with us that a revolution was needed, because they personally were grieved and not allowed to break any laws against robbery, looting, murder, etc.

CHAPTER XX

My cell had turned into a library because I was receiving so many books from the outside—from friends, through publishers, I got books on philosophy, economics, sociology, history and military and political science, plus newspapers. I systematically arranged my reading periods.

Meanwhile, I was receiving news by mail from such members of the Communist Party leadership as William Z. Foster in which they gave me the latest news in the Party, and the Party line—which I began to show a lessening interest in. I was already beginning to doubt their truthfulness, thanks to my chances for meditation. I also got a steady flow of mail from the American Civil Liberties Union and especially from Comrade Forrest Bailey, whom I knew to be a member of the Communist Party. He was the Assistant Director of ACLU while Roger Baldwin was Director. Baldwin never failed to confer with the ninth floor of the Party on any move of the ACLU. The ninth floor housed the inner sanctum of the Communist Party, the top leadership at National Headquarters at 35 East 12th Street and 50 East 13th Street. As a rule, no one but a trusted Communist Party member could enter the ninth floor. Baldwin was a frequent visitor.

My Mother's visits to me were like a dose of good medicine. She would stay four or five days in one of the rooming houses not far from the prison so she could see me every day. It was a hardship for this little old woman to travel by train from New York to Comstock, but my Mother spared nothing when it came to her children.

My Father's visits became more important as I began to doubt the wisdom of "Charlie" Marx and "Joey" Stalin. Whenever he got the chance, whether at home or in his visits to me in prison, he always brought forth his Golden Rule and belief in God, and in his visits to me he saw that some of it was beginning to tell, since my arguments

136

against his religious beliefs were weaker. He was shrewd and could see what was happening.

On October 2, I appeared before the Parole Board and Dr. Raymond F. C. Kieb, the chairman, wanted me to promise that I would abstain from my former activities, something I refused to do. I was held back the next month and then the third time on December 5 I tried a bribe. Through my brother Nathan and another man I payed $1,500 to Ed. J. Glynn. Part of this money reached a member of the Parole Board, Mrs. Celia Paton of Saratoga Springs, and she had obviously softened up the board by the time of my next hearing. But since I still wouldn't make the promise Dr. Kieb, the chairman, asked for, I was turned down again.

For the rest of my stay in prison I continued to read more and more early American history. Otherwise, life was cold, grim and brutal. There was no Mutual Welfare League, and no direct liaison between the prisoners and officials. The slightest infraction could bring a beating with a blackjack or an iron bar by the most cruel guards imaginable. Or you could wind up in the "cooler." This was a dark hole in the basement with no bed or chair. You were put in stripped naked. Rations were a gill of water and one slice of bread every 24 hours. A first infraction could bring you 30 days of this and loss of good behavior privileges for up to six months. A second infraction could double this and a third sent you to Dannemora. I was never a tractable prisoner. I couldn't overcome an instinct to fight back at injustice and bullying, and on several occasions landed in the "cooler."

I was permanently assigned to digging ditches for eight hours in frozen earth in ten degree weather. In the evenings, before going to my cell, I was permitted to visit the library. I discovered that our history is an amazing story—in spirit, in the quality of individuals and the measure of their accomplishments. Here was no socialist experiment. Quite the contrary. It was an individual effort, and was something new in the world. Socialism is an admission that the individual is unable to cope with his affairs; that it takes a group, supervised by some superior intelligence, to solve the ordinary problems of living. It is based on the same belief that motivated all systems prior to 1776 —that the individual simply can't go it alone. But here in America he had gone it alone, and the result was phenomenal. And more important than success or material benefits, the individual has emerged a dignified figure. The dignity has to do with a man standing up to life on his two feet. There is something ennobling about a man's living by that philosphy, which comes close to the Bible and that bit of hard philosophy which always guided my Father and gave him dignity even in defeat—that every tub must stand on its own bottom. My understanding of American pioneers brought me to respect and understand my Father more. And it brought more doubt about the wisdom of socialism.

For a long time, I had lived by never questioning. I had accepted the conclusions of my brother Joseph and the wisdom of V. I. Lenin, Leon Trotsky, Eugene V. Debs, William D. Haywood, Daniel De Leon and the others. But was it wisdom? I began to see these men as emotionally disturbed instead of gods spreading the fires of revelation.

The hard prison life went on monotonously, day after day. But at night I read. My mind, at least, escaped confinement. After three weeks at ditch digging, the guard received a note and I was given a job as tool checker.

In October, Mother wrote that she was coming to see me. She had contacted the union and had asked Irving Potash* to furnish her with a car to make the trip, but he had refused. I was a Trotskyite, he told her, and "the furriers are finished with him." Mother made the long journey by train, arriving late in the afternoon. Old and weary—she was 80—she slipped and fell while getting out of a bus and hurt her hip badly. But she stayed five days at a nearby boarding house and hobbled to the prison every day.

In December, 1930, the Parole Board called me in and without any questions, informed me that I was about to receive a Christmas present. I was going home on December 20th.

I thanked all the members of the Board and returned to my cell. I began rounding up my possessions—to give them away. To one old codger—a murderer serving 99 years—I gave my bedroom slippers, handy on the cold concrete floors at night, and a pair of pajamas. To another prisoner I gave my singing canary. To others, I distributed shirts, bed linen and my personal library, a good-sized collection of Marxist literature.

On December 19, 1930, the day before my release, I was called to the Warden's office and a piece of paper was put before me. I was

*See Appendix II, p. 241.

told to sign a statement that after my release I would never take part in radical activities. I refused to sign, and said that I would not even give such a promise verbally. He grinned and offered his hand. I kept my hands in my pockets. I had served every day of my time, counting the days I was locked in the Mineola County Jail, and I felt I had gotten a raw deal. I wanted everybody to know it, I had a chip on my shoulder.

"All right," he said, "if that's the way you want it."

He told me I would get $20.00 in cash and a railroad ticket to New York City, both to be handed to me by my escort when I boarded the train next morning.

I went to the state shop and was fitted for a suit of clothes. They were all the same, except for the size—dark grey with green checks. (Every New York policeman spotted you the moment you stepped off a train.) Next, a visit to the barbershop.

That night, there was little sleeping in my cell block. We had a "party" that went on all night, with the prisoners yelling from cell to cell. "Good-bye Bolshevik!" was the toast. I bribed the guards with five pounds of groceries and they let the men visit my cell for a little drink; something had been smuggled for the occasion.

Things finally quieted down, and I tried to sleep, but lay thinking about Mother and Father, how they were making out in their old age, and what I could do when I got out. I was still a Communist, but my heart wasn't in it. Finally, at dawn, a guard came and told me to get ready.

In the prison office was a package—a suitcase from Mother, containing one of my suits. I didn't have time to change, however, and left in the prison garb. It was bitter cold—six below zero. A guard went with me to the station where a local train was waiting. It would take me to Albany, and there I would change to the main line of the New York Central.

The guard walked with me to the nearest coach and gave me the $20.00 and my ticket. He looked at me with a grin as he handed over the money.

"I've been pretty nice to you," he said. "Ain't you going to see me?"

He was Ben Benno, the most brutal guard at the prison. I had seen men struck with an iron rod he carried for merely looking annoyed at him. I had been struck on several occasions.

"Yes, I'm going to see you," I said.

I mounted the steps. The train was about to start. As it began moving I turned and aimed a kick at his head. Then I dived into the coach. I didn't even bother to look back.

CHAPTER XXI

During the trip from Albany to New York, my thoughts kept churning as I tried to resolve the conflict between Communism and Americanism—between my involvement with Communism and my desire to strike out in new directions. I wanted to live a normal life. This desire, and my ability to see "normal" as being something outside the Marxian world, indicated the extent of my intellectual break with Marxism.

But how is one to break with an idea that has controlled his entire life?

I was sick of Stalinist Communism and of American Party functionaries who lived easy lives. But everybody I knew was in the movement and my term in prison had taught me one thing: you must have friends. You can't live alone. I don't mean to recommend the group living that Communists have adopted to break down and smother the individual. I mean the absolute necessity of having one friend—or two or three if you're lucky—to whom you can talk with frankness and receive understanding. Where, outside the socialist movement, was I to find such a friend?

The train sped down the east bank of the Hudson River, and I watched the play of winter lights on the slated water and the dull grey bluffs across the river. We passed Sing Sing, and the grey walls filled me with a sadness—but at the same time with the happiness that we feel when we awake from a nightmare. The prison guards I knew were frequently brutal—as bad as the criminals. But I had no romantic idea that Communist prisons were better. I had better sense than that. I knew that conditions in Russia were far worse. And the basic philosophy was different. The policy of free countries was to correct these conditions and to make improvements. In Russia, the cruelty was by official design. Soviet life became steadily more brutal.

I had come to no conclusion about my future when the decision was, in a sense, taken out of my hands.

As I came up the ramp and entered the station, I was seized by a pack of shoving and shouting people. A demonstration had been arranged to welcome me home! They waved "Welcome home, Malkin" placards and carried me on their shoulders. In the wild confusion, I discovered that there were two opposing groups in the demonstration—and I was the prize. One was fur workers from the fur union, but not the official union, and the other was the Trotskyist opposition, which had broken with the Stalin-controlled American organization. James P. Cannon, a former member of the Central Committee, had left the Stalinist forces to head this group. Among the Stalinists, none of the leaders were present. But there were many familiar faces from the rank and file whom I had known in the labor movement.

I turned my back on the Stalinists and joined the Cannon group. We left the station, followed by cheering members of both factions. We went first to the street in front of the Stalinist headquarters at 50 East 13th Street, where the crowd sang the "Internationale"—with Foster and some of the other leaders looking down from the windows.

The demonstration, with me captive at its head, then snaked down Fourth Avenue and eventually ended at the Presbyterian Labor Temple on 14th Street and Second Avenue.

After Cannon opened the meeting, Max Schachtman, one of his lieutenants, told the cheering crowd how I had stood up for the working class. He said that the Stalinists, on the eve of my departure for prison, had disowned and suspended me from the Party and had failed to exhibit the slightest interest in my welfare during my long incarceration. "Is this the kind of leadership the working class wants?" he asked. "No!" shouted many in the crowd to the applause of the left-wing Trotskyites—and the stony silence of the Stalinists.

I could not keep back a smile as I listened to the empty words—the pot calling the kettle black. I looked at the faces of the cheering mob, some confused, some adoring, all expectant—waiting for a miracle. Listening to the words, I felt that I knew more than the speakers, with their Marxian catch phrases and rehearsed tricks. All I wanted was to sit in dispassionate judgement of the facts—not to vibrate with emotion to the empty phrases of a trained rabble rouser.

142

I found myself in a confused and psychologically—as well as economi-cally—depressed world. It seemed that the system had broken down. Nearly everyone was saying so, including top opinion makers who had never been associated with the Marxist movement but were now talking a confused and emotional Marxism. Unemployed were eating refuse they had fished out of garbage cans. Nobody seemed to have the answer—except the Marxists. In Congress, the Democrats, long out of power, had come back strong with the 1930 elections and were now locked in a ridiculous stalemate with the Republicans. Any solu-tion waited on the 1932 elections, and in the interval, the socialists and Communists had joined forces to make matters worse wherever possible. They launched a drive to organize industry on a scale never before attempted.

During my first few weeks at home, I was unemployed and friend-less. Then one day I got word that Foster wanted to see me. When we met at his office, he had Bill Dunn with him. Between them, they tried to convince me that despite my disagreements with the Stalin-ist leadership, my place was in the mainstream of the labor move-ment. That mainstream was headed and directed, they said, by the Stalinists. This was true, in the element of labor I knew.

Foster showed me modifications of positions on the part of the Profintern. Certain concessions had been granted to the American branch of the Party, which had been put into effect at the Trade Union League convention in Cleveland in 1930.

Foster persuaded me to come back into the Communist move-ment. I threw myself into Party work in an attempt to purge my secret half-heartedness.

This was in the spring of 1931.

My first assignment after returning was to direct a raid on a mass meeting called by Norman Thomas, Carlo Tresca and others of the liberal-socialist leadership to protest the rise of fascist influence. They had not invited the Communists and Foster and his crowd decided to break up the meeting.

"J. Peters," who had replaced Pepper as the Communist Interna-tional representative while I was in prison, summoned me to the ninth floor of Party headquarters, where it was decided that I should mobilize a sizable squad of labor goons. I called for a mass meeting the next day in the fifth-floor auditorium, and more than 300 showed up from the Furriers' Union, the National Marine Workers Industrial

Union and other Red labor fronts. I told them we wanted a large, tough delegation at the socialist meeting, and all of them were to show up at the Irving Plaza Hall, 15th Street and Irving Place. They were to scatter about in threes and fours over the auditorium, with a sizable number finding seats in the balconies, near the rail, looking down on the main floor. They would be able to throw down chairs on the heads of the Socialists when the fight we were planning broke out. A steering committee was named to watch me for the signal.

I arrived at the hall ahead of the others and chose a seat in the center, toward the front of the auditorium. I knew the place well; I kept my eye on an exit to the right of the stage, where I could escape quickly into a backyard.

It was Sunday afternoon and the place was jammed. I waited for Norman Thomas, the main speaker, to take the floor. I then jumped to my feet. I loudly protested the exclusion of the Communists and organizations allied with them at this important meeting. As a Communist and a union member, I demanded that I be permitted to speak against the rise of Fascist and Nazi influence in Europe, which so greatly threatened the working class in America.

Thomas raised a hand and shouted that I was out of order. The crowd joined him, and I gave the signal by putting both hands above my head and yelling, "I demand to be heard!"

Hell broke out all over the auditorium and objects began raining from above. Thomas dived under a table. Quickly, a group of supporters leaped to the platform and stood ready to defend him from anything that might develop from the swinging and shouting mob. Lead pipes and even knives came into play. I had thoughtfully surrounded myself with a bodyguard, a group of waterfront toughs who drove a wedge toward the side door. As police poured into the hall, I escaped into the evening air and dashed across a small courtyard. Boosted over a fence, I came out in the street where an automobile was waiting.

I was driven quickly to Party headquarters, where I found that my shirt was bloody. I had suffered no wound, but apparently had been in contact with someone who had. I washed up, put on a shirt that someone handed me and went to Israel Amter's apartment on 13th Street. He was State Secretary of the Party and I told him briefly what happened. He sent me to Peters, who was waiting in the Mosco-

144

witz and Lupowitz Restaurant on Second Avenue near Second Street.

Apparently, Peters had already received a report. He got up and gave me a warm greeting. After I gave him a full account, he clapped my shoulders: "You have not lost your touch; you are better than ever. It was a job well done. Excellent!"

The success restored me to favor in the Party. A laudatory report went to Moscow, and I received a congratulatory message from the Kremlin. It was delivered by Harry Pollitt, Secretary General of the British Communist Party, who arrived in this country on a special mission to help restore the American branch to Stalin's line.

CHAPTER XXII

My next major assignment was to join Tom Mooney's mother on a fund-raising tour of the country. Mooney had been convicted of planting a bomb at a Preparedness Day parade in San Francisco during World War I. The Communists were quick to capitalize on the liberal agitation to get him out of prison, and also organized the defense of a group of its agitators who had been imprisoned in California for activities in the Imperial Valley vegetable region. Another cause was that of the "Scottsboro boys," nine Negroes who, in March, 1931, were accused of raping two white women aboard a freight train in Alabama and quickly became a *cause célèbre* among liberals.

Mother Mooney was a valuable theatrical property. Her presence drew the crowds, and the money came rolling in. After traveling the country with her from coast to coast, I returned to Party headquarters in New York with $19,000—a tremendous amount in those depression days. I was told to turn over the money to the International Labor Defense, Room 402, 799 Broadway at 11th Street. A woman clerk—her name was Helen Taub—gave me a receipt for $920. I looked at it in disbelief and asked her—"Why only $920?"

She answered that it was the Party's orders. Remembering what happened to the fund collected for my own defense—about $480,000 of which only about $50,000 was accounted for—I knew she probably spoke the truth. But I refused to accept the receipt on her word. I wanted some higher confirmation and she sent me to Amter at Party headquarters, which had been moved to 35 East 12th Street. He took me to Browder on the ninth floor, who complimented me on the work I had done. Then he explained that the Party could not begin to exist on the dues it collected from the members. It was necessary to raise funds through fronts and mass appeal to popular causes. He added with a wink that a little juggling of the books helped out. I asked about the $85,000 the Soviet Union sent each month and Browder said this went for other purposes, such as paying off union leaders and buying information.

I was not satisfied but knew that this was all the answer I would get.

Browder and Amter quickly changed the subject. They began talking about a new mission the Party had planned for me. I was to take a group of writers to the Kentucky coal fields.

I knew the Party had been trying for months to penetrate this region—and had gotten nowhere. When the question of organizing the Kentucky miners had first come up I had suggested that a particular Lenin School grad was just the man for the job. He got it, and was down there just two days before landing in a hospital with a fractured skull and other injuries. It took the hospital weeks to remove all the tar a mob had smeared over him before riding him out of the county on a rail.

A left-wing task force to carry food to the starving miners in defiance of capitalist mine bosses, was launched with a plethora of propaganda. During the spring and summer, newspaper accounts had given the impression that a full-size war raged out of control in connection with a miners strike in this often violent mountain region. Several newspaper reporters were allegedly beaten and driven from the area. Into this boiling cauldron plunged Theodore Dreiser, as chairman of the relief committee of 19 that included one of this country's greatest authors, John Dos Passos.*

Dreiser didn't live long enough to change his mind, as far as I know. At that time, in the autumn of 1931, he was in a literary calm after the success of *An American Tragedy*.

The relief mission was carried on in the name of the National Committee for the Defense of Political Prisoners, at 80 East 11th Street. But behind the scenes was the National Labor Defense, a strong arm of the Communist apparatus.

The Southern journey was launched at a dinner in Teutonia Hall, 153 Third Avenue, which was well reported in the New York papers. The next day the caravan headed down Highway One—two trucks loaded with food and clothing, preceded by three automobiles loaded with writers, Communists, socialists and dupes. Pre-

*Dos Passos later left the Party to become an avid fighter against Communism.

scheduled stops to harangue the gullible and pass the hat for loose change were made along the way.

Before consenting to go, I had demanded that the Party provide me with my own car and had been given a battered Model A Ford. I had the address and a letter of introduction to a former Pennsylvania miner and IWW member living in Pineville, Kentucky. I planned to make my stay in Kentucky as inconspicuous as possible by staying at his home.

Initially, I stuck with the caravan, giving what advice I could from my experience with Mrs. Mooney. We put on quite a show, and got a lot of newspaper publicity. From Wilmington, Delaware, we headed down to Norfolk, Virginia, with the idea of stirring up trouble among the unemployed shipyard workers. Then we cut across Virginia, zig-zagging toward the West Virginia-Kentucky mountains. I left the show at Front Royal, Virginia, and three days later, when the caravan pulled into town, was living quietly with the miner and his family in Pineville.

The newspapers took up the story from there. The local people found the writers ridiculous, even to the sound of their voices. I circulated quietly among the crowds at the street-corner meetings and listened to their ripe comments. The whole thing blew wide open when a vigilante group broke into Dreiser's hotel room and claimed that they found the novelist in bed with one of the women writers.

Newspapers reported the scandal from coast to coast on November 10, as a Bell County grand jury handed up an indictment charging Dreiser and Marie Pergain with adultery. Dreiser issued a statement denying the charge, and charging a frame-up.

On November 16 the same grand jury handed up a second indictment. Dreiser, Miss Pergain, Dos Passos, George Maurer, of the International Labor Defense, and six others were charged with violation of Kentucky's criminal syndicalism law. Others named were author Charles Rumford Walker and his wife, Adelaide; Samuel Ornitz, a writer who acted as Dreiser's first assistant; Celia Kuhn, a secretary; M. P. Levy, a writer; and "A. Gohna," a name the grand jury confused for Harry Gannes, a member of the group and representative of the National Miners Union.

The Bell County Circuit Court dismissed both indictments in 1933, but for a time, the incident made good newspaper copy and was even echoed in the halls of Congress.

The National Committee for the Defense of Political Prisoners petitioned Congress for an investigation. Among those signing the petition were Mary Heaton Vorse, novelist and poet; Malcolm Cowley, editor of the *New Republic*; Alan Taub, an attorney; Harold Hickerson, playwright; Doris Parks, a relief worker; Edmund Wilson, the critic; Jessie Wakefield, active in the ILD; and Anna Rochester, of the Labor Research Association. Most of the signers were Communist Party members.

In reply, Pineville citizens dispatched the following wire to Congress:

> The citizens of Pineville have for six months been pestered to death with Communists disguised as writers from New York, whose purpose was to obtain publicity for their doctrine and for books they intended to write. They have fomented trouble, discord and violence, and have brought about an intolerable condition. . . . If there is to be any investigation, we suggest it begin with New York and the nest of Communists there.

I lingered on pleasantly until after the first of the year. There was little I could do in Kentucky. The mountaineers were a rugged, independent lot, even in poverty, and just not ready for Communism. I returned to New York and found the Party brass buzzing with plans to send me to Russia for post-graduate work at the Lenin School.

CHAPTER XXIII

The Party leadership said that I was ready for higher instruction in all-round leadership. My natural abilities were good, but Moscow could give the polish that would enable me to reach a position of real importance in the Party.

Foster, Browder and the others had plans to send me right off to Russia. I would be enrolled in the Frunze Military Academy and instructed on the latest Soviet techniques of espionage and sabotage. But I was not crazy and not romantic. I was born in Russia—I lived there. I had vivid memories—and no desire to return.

My Mother's illness, resulting from the fall she had taken when visiting me at Comstock, had become worse during the winter. She was completely bedridden and in great pain. I explained to Party leaders that her precarious health made it necessary to postpone my departure. But in May there was a farewell dinner for me at the Hotel Albert, University Place and East 10th Street. One of two co-sponsors was Samuel J. Novick, former President and Treasurer of the Electronics Corp. of America, now one of the fugitive Soviet agents living in Mexico. Before Novick's activities and Party affiliation came out, he had also successfully sponsored the Johannes Steel radio broadcasts during the entire World War II period. The other sponsor, also a name in radio and electronics, was Irving Koenigsberg, alias Koenig. These two were selected to front for a dinner that would not have looked too good, considering my prison record, had it been an open Party affair. It might have aroused suspicion in some quarters, so two dummies were chosen. The guests numbered some 200 Communists, socialists and friendly liberals, and the talk centered on my departure and the Russian industrial plan, with frequent gleeful returns to the American depression and the prospect that things would get much worse.

The Party had obtained a fake passport for me and my departure seemed imminent when Mother's illness suddenly became critical.

For seven days and nights Nathan and I took turns next to her bed at 146 Monroe Street, where she had lain for so many painful months. On June 10 she died, with her head on my right arm. I was the baby, the last one she had looked after. She wanted me near and whispered that I should bend close. She kissed me and then lay back on my arm and died. A tear dropped from her left eye.

Mother's death settled the problem of my going to Russia. I simply informed the Party that Father, broken after her death, was too old and lonely to be left behind.

Later that summer, I went to Chicago secretly to take charge of District 8 which covered much of the Midwest, with headquarters at 208 South Wells Street. The one person informed of my position was Boleslaw K. Gebert, later in charge of labor unions in Poland.* He was then chairman of District 8, which included Illinois, Wisconsin, Indiana and part of Ohio.

Gebert, who was about thirty-five, had never troubled to take out citizenship papers. He was one of the founders of the Communist Party, and before that was a leading left-wing socialist. He had been a member of the Soviet secret police in this country since 1920, and wielded much power among Polish, Ukrainian and Slavic groups in the Chicago area.

My first act was to step up an organizing drive for the Trade Union Unity League, the Communist rival to the AFL, among stockyard and needle trade workers on the South Side. In this same area we invaded, without too much success, the Pullman Company, which was featured in the nation's big labor strike of 1894. That was the year Daniel De Leon briefly wrested control of the AFL from Samuel Gompers and President Cleveland called in the troops to keep the mail rolling.

On the South Side, much of it fast sinking into slums, was the University of Chicago, the intellectual Mecca of the Midwest. At the other end of town was Northwestern University, and Communist power in Chicago radiated between these two poles. A key man at Chicago University was Dr. Robert Morss Lovett. I worked closely with him, keeping his Party book and advising him on current policy. He lived at Hull House, where Jane Addams had created a reputation

*Until 1959. Today he may be in a Soviet concentration camp or dead.

as a social worker and do-gooder. She was a secret Party member, having joined under Arne Swaback, when he was district organizer there in 1928.

I remember one day, after I had been in Chicago for a short time, Dr. Lovett called at my office with a young woman whom he introduced as a student at Chicago University. She was Martha Dodd, daughter of Professor William Dodd, a member of the university faculty. Martha Dodd together with her husband, D. Stern, later figured in Soviet espionage. When they learned that they were wanted by the United States authorities they escaped to Mexico and from there to Czechoslovakia and through the aid of the O'Dwyer brothers, Paul and William, were able to take out their financial holdings with them.

It was during the visit of Henri Barbusse to Chicago in 1933 that I organized a propaganda stunt which won me international fame among Communist insiders.

Barbusse, a French Communist writer and leader of the pacifist *Carte L'International de la Pensee,* was one of the founders of the World Committee Against War and Fascism. Arriving in New York, openly proclaiming his Communism and calling for the destruction of capitalism, he was eased into the country by Edward Corsi, then commissioner of Immigration and Naturalization. He was feted across the country, primarily by intellectual dupes, at socialist-communist meetings. In Chicago, with Gebert and Dr. Lovett assisting, I arranged an anti-war demonstration for Barbusse at the Chicago Coliseum. The dramatic moment came when a squad of American soldiers in full uniform, but all wearing masks, marched onto the stage and in front of the gaping audience, pledged their loyalty to the Soviet Union in any war that might involve Russia and the United States.

Then they were whisked out a side door and into the street. They drove off in waiting automobiles before anybody could question them.

These men were part of a Communist unit in the Illinois National Guard. Gebert and I were the only ones at the meeting who knew their identities and their appearance created a sensation in the newspapers. It was reported gleefully in *Pravda,* which trumpeted that the American army stood ready to join the Soviets in any war that might arise against capitalism.

I received hearty congratulations from both the Comintern and the Central Committee of the Soviet Communist Party. The international representative of the Central Executive Committee in the U. S. in New York, Norman Tallentire, rushed to Chicago with a personal message from Foster, and his crowd. With him was Harry Pollitt, the British Party leader, and they came to my office with a young woman who was a student at Northwestern. They introduced her as Hertha Kouisinin, daughter of Communist Otto Kouisinin who was later named President of the Karelian "Republic" that the Soviets carved out of Finland in their war with that tiny country in 1939–40.

I returned to New York in January 1934 as chairman of the Chicago delegation to the first convention of the Friends of the Soviet Union. I had been nominated for the post by William Kruse,* of the famed Chicago electronics firm of Bell and Howell.

I had known Kruse since early 1922 when he had joined the Workers Party. He was at one time secretary of the Young Peoples Socialist League, and attended the second, third, and fourth Party congresses in Moscow. (And, was succeeded by Oliver Carlson as the National Secretary of the Young Workers League.) He was supposed to have been expelled with the Lovestone group in 1929, but when I was in Chicago he consistently worked behind the scenes with the Party, and has never testified about anything that went on while he was a member.

In New York I renewed old acquaintances, The Communists were out in the open as they had not been since 1919. The younger members were fired with excitement—revolution was just around the corner. But the old timers, who remembered 1920, were more subdued. It was the time of the Popular Front, the reunion of all Marxist factions, plus whatever dupes could be recruited; and it was the time of the New Deal, of Harry Hopkins and the Works Progress Administration.

The Friends of the Soviet Union had its convention in the Star Casino at Park Avenue and 107th Street. It was all ablaze with red banners and streamers and slogans decorated the hall: "Defend the Soviet Union!" "Long Live the Communist International!" "Down with American Imperialism!"

*See Appendix I, p. 234.

153

Alexander Trachtenberg* clapped me on the shoulder. I had done a great job in Chicago and the Party was proud of me. We were moving ahead on all fronts, he said. There was reason for rejoicing. With him, in a little group, which I joined in conversation, were Moissaye J. Olgin,* Jack Stachel* and Herman Goldfrank.* They each shook my hand warmly.

Trachtenberg told about Harold Ware, "Mother" Bloor's son, who was in Washington and had organized a Party cell in Henry Wallace's Department of Agriculture. There was promised real progress, at last, on the farm front where the Party had failed so miserably and had left itself open to repeated jibes from Moscow.

Trachtenberg then told me to have my group of forty-four delegates alerted to vote for a resolution that was to be introduced by Professor Corliss Lamont of Columbia University, and seconded by Stachel. The resolution would pledge American labor to the support of the Soviet Union and would be used as propaganda by Moscow to undermine the United States Government in Asia, Europe, Africa, the Middle East and Latin America.

I spent five days listening to speeches and resolutions, and each one left me more bored than the previous one.

The conclave ended with orders for the delegates to return to their homes, organize mass meetings and popularize slogans to create a pattern of thinking that would make Marxian designs more acceptable to the American people. Hunger and stories of apple salesmen and the "army of unemployed" were to be played up to help reinforce the impression that capitalism had completely collapsed. Federal work projects like the Civil Works Administration were a must, but the Communists were told to open an attack on the National Recovery Administration as being a fascist measure for the enslavement of the workers.

*See Appendix I, p. 235.

CHAPTER XXIV

Shortly after the convention, I was transferred from my duties in Chicago and told I had been selected for a new, important mission. From then on I was to be occupied with labor, particularly in the communications fields. I was one of the four red chiefs assigned to organizing new unions within existing labor organizations.

My first project was the Newspaper Guild, which had gained a lot of publicity and had made some headway since Allen Raymond, of the *New York Herald Tribune*, was elected the first president at a meeting in the Hotel Algonquin on November 15, 1933. Shortly thereafter, Heywood Broun, elected a vice-president, supplanted Raymond. Broun and Morris Watson, of the Associated Press's New York Bureau, became the powers in the Guild. Both were Communists.

I first knew Broun as an old-time socialist, who was then working on the *New York World*. According to communist records that I handled, Broun had been a dues-paying Party member since April 1933.

The first evidences of a split in the Guild—an indication of the Communist influence—came at the national convention in Cleveland in June 1935. The Guild had started as an independent union, but a movement developed to take it into the AFL. This was strongly and successfully opposed by the left-wing and Communist members, who eventually took it into the CIO when John L. Lewis set it up with Communists as the chief organizers.

An attack on the NRA was sounded by left-wing and Communist delegates. The NRA symbol of an eagle was called the "black crow," and the administrator, General Hugh S. Johnson, the leader of American fascism. But Broun, as president, had to admit that if it had not been for Section 7-A of the NRA code, there would have been no Newspaper Guild. It was this law, expanded into the Wagner

Labor Relations Act, that gave power to organized labor. Before NRA, organized labor had dwindled to about 1,500,000 dues-paying members. A year and a half after the adoption by the New Deal, the AFL membership alone had jumped to about 6,500,000 and there were also many unaffiliated industrial union groups.

Morris Watson came into the news when the Associated Press fired him in October 1935. The resulting furor echoed from the court rooms and newspaper headlines for two years. The AP retained John W. Davis, 1924 Democratic presidential nominee, as defense attorney, charging that the NRA clause that required it to rehire Watson, as directed by the Labor Board arbitrator, was unconstitutional.

I remember a dramatic court-room scene that involved Broun as a principal character witness while the case was being heard in U.S. District Court of Southern New York, before Judge William Bondy. Judge Bondy had ordered an adjournment after an hour long argument, but suddenly Broun was on his feet. He wanted to make a speech. Judge Bondy replied that the Guild's case had been ably presented by Morris L. Ernst, but this didn't satisfy Broun. He asked for five minutes on "behalf of the thousands of newspaper workers of the country." To this Judge Bondy replied that "to be brutally frank," he didn't see what could be accomplished by listening to Broun except "to make news for the papers tomorrow."

Broun again rose to his feet. He wanted to know if he could have "just two minutes." Shaking his head, Judge Bondy replied that he knew the history of unions, and was personally "in sympathy with the labor cause," but that the only question before the court was one of law and no purpose could be served by listening to Broun.

At this point, the toussle-headed Heywood Broun, who had sat down, jumped up with a sheaf of papers in his hand. He asked if he might read a few words, and without waiting for an answer, began reading:

"John W. Davis is asking you for permission for the AP to run a yellow-dog shop."

Broun sat down with a satisfied smirk, and now the grey-haired Davis was on his feet, demanding, in a voice quivering with anger, that the remark be stricken from the record. Judge Bondy so ordered.

But Broun was not finished. He grabbed the floor once more and addressed the court.

"But you are arguing economics now," Judge Bondy objected.

"Doesn't economics belong in a court of law?" Broun inquired.

"No," replied the judge, "and it would be better for our government if it would desist from entering into economic problems in which there is so much diversity of opinion."

The case, along with similar ones, eventually reached the Supreme Court. This body, on April 12, 1937, in a 5 to 4 split decision, ruled against the AP. Watson was ordered reinstated. But by this time, he was rolling high as the international vice-president of the Guild and had no further interest in getting back his job as a news reporter. His Soviet sympathies led him to take the side of the Kremlin in its war on tiny Finland, and from there he went on to become an editor of the *People's World*, West Coast organ of the Communist Party.

In December, 1935, I was called to a Central Committee meeting on the 9th floor of Party headquarters at 35 East 12th Street. Here I found Browder, Stachel, Peters, Al Marini,* William Weiner** and Max Steinberg, organizing secretary, sitting around Browder's desk, waiting for me. Steinberg began the discussion by saying an important new assignment had been worked out for me. Peters explained what they had in mind.

I was to coordinate Communist organization in the transport and communications industries. My responsibility covered a wide field: railways, shipping, subways, longshore operations, telegraph, radio, telephone, etc. We were to take over the unions in these fields, and organize employees who did not yet belong to one. We were to muscle the AFL out of the picture wherever possible.

The Communists, hiding behind "liberal" fronts wherever possible, were leading an attack on William Green and the AFL for failure to organize the great mass of unskilled workmen. This was a new approach to the old problem of the industrial versus the craft union. But nothing was said in the open about this; the Communists were to let sleeping dogs lie. The attacks were based on the broad hypothesis implied by the NRA, and sanctified by the Wagner Labor Relations Act, that every man should belong to a union. The nation was sympathetic to the cause of organized labor, and the Communists simply capitalized on the popular emotion.

There was a natural gap between John L. Lewis and Green, one

*Alias Brown. He was the Communist International representative in the U.S.
**Alias William Blake. His real name is Velvel Varshaver. He served a prison term for passport fraud in 1940–41.

of jealousy on the part of Lewis towards a man he considered his inferior. The Communists were adroit in widening this split. The result was Lewis' decision to back the Congress of Industrial Organizations and a rash of labor disorders, including the famous sitdown strikes of the Detroit auto workers.

An Irishman who had been selected to head the New York subway workers was introduced to me a few days after the meeting at Party headquarters. He was Michael J. Quill, whom I had first met in 1933 at the Red Trade Union Unity League, 799 Broadway. Quill, on that occasion, had talked about his activities with the Irish Republican Army fighting against the Black and Tans in 1920. He claimed that he had been wounded, which accounted for a limp and his use of an Irish blackthorn cane. I had said nothing, but remembered having heard a different story about Quill from an Irishman who knew him in Ireland.

When I saw him this second time, he was accompanied by Rose Wortis, Samuel Nessin (both charter members of the Communist Party and CP functionaries), and John Santos.* Quill had just been chosen to replace Tim O'Shea as president of the newly founded Transport Workers Union.

I started out by challenging Quill on his past.

"Mike, I know something about you. Frankly, we've investigated your background and the facts seem to be that you didn't fight with the Republican Army at all. You fought with the Orangemen and the Black and Tans. This information came from people in your own country in Ireland."

His face turned red and he began sputtering a denial.

"How about 1916?" I said. "I find you were active in the Orange Free State smuggling for the Germans." Quill denied any such connection and although I didn't believe him, I approved of his heading up the union. I think Quill's gift of gab, plus his cultivated Irish brogue, turned the trick. I considered him a natural to line up the Irishmen dominant among the subway workers.

Another man elevated from obscurity was Joe Curran, who has headed the National Maritime Union for many years. He came into the picture as leader of a wildcat strike aboard the S S *California* in San Pedro Harbor in 1937, which earned newspaper headlines across

*See Appendix I, p. 235.

158

the country. He replaced George Mink, who had been ordered to Europe as a Comintern courier, in the fight we had opened against the AFL's International Seamen's Union. Curran was introduced to me by "Joe Brandt," a Communist Party labor organizer whose real name was Joseph Bruinstein, and who later served in the Communist-controlled International Brigade during the Civil War in Spain. We were at a meeting of Section Two of the Party at the old Manhattan Lyceum. With Curran were Tommy Ray, a Soviet courier, and Roy "Horseface" Hudson, a Communist waterfront organizer. A look at Curran—a solid six-foot-two and ham-fisted—convinced me that he was the leader we were looking for. I handled his Communist membership book for a while, which was listed under his Party name "Joseph Narruc," which is Curran spelled backwards.*

All this time, I watched with increasing uneasiness as Soviet Russia turned towards almost open human slavery. There was no longer any denying that the march was in this direction. The so-called treason trials of 1936 ended any doubts for anyone with the intelligence and honesty to question. I realized that I had made a mistake in getting back into the Party. I remembered how I felt when I got out of prison, and once more I turned to American history—reading at night in my apartment from books I borrowed from the public library.

I lived in a two-and-a-half-room apartment in a tenement on 23rd Street, between Second and Third Avenues. It had a steel door and bars on all the windows. The Party had ordered me to make it as burglar proof as possible because in my bedroom was a steel file cabinet full of names and records of important Communists and those who cooperated with them in the labor movement. I had a special combination lock on the cabinet.

In my living room were shelves stocked with books from floor to ceiling. I had one of the best private collections of original Marxist books and documents in the country.**

Buried among the Marxist books and Communist papers was also a very good collection of Jewish religious literature. I turned to this more and more in the summer of 1936, after I moved to One Charles Street in Greenwich Village.

*See Appendix I, p. 235.
**Eventually I turned it over to the House Committee on Un-American Activities.

That fall, Father became ill. His condition worsened, and he was taken to Gouverneur Hospital on the Lower East Side with pneumonia. After a six-day battle under oxygen, he died on October 15, 1936. I felt my guide and mainstay on earth had passed from me.

Father's last words were to inquire if I had heard from Joseph. All these years, he had never once forgotten the bright-eyed little boy with the blond curls he had hoped would grow up to be a rabbi. Until the very end, he never quite gave up hope of seeing Joseph.

I had not heard from or of Joseph since 1935, when he had written from Geneva, where he was serving as assistant to Maxim Litvinov at the old League of Nations. Joseph had wanted me to come to Soviet Russia. It was an embarrassing request because I couldn't go, but neither could I write and tell him what was in my mind. I felt he was still a fanatical Marxist; that had not lived long enough in America to understand what I was dimly and painfully groping for.

When Papa died, my heart was cleansed and I knew it was a wonderful country. I knew Papa was right—and had been all his life. I went out of his room in the hospital with tears streaming down my face and with sadness in my heart. But there was one bright spot; I had found the right way while there was yet time—while there was still a chance to make amends.

CHAPTER XXV

The difficulty of breaking with the Communist Party, as I had discovered when I got out of prison, is the bleak loneliness one must face. No door is open to the world you seek to enter. You have branded yourself an implacable enemy, and the least you can expect is suspicion. It was even more difficult in the 1930s than it is today. In 1937, with sitdown strikes the mark of the times and with labor violence promoted, condoned by the elected officials of government, a man breaking away from the Communist Party invited the open hostility of all liberals and even attacks on his life.

I began by inviting to my apartment people in the Party who were deeply disturbed over the way things were being run from Moscow.

Cautiously, at first, I drew these people to me with a word here and there. Gradually, we came to exchange confidences, and I developed a small group of friends, who were willing to admit in the privacy of my apartment that the Communist Party, as it was being operated, held little chance of success in America. The people who were giving the orders from inside the Kremlin hadn't the slightest idea about life in the United States. Their views were idiotic.

I don't believe that when these meetings began, I had fully come around to accepting the complete failure of Communism. When I came out of prison I had begun to reject Marxism, but my vision had become clouded during the depression by intellectuals on every hand, writing and saying what Communists and socialists had been saying for years. My hesitation—or stupidity—is perhaps a little pardonable in light of the intellectual confusion in which we lived.

I also began meeting secretly with a few expelled Party members whom I'd known intimately in the past. One of these was Joseph Zack Kornfeder, who had spent several years in Moscow and who, as a Soviet courier in Latin America, was arrested in Venezuela in 1932. As a United States citizen, he was released on protest from Washing-

161

ton. Returning home, he had started preaching a program of militant labor action that conflicted strongly with the popular front idea then in vogue. At the Eighth Party Congress in Cleveland in 1934, he was severely criticized for "left-wing deviation" and was ousted. The convention was alive with such terms as "right centralist deviation" and "left centralist opportunism." I knew Marx as well as anybody in the Party, but I didn't know what they were talking about—and I'm sure Foster and Browder never knew what they were talking about. What happened, of course, was that Stalin had ordered a purge and these mysterious terms were seized on as an excuse for shaking off troublesome members who had not taken too well to Party discipline.

Browder, of course, never really understood Marxism. In 1927, when he returned from a Moscow-ordered mission to China, he penned a lengthy and confused paper to explain, from a Communist viewpoint, what was at stake in Asia. I was present at a special meeting of the Central Executive Committee at Party headquarters, then at 43 East 125th Street, to listen to Browder give his report. It was received in embarrassed silence. Bill Dunn made a motion to table it, which was approved, thus dumping it into the waste basket. But while Browder was reading, an idea struck me and I was unable to suppress it. I picked up a pencil and quickly scribbled a few lines of doggerel that passed from hand to hand among the Party's amused hierarchy. It went something like this:

> There is an old man named Browder
> Who keeps sputtering louder and louder;
> He travelled the seas,
> Saw millions of Chinese,
> But can't tell chow mein from clam chowder.

Joseph Zack Kornfeder was ordered expelled unless he submitted a statement to the Central Committee, completely retracting his views and agreeing henceforth to submit fully to Party discipline. Kornfeder was a proud man and he walked out of the Cleveland convention and joined Cannon's Trotskyites. Failing to find what he wanted there, he soon quit and joined what was left of the IWW. But, eventually my good friend Joseph Zack Kornfeder came full circle, and for many years—until his death in 1963—performed heroically by testifying before government bodies as to what he actually saw and experienced while a top Communist.

I was so disgusted at the Cleveland convention that I began plotting some move that would assert the Party's independence of Moscow.

With friends who felt the same, I discussed the Soviet line, past and present, the Kremlin leaders and the character of the American hierarchy, who were nothing more than Moscow's stooges. My friends concurred that we were helping to build a monster which would extinguish the last spark of human liberty and dignity. We agreed on a plan—a desperate plan. We decided to raise funds to publish and distribute literature among Communists and socialists that would call attention to to the things that bothered us. We were perhaps naive and foolish, but we envisioned Marxists re-examining their theory of the good life and how it was to be attained. We thought we might exercise an influence because we all knew so many Marxists who felt as we did. The question was could they be counted on to stand up and assert themselves?

One of my friends turned out to be a secret agent who reported everything we said to the Party leaders. She was a professed Bohemian, who had made a good thing of marrying and divorcing four or five wealthy men and holding them up for alimony. I will simply identify her as F.G. She was then about forty and lived on MacDougal Street. She was an amateur actress and a member of the Provincetown Playhouse group.

Long ago, I gave her full identity to the FBI.

As a result of the information she gave the Party, I was called before the Central Control Commission, of which I had once been chairman. I was charged with counter-revolutionary activities, including fractionalism, right centralist revolutionary opportunism and left centralist deviation; of being an enemy of the working class; of fighting the Comintern, aiding imperialism, Trotskyism, Lovestoneism and Bukharinism. I was even accused of being an agent of the Gestapo and the Japanese.

The hearing was in Browder's office, Room 904 at Party headquarters. Present, besides Browder, were J. Peters, Alexander Trachtenberg, Fred Alpi (alias A. Marini), Charles Dirba, Rose Auerbach, William Weiner, Alexander Radzi, who was a GPU agent, and a scattering of others.

163

I was ordered to surrender my Party membership book, a standard procedure when anyone was brought up on charges—a rule which I myself had instigated years before. The purpose was to deprive the accused of evidence that he was ever a Party member if he decided to go before a grand jury or Congressional committee.

I refused, claiming that my card was my private property: I had payed dues for it and had worked harder than any of them to earn the right to it. I stated that I refused to acknowledge the authority of a "group of opportunists" to sit in judgement of me.

They told me a Communist has no private property. This, I said, was nonsense, and began reeling off the names of secret Party members whose private wealth was an established fact: Frederick Vanderbilt Fields,* Grace Hutchins, a GPU agent and millionaire angel of the Party; Grace Mailhouse Burnham,* owner of the building at 799 Broadway, where many Communist fronts were housed.

Trachtenberg and Dirba began yelling, and I told them to "drop dead."

Dirba, Secretary of the Control Commission and six-foot-three, tried to intimidate me. He shouted that I would be sent to Moscow to stand trial. I told him to stop being silly—and reminded him that I myself had him expelled in 1926 for robbing the Party treasury of $8,500. I dared him to step forward, if he wanted to make anything personal of our feud, and threatened to throw him out of the window.

J. Peters got up from his chair as if to take hold of me, and I shoved him hard. He hit the chair with a thud. I told them I would mail my reply to their charges. Bowder answered that it would be sent to Moscow. I said that would be all right with me. Then I warned them against any rough stuff, such as having me beaten up while I was preparing my reply. "I'll hold every damned one of you accountable —individually and collectively!"

I walked out of the room and slammed the door.

In my apartment, I worked on my statement for two and a half days, and finally completed the 16-page document. I expressed the view that modern Communism leads inevitably to the totalitarian state in which all but a few Party bosses become slaves; that Marx had drawn up what had become a blueprint for conquest; that the Bolsheviks under Lenin had put the system into operation and there was

* See Appendix I, p. 236.

no longer any need for speculation as to how it would work out. It made a mockery of everything that civilization stood for. It denied human dignity and the freedoms for which men had struggled and given their lives—freedom of religion, speech and assembly—and deprived the people of the right to hold free elections, to peacefully change political leaders. The Soviet Union had rolled back these precious freedoms and its people were living in Oriental bondage such as the Western world had never known. Concentration camps were the symbol of Soviet power; the firing squad and prison dungeons haunting spectres. A man would have to be out of his mind if he continued to work for and give his loyalty to such a system.

I pointed to Mussolini, a devout student of Marx, who had tried to improve on the Soviet system by setting up his own brand of socialism—Fascism, or national socialism. But there was little difference, both were based on the theory that man was created for the state, not the state for man.

Hitler had merely copied Lenin and Mussolini. So far as I could see, there was no difference between Communism and national socialism—between Communism, Fascism and Nazism except that Stalin preferred the color red, the Fascists, black and the Nazis, brown.

My conclusions were brief: the only specific cure for the ills of the twentieth-century was a return to rationality and constructiveness. We needed a method that builds, not destroys freedom and individual dignity.

I ended my report with a slogan of my own: "Down with Marxism, Fascism and Nazism! Up with freedom!"

I decided against mailing it and carried it to Party headquarters instead. I wanted to see the reaction.

I entered Peters' office and slapped the report on his desk. Charles Dirba was sitting there, as Peters fingered the report without reading it, and told me coldly to wait for the decision of his commission. Then, as I was leaving, Peters informed me I had been deprived of all posts in the Party, but could continue in the mass front organizations.

This meant I might remain a member of the American Committee for the Protection of the Foreign Born, the International Labor Defense, the American Writers Union (of which I was chairman of the membership committee) which the Party had set up, the WPA Writers Project, and others.

Word had gotten around, of course, that I had been expelled and wherever I went, there were people who turned and hurried off when they saw me coming. Some refused to talk with me when we met, while others would, their decision usually dependent on their own isolation from the Party leadership.

In April, 1937, John J. Ballam, charter member of the Communist Party and a member of the National Committee, told me of my expulsion.

CHAPTER XXVI

One day in the summer of 1939 Ben Stolberg, the anti-Stalinist writer, called and asked me to have lunch with him. We met the next day at the old Chelsea Hotel, where he was living, on 23rd Street just west of Seventh Avenue. We talked in generalities and then he told me that someone wanted to meet me. We made an appointment for the next day at 2:00 P.M. in Room 315 of the New York Public Library at Fifth Avenue and 42nd Street.

When I got there, Ben was sitting with two men I had never seen before. He got up with a smile as I approached. "Walter," he said to one of his friends, a nervous little man whose eyes darted at me quickly, "I want you to meet Maurice Malkin." We shook hands. He covered the room with quick probing lances, and then told me—in Russian—that he was glad to meet me.

He was General Walter G. Krivitsky, former chief of Soviet Military Intelligence in Western Europe, who had defected in 1937. He wrote a series of articles for the *Saturday Evening Post,* and a book in which he predicted the Soviet-Nazi treaty and the beginning of World War II.*

The other man was Boris Shub, our intended interpreter, but we didn't need him and after a bit he excused himself. Krivitsky and I went on talking in Russian in the library for over an hour. He questioned me sharply about my career and I was surprised to find he knew more about some of it than I did myself.

Suddenly he asked me when I had heard last from my brother Joseph. I told him about the letter I had received from Geneva in October, 1935, in which he had tried to persuade me to visit Moscow. Since then I had heard nothing.

The General glanced nervously around the room, then began

*See Appendix I, p. 236.

speaking slowly. He told me that Joseph and his wife, Maria, had been close friends of his. Joseph had been murdered, he said; he knew this to be a fact.

We were both silent for a moment. I don't think I was shocked because I knew this had probably happened in the madhouse that was Stalin's Russia.

Krivitsky told me that he had been in Moscow in 1936, attached to the intelligence section as an instructor at the Frunze Military Academy. Joseph and Maria had returned on orders from the Kremlin, and were met by GPU agents at the railway station. They were not even allowed to go to their apartment in Teatralny Ploshchad (Theatre Square), half a block from the Moscow Arts Theater. The agents took them to Number 11 Lublyanka Street, the GPU Headquarters. Twenty-four hours later, their bodies were found in the street, riddled with bullets.

The General told me that the reason Joseph was not tried and submitted to the humiliation of a public trial was because he refused to sign a confession to save himself or his wife. Stalin knew that without the confession it would be impossible to hang anything on a man who had enjoyed the friendship of Lenin, had served with distinction as intelligence Commissar of the Red Army throughout the Civil War, and as Consul General to Japan in 1925 and to Germany in 1926–27. After his murder, they simply claimed he was a member of the alleged spy plot which later brought about the liquidation of Marshal Mikhail Tukhachevsky and the thousands of Red Army officers.

As he spoke, Krivitsky glanced nervously about the room. After almost every word, he would turn to look. As we prepared to leave, he asked me if I could join him for further talks the next day, and we agreed to meet at 11:00 A.M. in Central Park near the 72nd Street entrance.

Outside, as we shook hands on the street before parting, he asked me if I carried a weapon. I told him I did not. With this, we parted, he and Stolberg leaving together. Next morning I met him at the appointed place, and he suggested we take a stroll through the park. We finally sat on a bench at a children's playground. As we watched the children at play, he told me he had a young son he had managed to bring out of Russia with him. His wife and child would certainly have been murdered, he said, if he had left them in Stalin's grip.

Then he began questioning me about my attitude toward Communism and the Soviet Union. I told him the entire story of my break with the Party, and my disillusion and disgust with Marxism as a creed or theory of government. He replied that he had met a number of former Communists in this country who felt the same way. I mentioned Ben Gitlow and Joseph Kornfeder, and told him he would also find them interesting to talk with.

He then asked me what I meant to do with the knowledge I had of the Communist conspiracy. I told him this was something that troubled me deeply. The American people—and free people everywhere—should be warned of the danger threatening them before it was too late. There was only one forum that would permit us to be heard, I said. It was the House Committee on Un-American Activities, headed by Texas Representative Martin Dies, who had become the stormy petrel of the day in his rows with Mrs. Roosevelt and the New Deal. The criticism leveled at the Committee had convinced me that it was all right and could be trusted. Most of its enemies were people I knew as Communists, friends of the Party or dupes. The work the Committee was trying to do, I suggested, could be vastly strengthened if some of us who knew what we were talking about would come forward and tell our story.

He said, "Malkin, if you could convince the others to do this, I would go along myself. But are you willing to face the danger?"

He said the American government could offer us little protection against Stalin's long arms. "Are you willing to take the risk?"

I told him I would rather be dead than live in silence with what I knew.

"You know the Party," he said. "You know its agents. I need not tell you that people have vanished, right here in New York City. You can never tell what may happen to you. And the best of intentions can bring you only enemies where you might expect friends. This I know," Krivitsky said seriously. "Don't think you are going to be a hero to all the people you are trying to save."

We parted after agreeing that I should contact other former Communists and feel them out about telling their story before the House Committee. He made me promise not to mention to anyone that I had talked with him. I watched him walk toward Fifth Avenue, glancing nervously about as he went up the path.

I got in touch with Ben Gitlow immediately and he agreed to join me. The same afternoon I reached Kornfeder, and Joe was also enthusiastic.

The next day I called Ben Stolberg and told him I wanted to meet Krivitsky, who, in his caution, had refused to tell me where he lived. I could only contact him through Stolberg.

Ben told me that the General had just left on a trip to Canada or England, I can't recall which. It was six weeks later, in September, before he returned. The war had already broken out in Europe and the world watched the Nazis and their Soviet allies invade Poland. The Communists had joined forces with the Nazis—just as Krivitsky had predicted—and were drumming up a campaign to keep this country out of the war by any means possible.

I received a telephone call from Ben Stolberg that the General had just returned and wanted to see me. I met him in Stolberg's Hotel Chelsea apartment and I told him of my talks with Gitlow and Kornfeder. He asked me if I had questioned them as to their willingness to stand all the vilification that would follow their acts. I assured him that these boys were old-timers and were not afraid of anything. We agreed that each of us should contact the Dies committee separately and offer to testify.

Two days later, on September 22, I decided to send a telegram to the Committee offering my services. That evening I met Krivitsky for dinner in Luchow's Restaurant on 14th Street at Irving Place. I told him what I had done and he kissed me on both cheeks.

"Maurice," he said, "you are doing one of the most heroic things you could do because from the American Party you are going to get the full wrath of Communism. You'll get the brunt of abuse."

After my meeting with Walter I thought about his advice and his warning concerning the effects and possible repercussions because of the steps I was about to take in my final break with Communism. I was troubled because I thoroughly understood what I was about to face—a lifetime of mental conditioning and brain washing isn't easy to change.

I was a worker, and had been taught that as a member of the "working class" all representatives of the State are tools of the enemy, the capitalist class. There should be no cooperation with the "exploiters of the proletariat."

So my mind was troubled: I was about to break with training, tradition and habit and embark upon an entirely new life. And I wondered what it would be like—making a new life in a new world.

The break also meant an economic struggle to find employment in a profession free from Communist control or influence—free from fear of retaliation from frame-ups, filthy press and Mafia goon squads —and, as the last resort, kidnapping and murder.

After a night-long inner turmoil, I decided to take this final step to help my adopted country—the nation which gave my parents a chance to live their lives in peace and freedom, without fear of police raids on our home: freedom for my father to go to his synagogue daily and pray to his God, knowing he would come home to his family; freedom to work without molestation from anyone; freedom to bring up his children in a country that offered equality for all.

With these thoughts on my mind, I also thought of the socialist and Communist monster that I had helped to create, which was spreading its venomous ideology, endangering my country's existence, as well as my very own. I went to the Western Union office on Broadway and 13th Street, a few doors from Communist Party headquarters, and sent the following wire to the House Committee on Un-American Activities:

Hon. Martin Dies
Chairman of the House Committee on Un-American Activities
Old House Office Building
Washington, D.C.

I am willing to give full testimony on aims, objectives, program and activities of the Communist Party of the United States and its parent body the Communist International, including the activities of the Soviet Government agencies in the U. S.

(signed) Maurice L. Malkin

A few hours later I received a telegram from Rhea Whitley, counsel for the Committee, on behalf of Mr. Dies, instructing me to appear at the hearing room of the HUAC at the Old House Office Building, Washington, D. C. on Friday, October 13, 1939, at 9:00 A.M. —and to be ready to testify about my knowledge of the Communist Party and its activities.

With the wire in my pocket I went to the National Headquarters of the Communist Party at 50 East 13th Street for a last look at this

171

link with my former life. I already felt that I was beginning to breathe freely and see clearly.

The first one I met there was Charles Krumbein, whom I had known in the Party for 20 years. He had been a close friend. Krumbein served Moscow well as a Soviet agent throughout the world, and had been in prison—in the U.S. after his arrest at the Bridgeman Convention during the 1922 Palmer raid, and in the 1930's in Great Britain for using illegal passports and entry as a Soviet agent. And again in the United States when he spent three years in a federal penitentiary for misuse of American passports and fraud.

He tried to convince me to get back into the good graces of the Party using the age-old socialist-Communist argument that "there is only one place and one road for a worker-revolutionist" like me— "the revolutionary road in the ranks of the Party." I felt that he did not really believe this himself. I left him with the words "We shall see," and two days later he heard my answers on the newscasts and saw it in the press.

After a sleepless night I packed my traveling bag and a briefcase, which contained all my Communist Party membership cards and leftist credentials. These included Workers Communist Party and other Communist front cards, plus personal letters from William Z. Foster, Chairman of the Communist Party, Roger Baldwin, National Secretary of the American Civil Liberties Union, and two Communist officials of the ACLU, Forrest Bailey and Robert W. Dunn. I took these credentials so that the Party could not seriously deny my Communist background—as they did in the cases of Juliet Stuart Poyntz, Ben Gitlow and others. The Red fascist leadership denied, disclaimed and disavowed any knowledge of their misdeeds or actions, and had even tried to deny that these people ever existed!

Early on October 13, I left my apartment for Pennsylvania Station and boarded the train for Washington, D. C. Throughout the four-hour ride, my father's lifelong warnings were in my thoughts—that the road his children were taking was not the good road, and evil would follow unless they changed their ways.

Joseph and I had followed the teachings of Marx and Lenin—that the Party member must be ready to sacrifice everything and give all his time and energy to the Party. He must be a professional revolutionist whose life belongs to the Party.

We carried out these teachings with all that was in us—and we suffered imprisonment, torture, abuse and hunger throughout our lives. And my father's prophecy came true; Joseph, suffering imprisonment in Russia under the Czar, then witnessing far worse brutality and murder under the Marxist "workers paradise" before facing as payment for his devotion to the regime, his own execution. Maurice, his youngest son, also imprisoned and beaten by a free society that expected loyalty but received betrayal, a land which gave him equal opportunity, freedom of worship and freedom of speech.

Together with these thoughts, I remembered what I had read in prison of our American history, our Bill of Rights, the Constitution and its Framers—and I remembered the hardships and struggles of all the pioneers who had made our country what it is today, a real *Ir Miklat* (Hebrew for City of Refuge) and *Eretz Zavas Cholov Udvash* (Hebrew for Land flowing with Milk and Honey) with opportunity for all.

And what had Communism produced? Under the Czar, Jews were permitted places of worship and schools where they were allowed to teach their children the ways of God. Even public schools and universities admitted a certain number of all nationalities, including Jews: writers, artists and other professionals had limited freedom. But under the totalitarianism of Communism there was no freedom of worship for the Jews, no religious teaching, no free press and those opposed to the system were liquidated.

The final blow was the alliance of fascism and Communism in the Soviet-Nazi Pact. This convinced me that there is no real ideological difference between Red totalitarianism, Nazi Brown totalitarianism and other fascist dictatorships. They all believe that the individual is a serf of the state, and that the state has no responsibility to the individual.

The more these thoughts went through my mind, the more determined I became to make my final break and give all my knowledge of the Red danger to the free Congress of my adopted country, which gave my Father, Mother and me all the freedoms I had spent a lifetime disrupting and betraying. My determination did not weaken, even at the thought of Krivitsky's last words to me, that Communism does not forget those who turn away from it—that it will be quick to seek vengeance.

Upon arriving in Washington, I felt physically tired, but mentally strong. I registered at the Dodge Hotel overlooking the Capitol and,

173

after a refreshing shave, shower and change of clothes, I took my briefcase and walked over to the committee's offices in the Old House Office Building. The first person I met there was Dr. J. B. Matthews, research director of the committee. A former leftist who had turned against the Communists, he had freely admitted to having been active in many Communist fronts, but never revealed his previous Party membership. He simply told me to forget about the past and think only of the present and future.

My appearance and testimony for the Committee was two days after Krivitsky's about Soviet espionage and intrigue throughout the world—especially in the United States.

With all committee members present, Chairman Martin Dies of Texas called the meeting to order. The members were Congressmen John J. Dempsey, New Mexico; Joe Starnes, Alabama; Joseph E. Casey, Massachusetts; Noah M. Mason, Illinois; J. Parnell Thomas, New Jersey; and Jerry Voorhies, California.

After being sworn in by Chairman Dies, I was questioned mostly by Dr. Matthews, but members of the committee also questioned me. I was first asked about my history in the revolutionary movement, based on my membership books in the Socialist Party and the Industrial Workers of the World (IWW), beginning in 1915, and the Communist Party, as a charter member, from 1919–1937. Then followed questions on correspondence and credentials concerning dozens of Communist fronts and organizations, and all positions that I had held in the Communist Party for nearly 20 years.

Throughout my testimony, especially on Communist penetration of the trade unions and capture of the CIO by the Red fascists. Rep. Voorhies said that such people as David Dubinsky, and others like him, didn't know what was happening. He also tried to imply that Communists were not all bad—and claimed that they had helped the American workers. Voorhies, whom the people of California sent to Congress to represent them, called himself a liberal—but was frequently far to the left. When this was discovered by California voters, they removed him from the political arena and elected a man who was to make history for our country as a member of the House, Senator, Vice-President and President—Richard M. Nixon. Mr. Nixon was not color blind. He knew Red when he saw it—in Alger Hiss and others—despite all obstacles put in his way.

CHAPTER XXVII

Reaction to my testimony about Communist Party graft, corruption and alliances with gangsters and of Communist control of trade unions in the CIO and AFL, especially in the Furriers' Union, drove the leadership to desperation. One of the first moves they made was the Soviet tactic of family pressure—trying to extract statements from members of my immediate family labeling me a traitor to The Cause, a counter revolutionary, an agent of Imperialism, etc.

The leaders of the Furriers' Union, Ben Gold and Irving Potash,* called my sister Elsie, a fur finisher, and my brother-in-law, William Wolliver, fur worker and member of the joint council of the union. They ordered them to make statements condemning me. Elsie consulted my brother Nathan, and he said she and William should tell them to go to hell—and that if they gave in to the pressure, he would issue a statement telling the truth—that the statements had been forcibly extracted by threatening their jobs and union membership. That finished that—no statements were published.

Nathan was then called to the District Headquarters of the Communist Party at 35 E. 12th Street, and Israel Amter, the District Chairman, ordered him to issue a statement denouncing me. They were asking the wrong person because Nathan was a rebel and revolutionist before the Golds and Amters ever heard of Karl Marx. Nathan told Amter to go to hell, then stated he was sorry he didn't have the nerve to follow me and tell all he knew of the filth of the Communist movement. Then he took his membership card, ripped it to pieces and threw it in Amter's face.

The Party's next move was to send thieves to ransack my apartment. Communist leaders knew that I had one of the largest collections of Party membership lists, meetings, minutes, books, period-

*See Appendix I, p. 237, and Appendix II.

icals, pamphlets and records in New York. They had hoped to get the material and also find something incriminating which would enable the Communist Party to discredit my testimony before HUAC. They even ripped open mattresses to look for documents, but I was one step ahead of them. On October 14, the day I returned from Washington, I moved all my files and documents to a friend's apartment, a journalist for the Hearst publications. I kept only books by Lenin, Stalin, Marx and those from the Communist Party U.S.A., which I knew no one would take.

While newspapers headlined my revelations of the Arnold Rothstein deal with the Communists and the Furriers' Union, and my testimony on police collaboration and graft, New York City Police Commissioner Lewis Valentine sent an inspector to check my statements and found them to be true. In answer to my charges that the Communist Party had units in the Brooklyn Navy Yard, Rear Admiral Andrews, naval commander of the 3rd Naval District, made a statement to the press that they formerly had a few Communists among the WPA workers, but he failed to say—or did not know—that there was a permanent group of 18 Party members. This group was under the leadership of a welder, Irving Velson, also known under his real name of Irving Shavelson. Peter Cacchione, who later became a Communist Party Councilman from Brooklyn, was the go-between. These Communists knew many naval secrets, including the coming and going of battleships, cruisers, etc.; details about the ships; the layout of the yard and its workings; access to this knowledge of ship movements may have been passed on to the Japanese who knew exactly where our Pacific fleet was when they attacked Pearl Harbor.*

All this information, picked up from the shops by the Party unit, was passed on to Pete Cacchione, the Communist Party Organization Department, Max Steinberg, District Organization Secretary, and finally to J. Peters, Party official and Soviet espionage agent. It was then transmitted to Moscow through the Control Commission, Charles Dirba, its Secretary, and Gerhart Eisler.**

This the Admiral did not know, and I could not blame him because

*The Communist-Axis treaty was in effect for much of the time that this information was going to the Soviet Union.
**See Appendix I, p. 237.

even our President, Franklin D. Roosevelt, did not want to know. This was evident in 1938 when Whittaker Chambers submitted proof to Roosevelt that Alger Hiss was a Soviet spy.* The President did not want to believe it, or know about it, perhaps because there were leftists and Communists among his advisors and cabinet: Harry Hopkins, Albert R. Williams, Harold Ickes, Lauchlin Currie, Nathan Gregory Silvermaster, Harry Dexter White—not to mention his chiefs in the WPA, where Communists were in charge or control of the most important projects: Hallie Flanagan, of the Federal Theatre, and Henry Alsberg, of the newspapers. Alsberg was a homosexual who was blackmailed by the Communist Party, in my presence, into placing Orrick Johns, former editor of the *New Masses,* in charge in New York, and putting a waterfront goon, James McGraw, on the newspaper project. These weren't the only ones placed in such positions; most national projects were under Communist supervisors. During the international crisis FDR was too busy with his leftist advisors, building up his reputation as the "savior of our country," to notice that the Communists had infiltrated most departments, including the National Labor Relations Board, the Justice Department, the State Department, the Treasury Department and even the Army, Navy and Defense Departments. The First Lady of the land, Eleanor Roosevelt, was busy sponsoring Communist agents, such as Kurt Rosenfeld,* Ambrogio Donini*—whom I exposed in 1939—Andre Katz, alias Andre Simon, and a host of others.

I also named the Communist International representative Frederico Alpi (alias Marini, alias Fred Brown) and Reverend Reissig. Even after I named them as Soviet agents they were still defended by the First Lady who also sponsored Hans Eisler and many other Soviet agents. These people were allowed to remain in the country and work for the USSR.

A few days after my return from Washington, and while under subpoena from the Committee, I went to a restaurant in Greenwich Village. As if by magic, I was suddenly surrounded by a gang of Communist goons. Knives flashed and I felt one penetrate my midsection, but my training in the Communist goon schools paid off—I broke through and ran out of the restaurant into the cold, leaving behind my overcoat with my house keys in the pocket. Accompanied

*See Appendix I, p. 238.

by an artist friend named Sam Hartman, I went to the Charles Street Police Station and reported the incident. Two detectives returned to the restaurant with me, but of course we found no one there. That was as far as the investigation went, because the police were furious about my testimony on police graft; it was a closed case from the beginning.

Since my apartment keys were in the pocket of the overcoat I had left in the restaurant, I did not go into the apartment immediately —not wanting to give them an opportunity to finish the job. Instead, I went to a friend's apartment, that of Charles Jaffe, a journalist on the *Jewish Morning Journal,* who had an apartment at 22nd Street and Second Avenue. My jacket and trousers were caked with blood and he immediately made me take off my shirt, and washed and bandaged the wounds in my abdomen and right side (though I had only felt one, I had been stabbed several times), and put me to sleep. The next morning Jaffe took me to a supposed friend of mine, Dr. Abraham Sakin, on Eastern Parkway in the Brownsville section of Brooklyn. He wrote articles for the *Jewish Freiheit,* the Communist Party newspaper, and was friendly with many top Reds. He was very nervous and I thought he was going to faint at the very sight of me. He knew all about my testimony, and he did not even want to examine my wounds or treat me, so Jaffe took me to Unity Hospital, where doctors re-dressed and treated my injuries.

Someone at the hospital must have notified the press, for within half an hour the place was swarming with news reporters and photographers. I must admit they were alert, dedicated newsmen, far more so than the liars and propaganda hacks I worked with on the Communist press.

After being discharged from Unity Hospital, Jaffe and I went back to my apartment in Manhattan. When I entered, I found everything in shambles—books taken from shelves and thrown on the floor, desk drawers ripped open and their contents strewn all over, etc. The Red storm troopers had paid another call, trying to find something they had missed on their first visit.

Then and there I decided to make good use of all my books, pamphlets and other radical literature—a collection of nearly 3,000 publications and important documents—and give the material to the FBI and the HUAC because I knew they would put it to good use.

I also decided to look for a new apartment, but I had very little

178

money in reserve, was without a job and very little prospect of getting one. The Communists were in control in the industries that I knew through the trade unions; they would try to make sure I remained unemployed.

CHAPTER XXVIII

While looking for a job and a new apartment in New York, I received a letter from the Royal Canadian Mounted Police, asking if I would come to Ottawa to assist Commissioner Bevan. Through my testimony and press reports they knew of my experience in the Communist Party—and my break with it. I didn't waste any time, and in a few days had stored my apartment furnishings, clothes, correspondence, records and books and left for Canada.

In Ottawa, I registered at a small hotel near the Parliament Buildings under the name "Maurice Roberts." The Communist Party had temporarily assigned me the name in 1931, during my activities in the needle trades and fur strikes, because I was still on parole after release from State Prison and the name Malkin was too well known. I knew the American Communist Party must have alerted its brother Parties about my testimony; when the Canadian Party discovered my presence it would try to carry out my sentence for betrayal.

I walked over to the impressive courtyard of the Parliament Buildings, with its old European architectural beauty. There I saw my first "Mountie," a member of the Royal Canadian Mounted Police, resplendent in his colorful uniform: wide-brimmed campaign hat, red tunic, blue riding breeches, with a wide yellow stripe down the sides, and cavalry boots. I asked where I could find the Central Headquarters of the RCMP and he pointed out a building only about 50 feet from where we were standing. Inside the headquarters, another member of the force, after calling on the inter-office phone for permission to admit me, escorted me to an office on the second floor. There, I showed a secretary the letter I had received from the RCMP and she took me to the office of the commissioner.

Commissioner Bevan, the chief of this famous law-enforcement group known for its motto "We always get our man," was a middle-aged gentleman, dressed in civilian clothes, but with a brisk, military manner. After greeting me, he called in his expert on Communist activity, Sergeant Major Templeton. He had attained this rank because, as a green emigrant from Latvia, he had joined the Canadian Communist Party as an undercover agent of the RCMP and was able to help convict Tim Buck and many in the Canadian Party leadership on sedition charges.

After discussing my background and answering some questions, I was assigned to the anti-subversive division of the RCMP as Special Agent 937X, to work in Toronto with Chief Inspector Mervin Block. The Inspector was a picturesque gentleman, about 60 to 65, with manners and tact. Mr. Block was later put in charge of security for Igor Gouzenko, the code officer who defected from the Soviet embassy in Canada and revealed the activities of a Soviet spy ring, which was in contact with Klaus Fuchs, Julius and Ethel Rosenberg, and other Communist agents. Block was of the highest calibre —he spoke fluent Russian, having been attached to the British ambassador's staff in Russia during the Bolshevik Revolution—and thoroughly understood the Communists. We formed a friendship which I value to this day. We worked together for about nine months, analyzing Communist betrayals of wartime Canada and the United States during the Stalin-Hitler pact. When it appeared that the U.S. was about to enter the war, I told my friends that I was going home to try to help my country. I was given a sincere farewell, and returned to New York.

Once home, I immediately went to work investigating Soviet espionage in the U.S., for our country was making an all-out effort to rebuild a military structure neglected since World War I. Factories were being converted from peace-time to war industry, to produce supplies both for our allies, under attack by the Nazi blitz, and for our own newly drafted military forces.

We perfected a new bombsight which enabled our fliers to effect greater precision bombing of the enemy. Known as the Norden Bombsight, it was manufactured by the Carl B. Norden Precision Tool Company, the Sperry Gyroscope Corporation, and by the Manufacturers Tool Company.

The Communists, who had cells in these companies, worked with the Nazis to obtain blueprints and plans for this bombsight and ship them to the USSR. This was during the Nazi-Soviet pact when the Reds and Brownshirts were sleeping in the same bed. Stalin said that each was entitled to his own ideological beliefs and "Capitalist Imperialism," not Fascism, became the main enemy.

During my investigations I uncovered the big steal, and exposed it in a series of articles called "Communism Goes Underground," published in February, 1941, in the Sunday supplements of the King Features Syndicate and Hearst Press.

During this period, I met and married Laura Dick, who was to encourage me in helping our Government rid itself of the Communist menace. Laura bravely withstood the threatening telephone calls which we received night and day. I had abuse hurled upon me by the Communist press; later, my two daughters, Arlene and Lana, had to fight back when heckled by Communists' children in high school and Brooklyn College. My wife and children have been and are still my joy. All have helped in the struggle against the Red Frankenstein.

While in the process of writing a book, I was contacted in New York by the British intelligence service and asked to go to the offices of the Imperial Purchasing Commission at 20 Exchange Place. I was introduced to Mr. C. J., who was in charge, and after discussing my membership in the Communist Party and my previous work with the Royal Canadian Mounted Police, it occurred to me that the RCMP had lost no time in notifying them of my presence in New York. They asked if I would be willing to work for them, and I agreed—providing the American Government gave the O.K. They assured me that this had already been arranged before I came to see them, a fact that I was able to verify.

Until five days after Pearl Harbor I worked with the British, investigating Communist and Nazi activities in the United States. All the information I uncovered was shared by the British and U. S. governments.

After Pearl Harbor, I went to school to learn the trade of machinist, then served an apprenticeship in the Sperry Gyroscope Corporation shops in Brooklyn for three months. From there I went to the Brooklyn Navy Yard for about nine months, where I worked under the direction of Naval Intelligence. Until 1946 I worked at the Bethlehem Steel Company shipyard in New York at 56th Street, getting my instructions from Lieutenant-Commander Robert Morris, Naval Intelligence, Third District. He later became a Judge and Chief Counsel for the Senate Internal Security Sub-Committee.

During my activity in the Navy Yard, I was able to help check on a group of "comrades" who were working there under the leadership of Irving "Velson" (real name: Shavelson), a welder. The Navy Yard tried to get rid of him, but couldn't because, according to President Roosevelt and the Assistant Secretary of the Navy, Adlai Stevenson, the Communists were our allies and friends. Finally, Velson was discharged for breaking Navy Yard rules.

After his ouster, Velson went to work at the Bethlehem Steel Company's shipyard and became president of Local 16 of the Industrial Union of Shipyard Workers. I immediately joined this union and went to work as a machinist at the same shipyard. I began agitating for Velson's removal—exposing his Navy Yard record and Communist Party connections. In a short time a group of patriotic rank and file workers and recently discharged veterans had him expelled from the union—and he was drafted into the Navy.

During this time a peculiar thing happened in the headquarters of Naval Intelligence in New York. One day Commander Morris came into the offices and found the files on Communist activities were missing. This was after Adlai Stevenson ordered harassment of Communists discontinued. It has remained a mystery to this day.

In 1946 I left the Bethlehem Steel Company shipyard, and went to work rebuilding lithography and printing machines, which were very scarce. Few new printing machines had been built for several years, since all tooling had been converted to wartime effort. So rebuilt pre-war machines were at a premium until new ones could be manufactured. The shortage of these machines was worldwide, not only in the United States, and the market almost unlimited.

I established myself in the rebuilt lithograph machinery field and soon had a thriving business. I began sending the machines as far away as India, and orders kept my shop working 24 hours a day for about two years.

All during this time I was quite uneasy about the world situation —our sellout of the smaller nations to the Kremlin and the penetration of the Communists into all walks of our country's life.

The first betrayal was at Yalta when we gave them Poland, Estonia, Latvia, Lithuania, etc. Then we ordered our troops to stop and allowed the Russians to take Czechoslovakia and large areas of Germany, including Berlin.

This was due to the Roosevelt-Truman policy of allowing Moscow a nearly free hand, believing that they were different from their former pact partners, the Nazis. FDR and Truman were fooled by the Soviet announcement in 1943 that they had liquidated the Third International, and believed that the Communists had become "good guys" and believers in democracy. But the Red cells kept on multiplying.

Our government seemed to throw open the doors of many agencies, such as the State and Treasury Departments, to Alger Hiss & Co., Harry Dexter White and his cohorts, and other Communist traitors. Communists in the Treasury Department even gave the Russians our plates to print American occupation currency, which could have wrecked our whole economy.

I wasn't the only one uneasy about the situation, especially after the revelations of Igor Gouzenko in Canada and the arrest of Ethel and Julius Rosenberg, and other Communist spies in the United States.

The demobilized GIs began to see that our country was in deep trouble. Kremlin agents influenced the Government and controlled sections of the organized labor movement, and we were having trouble converting our country's industry and commerce from a wartime to a peacetime economy because of strikes, slow-downs and sabotage.

Then a few young American war veterans, such as Richard Nixon and the late Joseph McCarthy, were elected and began to raise their voices in Congress to rid our government of the enemies who were working for the disintegration of our way of life. They found a great leader in the veteran Nevada Senator, the late Pat McCarran, and—slowly, but surely—the country was aroused and things began to happen: the investigation and arrest of many alien Communist agents, such as Gerhart Eisler, and the trial of some leading Communists, who were citizens, under the Smith Act as agents of a foreign power.

CHAPTER XXIX

One of our enemies the government was investigating was a Hungarian who came to this country during the influx of a great many refugees in the early 1920s. He was a little, dark, curly haired young man whom I had known as Schwartz in the Hungarian Section of the Party. He worked on the *U. J. Elore*, the Communist Hungarian-language daily newspaper, at 33 East Second Street, in Manhattan. As organizer for Section 1, which covered from South Ferry to 59th Street, and from the East River to the Hudson, and as a member of the District Executive Committee, I had handled his Party credentials. He told me that he had been a member of Bela Kun's secret terror squads during the Hungarian Red Revolt in 1919.

One day in June, 1948, two young men visited my shop. They introduced themselves as Laurence Parr and Murray Boriskin, investigators for the Immigration and Naturalization Service of the Justice Department.

A little discussion showed that Parr had done considerable study and research of Communist literature. I took an immediate liking to him and later we became very good friends while working together in the "I & N" (Immigration and Naturalization Service). Over a cup of coffee, he showed me a photograph of a man and asked me if I could identify him. I immediately recognized Schwartz, who had become a big power in the Communist Party—both in its organizational structure and in spreading its tentacles through the United States. He wrote the Communist Party manual on organization, but his main function was recruiting and directing espionage agents for the GPU. He was the contact man for transmission of information among Soviet agents in the United States, and was also active in forging American passports. He used various names for these operations, including Kaufman, Goldberg, Stevens, Roberts, Miller, Schwartz, and, in the Party, J. Peters.

I gave a brief description of Peters' background to Parr and Boriskin, and they burst into pleased laughter, because the information I gave them was so much more than what they had had in their current file.

Parr asked me if I would be willing to sign a statement for the I & N and appear as an expert to identify witnesses in the Peters' case when it came up in August. I said that I would be more than happy to help—but I also had to think about my newly-established business, because I knew as soon as my name appeared in the newspapers again I would be through. The comrades would see to that.

The investigators kept urging me to appear as a witness because they considered my knowledge of Peters most important to his deportation from the United States. My conscience was bothering me—I had an opportunity to help the Government get rid of a dangerous enemy, but the cost would be the loss of my livelihood. I'd be forced to liquidate my business because of the notoriety I would receive—and I had a family to support. I remembered the grim situation following my testimony before the House Committee on Un-American Activities in 1939.

That evening I talked over the situation with my wife, Laura, who had learned to hate the Communists and socialists during her childhood in Poland, and since her arrival in the U.S. in 1925, when she refused to join the Milliners Union, while working at that trade. She has always loved this country very much, and advised me to sell out my business. She said we could always find some way to get along, even though we had two children. Laura has always encouraged me, especially when it concerned my helping the government.

The next day I went to I & N headquarters, at 70 Columbus Avenue, and gave a full sworn statement to Larry Parr. I also promised to testify at the deportation hearing for J. Peters scheduled for August 28, 1948.

As an expert on Communism, I would testify, among other things, that Peters was a top-echelon Soviet agent and leader of the Communist Party structure which advocated overthrow of the U. S. Government by force and violence.

Edward Emanuel served as examining officer and Ralph Farb, presiding officer. Carol W. King, an old Party war horse, was attorney for Peters.

On arriving at the I & N office on the morning of the hearing, I went to Emanuel's office, where I met George Hewitt, a Negro ex-communist who had graduated from the Lenin School in Moscow. He was also a witness for the government, ready to identify Peters as a Soviet agent.

While we were talking, Emanuel's office door suddenly opened and a man looked in. I recognized him immediately as a man I had seen around Communist Party headquarters during the 1930s, and Hewitt remarked that he looked familiar. When asked whom he wanted to see, the intruder replied nervously, "no one—no one," and quickly retreated. I was certain that he was looking to see who the witnesses were to help the Party prepare its defense—as is always done by communist infiltrators in our Government agencies.

I lost no time reporting the incident to John Boyd, Deputy Commissioner of I & N, who had come to New York from Washington to supervise the hearing. Boyd asked me to look around a few offices and see if I could find the man. I finally spotted him sitting at an empty desk in the back of a large room. Later I found out his name was Jacob Auerbach, the assistant warrant and exclusion officer, who had his own office in another part of the building. He worked under Rublio A. Esperdy, then chief warrant and exclusion officer, a good, loyal American, and retired District Director of I & N.

Auerbach had worked at the Immigration Office in Ellis Island in the 1930s and had been under Government suspicion because of his overt militancy among WPA workers and in various organizational activities. He was suspended for some time pending a hearing by the Loyalty Review Board of the Civil Service Commission and other agencies, but I believe he was later reinstated, though in a less important position where he would not have access to confidential data. Eventually, he retired from government service.

The morning of the first day was taken up with motions and countermotions. In the afternoon Hewitt was called as the first witness. After answering detailed questions about his personal background, Communist Party membership and activities, he identified Peters as a Soviet agent. He testified that while studying at the Lenin School in Moscow he had dealings with the defendant and gave details about Peters' activities.

Among other witnesses identifying Peters as a Soviet agent and the real chief of the Communist Party in the United States, were Whittaker Chambers and Louis Budenz, former editor of the *Daily Worker.*

I took the stand on the third day, and the hearing room was

crowded with Communists and their sympathizers. Outside, a mass of pickets noisily shouted condemnations of Budenz, Chambers and me—screaming such names as "renegades" and "Counter-Revolutionists"—and demanding that Peters be released.

I saw Peters sitting next to his attorney. He looked like an innocent child, with his large, blue eyes and dark curly hair. A stocky, five foot seven, he had a dark moustache, and was well dressed. With his polka-dot bow tie he looked like a grown up Eagle Scout who helped old ladies cross the street.

Edward Emanuel, the examining officer, spared no detail in his questioning—beginning with date and place of birth, my present citizenship, on through my positions, education, and tenure in the Party. He asked me to identify innumerable texts, periodicals and pamphlets published and used by the Party in its schools and cells, including Peters' *Manual on Organization.* Published by the Party, as a "must" text for every member, it fully describes the organizational structure of the American Section of the Communist International, with headquarters in Moscow. Emanuel then asked my expert opinion as to whether such publications truly represented the views of the Communist Party, and especially of J. Peters. I answered yes, that all these publications were taught at the Communist Party schools and I used them as textbooks myself while a Communist, acting for the Party, as a teacher in its schools. He asked whether these publications did, in fact, advocate violent overthrow of the United States Government and the establishment of a dictatorship of the proletariat in the United States after a Communist-led victorious revolution as it was done in Russia by the Bolsheviks in 1917. I again answered yes, that I had been taught that the American workers would never capture power peacefully, but only by force and violence would the Communists be able to take over the country. I stated that I had taught the same, on instructions, when I was teaching in Party schools.

Examining officer Emanuel asked me whether other Party publications, some written by N. Lenin, J. Stalin, Earl Browder, W. Z. Foster and J. Peters, also advocated the overthrow of the U. S. Government by force and violence. I answered that sometimes they openly did, but most of the time they used Aesopian language; they taught subversion in such a way as to use a cover language to fool the American authorities, as Lenin used to fool the Czarist police. When

they wish to speak of force, violence and dictatorship they u
phrase "workers' democracy"—meaning the dictatorship of t
letariat set up after taking power by force and violence. The C
nists use the phrase "workers' democracy" because it sounds
cent enough to the average person, but to an educated
member it would mean a Soviet dictatorship as in Russia afte
Czarist Government was overthrown by force and all opponents
liquidated. I also explained that amongst ourselves, when I was in the
leadership of the Party, we spoke only of bullets and barricades—and
not ballots—to be used to gain control.

I was then asked if I knew a person by the name of J. Peters, and
whether or not he was in the room. I went over and pointed my
finger at him, sitting next to his attorney, Carol W. King. I was asked
how I knew him. I answered that I had known him since he came to
the United States in 1921–22, and I was one of his nominal superiors
in the early 1920s when he was a leader and one of the top editors
of the paper *U.J. Elore*, the Hungarian Communist newspaper. I
testified that I also knew him from 1924 to 1928 as a member of the
New York District Executive Committee of the Workers Communist
Party, and in the Party leadership, after my release from prison, from
1930 to 1937. And when I left the Communist movement he was one
of the top Moscow agents in the United States, and in the Communist
Party organizational structure as an organizer of guerilla squads,
action committees and sitdown strikes of the type used to capture
factories, as was done in the 1930's in Detroit and other parts of the
country.

When Carol King attempted to cross examine me as to my
theoretical knowledge of Communism she blundered, because the
more she questioned me the more I strengthened the government's
case by my knowledge of Marxism-Leninism. Finally, Peters pulled
her to the side and ordered her to stop because she was helping to
bury him. Peters realized that I was a well-trained veteran Communist with a good memory—and she, with her questioning, was doing
him more harm than good.

She stopped that line of questioning and went to the Communist
tactic of attempting to degrade or besmirch my character. She asked
me whether I lived with women in the Party, in an attempt to vilify
me. I answered that during my Party career I was never married
and never lived with women, although that made me an exception

to the Communist rule—many leaders lived with and off women.*

And then I told her to read Party literature on promiscuity: *Free Love and Red Love* by Alexandra Kolantai, the writings of Clara Zetkin, the "Mother" of the German Communist Party, on the subject and the Communist position of doing away with morals and enlarging Party membership through promiscuity. I ended up by saying that if she had been half decent looking, and not as she was, she also would have participated in the free love at the Communist camps—but no one wanted her!

That ended the hearing. She threw up her hands with a statement that she did not care to go on further with a "Benedict Arnold."

From the hearing room I was immediately whisked into a room where I repeated my identification of J. Peters for the news.

Throughout the hearing, Peters had continued to claim he was "Alexander Stevens," but in the face of the evidence the Government presented, he finally admitted to being J. Peters.

Peters was deported to Hungary, where he functioned in the news censorship apparatus and as a propagandist—and bitterly denouncing everything American. I haven't heard of him for the past few years, and wouldn't be surprised if he is in one of the workers' fatherland's concentration camps. This often happens to the staunchest supporters and upholders of "workers' democracy," where the revolution and Communism devours its own children; just as Stalin killed off all those who made the 1917 Soviet revolution.

*See Appendix I, p. 238.

CHAPTER XXX

In 1956, our government—continuing the soft line towards the Kremlin inherited by the Eisenhower Administration from the Roosevelt-Truman policy of appeasement—liquidated all anti-subversive sections in the Immigration and Naturalization Service and halted deportation and prosecution of known alien Communists. We then stopped prosecutions of communists under the Smith Act, giving the Party a chance to regroup and organize new mass fronts. The Roosevelt-Truman foreign policy first allowed the Russians to take over in Czechoslovakia and Berlin by ordering our troops to let them enter, although our armies were there first. The betrayal and sell-out of East Europe, giving these countries to the Russians, was followed by a policy that turned China over to Mao Tse-tung in 1949. This line was followed strictly and on schedule as if Mao was the Secretary of State instead of Dean Acheson, because our State Department had his supporters—including Owen Lattimore and Alger Hiss—helping to shape our policy, and they made sure that we carried out the Red line that Chinese Communists were "agrarian reformers" and lovers of democracy. And before the invasion of South Korea, our Secretary of State had announced to the world that the United States did not consider Korea part of our defense perimeter. This told the Reds, in plain English, that we had no intention of defending Korea and thus making it safe to launch an attack. The Korean "police action" cost the United States 123,000 casualties and we lost the war. We could have won and clipped the wings of Red China if President Truman had allowed General Douglas MacArthur to use his strategy against the Communists as he did against the Japanese. Instead, he recalled and attempted to disgrace the General, lost the Korean War and helped to build Mao's China into a great power.

Policy at home was no different. Communist infiltration of our government agencies—the State Department, Treasury, and others become so alarming that Senators Joseph McCarthy, Pat McCarran and others launched investigations. The President called these investigations "Red Herrings." Instead of helping these patriotic Americans, he hampered them by refusing to cooperate and slandering those who were trying to defend the country. In this way, the Red Fascists were able to strengthen their organization. From 1948 to 1956, because of the prodding of patriotic legislators, the government was investigating and prosecuting the nation's enemies under the Smith Act and through the Immigration and Naturalization Service. There were anti-subversive sections established by I & N in the most important districts throughout the country to investigate and deport alien Communists. This department of I & N was so effective because most of the Communist Party leadership were aliens—Alexander Bittelman, Jack Stachel, Betty Gannet, Beatrice and George Siskind, Irving Potash, Johnny Williamson and dozens of others.

In 1956, I & N had over 10,000 cases of alien Reds ready for deportation. But something had been happening. Even President Dwight D. Eisenhower was suffering from the virus of appeasing the Communists. He appointed, as a payoff for election favors, Earl Warren as Chief Justice of the Supreme Court. Then followed the stoppage of prosecutions of the Communists under the Smith Act. Next came the liquidation of the anti-subversive sections of I & N and the dropping of all deportation cases against Moscow agents in the United States. They were given a chance to regroup and reorganize into new fronts and penetrate civil rights and peace organizations.

I had been a consultant to I & N from 1948 to 1956, and participated in most of its important cases and hearings. In 1956, when the order to liquidate the anti-subversive sections came through, my services were curtailed. I immediately started to look around for a way to resume my former printing machinery business which I'd given up in 1948 to accept an appointment with the Immigration and Naturalization Service as a consultant. Talking to some of the dealers led me to believe that Mexico was a good market for both new and rebuilt printing and lithography machinery. A trip to Mexico City confirmed that there was a market for such items. I opened a plant in Mexico City and began bringing American machinery to Mexico.

After arriving in Mexico City I spent some time among the ...y, one of whose members was Daniel James, a correspondent for the Hearst Press. He was a former editor of the *New Leader*, and I first met him through Isaac Don Levine, who was in Mexico researching a book on the assassination of Leon Trotsky. One night James asked me to meet him at the Hilton Hotel bar. Over drinks, he asked me to enlighten him on a few things. The first was the background of Carlos Contreras. I knew him very well and had even shared an apartment with him in 1925–26. I told James that Contreras was also known as "Vittorio Vidali" and "Vittorio Grande" and that his real name was Eneo Sormenti. He originally came from Trieste, Italy, and arrived in New York in 1923 as a stowaway. He was wanted in Italy for murder and other crimes commited as leader of the Trieste Young Communist League and had been a member of the Municipal Council in Trieste before Mussolini came to power. He was a Communist Party expert on gangster tactics and street violence, and had a gang of Italian cut-throats at his command to carry on his "profession." He was also the Party's contact man with the Mafia until his deportation from the United States in 1927. From 1927 until 1938, he traveled to Brazil, Argentina, Peru and elsewhere throughout Latin America as a Comintern agent and hatchet man. In 1936–37, he was the political commissar of the Garibaldi Brigade in Spain during the Spanish Civil War. He was also responsible for the killing of Andres Nin, leader of the POUM during the Spanish civil war and during the Catalonian uprising against the Communist terror in Spain. Sormenti now is in Cuba as an advisor to Castro on guerilla warfare. James took notes for about two hours, and never got to his second question because it was too late.

A good source of information in Mexico City is the Hotel Geneve, which caters to Americans. The back of the lobby, known as the Jungle because of its floral and tree decorations, is a gathering place for a great number of Americans, including those living in Mexico. One day while I was having a drink, I noticed that the next table was occupied by three American young men. Seeing me sitting alone, one of them came over. He asked me if I would like to join them and introduced himself as Jack Vitt. I accepted. After the usual formalities of introduction and brief exchanges of our backgrounds, they began a conversation about Haiti and Cuba. Through their conversation, I gathered that Vitt was an ex-marine sergeant. Another, named Bill, was a combat pilot, who had lost an arm in the war in the Pacific. The third was a former lieutenant in the submarine service, who was employed by Revlon but was looking for adventure. Vitt seemed the most knowledgable about Latin America and led the conversation, frequently mentioning the names of Castro and others involved in the Cuban revolt. He also claimed to be a close friend of DeJoie, Haitian exile leader, and his sister, Jessie. She later married Daniel James. Vitt ordered often, and drank liquor as though it were plain water. His conversation struck my interest and I decided to get closer to him. He apparently was a recruiting agent for both Castro and DeJoie, who was organizing a revolt against Francois Duvalier, the president of Haiti. He mentioned that both Cuban and Haitian exiles had large sums of money at their disposal and were recruiting men with military experience, especially former American GIs. Vitt kept drinking until he looked like he was going to pass out. He finally decided to go to his room, which was in the Hotel Geneve to sleep it off. He was trying to sober up for a party that evening at the National University apartment of a friend, to which he invited me. I told him I would meet him at the Geneve at 8:30 P.M. After Vitt left, I walked to the Carmel restaurant on the corner of Londres and Geneve Streets, which was owned and operated by Abraham Glantz, a Jewish poet who fought in the Red Army during the Russian Revolution of 1917, whom I had met in New York in 1939. He tries to imitate Trotsky—including goatee, bushy hair and the nickname of the Russian Revolutionary. He has denied that he ever was a Communist, but admitted his Communist Party membership from 1917 to 1951 to me. I have strong doubts about his being an ex-Communist, since his associates in Mexico consisted of known Communists. While drinking coffee, Glantz introduced me to a man of about 65, who became a good friend and helped me to get acquainted with the Jewish community and others in Mexico City. His name was Dr. Abraham King, an American dentist, who had been a resident of Mexico for 35 years. Glantz told him that I was an old time radical and very well acquainted with the literati in New York. Dr. King asked if I knew an anarchist, Harry Abrams, and his wife Molly. I told him that I knew the Abramses before their deportation from the United States in 1920, with Alexander Berkman and Emma Goldman, to Russia. They later had to flee the Soviet Union. Dr. King said that he was a good friend of Abrams, when he had lived in Mexico, and was with him on the Anti-Communist Jewish Refugee Committee during the late 1930's and early 40's until Abrams' death. We

194

became very friendly. Dr. King gave me his address and telephone number and asked me to call him anytime. He offered to show me Mexico. We parted and I returned to my apartment.

After a few hours rest and a good cold shower, I went to Sanborn's restaurant and had dinner. From there, I walked to the Geneve Hotel and my appointment with Vitt. He was still half drunk when I met him. However, he was able to carry on a coherent conversation while riding in the taxi to the university. Vitt told me something of his life. He was born in San Francisco, was a high school graduate and had joined the marines, where he saw active service in the Pacific in World War II. Since his discharge, he had been an adventurer, training guerrilla forces in Boliva, Brazil, Argentina and other Latin American countries. He also asked me if I knew how to procure armaments such as mortars, machine guns and grenades. I did not want to commit myself, so I told him that I might be able to help if the price was right but wanted to know where and to whom this material would be going. He asked me if I had time the next day to meet someone. I told him I could arrange my time as necessary, and we arranged that I meet him at his hotel on the following day. We reached the university, and the party where I was introduced to the host, an American named John Wills from New Jersey. An art student at the university, he immediately asked me to have a drink. I found out that most of the men present were students attending the Mexican university on the G. I. bill. The only other person I met was Joseph Hoppe, who was married to former silent screen star Nancy Carroll. He was a pleasant fellow, who had spent four years in a Japanese prisoner of war camp in Malaya. The party was pretty dull, with everyone getting drunk and boisterous, so I found an American journalist, Harriet Weaver, who worked on the English language paper, the *News*. She had a car and was going into the city. I gladly accepted her offer of a lift and she dropped me off at my apartment. I called it a night.

CHAPTER XXXI

On another occasion, a few days later, Vitt invited me to a "party" that was much more interesting. I was to meet him at the Geneve Hotel, and when I arrived Jack was sitting at one of the tables drinking his Corona Beer and looked as if he already had quite a few under his belt.

As soon as he saw me, he finished his drink and we walked outside and hailed a taxi. Vitt gave the driver an address in Lomas, an exclusive residential section on the outskirts of the city where only the wealthiest people live. It took the cab about three-quarters of an hour to reach our destination, one of the most modern private houses in the neighborhood, surrounded by a white brick wall.

As soon as the taxi drove out of sight, Vitt made it clear that he was familiar with the area. He rang a bell in a concealed part of the gate and almost immediately a servant appeared who recognized him and told us to come right in. "Mr. DeJoie is expecting you." By "you," she apparently meant both of us. Vitt must have told him about me in advance.

As soon as we entered the house, we were greeted by a young man in his early thirties, dark brown skin, short clipped black hair, with a small black moustache, 5' 10" and about 165 pounds. He greeted Vitt with a warm "hello" and they shook hands. Then Jack introduced me to Louis DeJoie.

We were ushered into a spacious living room with modern furnishings and large windows from floor to ceiling which faced the garden. We were given cocktails as soon as we were seated, and were joined by a very attractive blond young woman about 25 years old, followed by a tall, slender, beautiful brown-skinned girl in her late twenties. They both came down from upstairs living quarters. The blond was introduced to me as DeJoie's wife and the dark-skinned girl as his sister, Jessie. The latter excused herself shortly, claiming an appointment in the city and left.

Vitt immediately started a conversation about Haiti and DeJoie asked me if I was familiar with the situation in that country. I replied that I only knew what had appeared in the press. DeJoie then heatedly declared that his father was the "rightful president" of Haiti and that we must invade it and depose Dr. Duvalier by force. He kept on repeating himself on the need for an invasion and that "money is no object." Vitt talked about the type of armaments that would be needed for such an invasion, and DeJoie asked me my opinion. I told him that he would need military instructors in guerilla warfare, training camps, at least 250–300 men, about 1000 rifles—the extra ones to be distributed in Haiti—plenty of ammunition and grenades, landing boats and—above all—good timing.

When I was through, DeJoie dismissed my estimate and confidently insisted that he could carry out an invasion with only 30 men. I wondered what kind of an ass I was dealing with. Generalissimo Trujillo, dictator of the neighboring Dominican Republic, kept 500 crack soldiers in barracks in Port-au-Prince as protection for his friend Dr. Duvalier, not to mention Haitian troops. DeJoie kept on drinking, with the help of Vitt—who was always ready for another drink—and the more that Louis drank the more he babbled about a 30-man invasion. He also told me that his father was touring Venezuela, Puerto Rico, Peru, Costa Rica and Cuba raising funds and recruiting men. He had the help of Romulo Betancourt in Venezuela, Munoz in Puerto Rico and Raul de la Torre in Peru. During his babbling, DeJoie said that 50 men were already being trained in the Sierra Maestra of Cuba and Fidel Castro was helping them.

He promised that as soon as he and his father took over in Haiti, all those that helped would run the country and have anything they wanted: position, power and anything that money could buy. After listening to him for as long as I could bear it, I said that I did not want anything to do with his plan because I realized that I was talking to a dreamer (I could have said lunatic) in his insisting upon an invasion with 30 to 50 men, though I would have been glad to see Duvalier overthrown. After my declaration, Vitt and I bid him good-bye and we went back to the city, Jack to his hotel and I to my apartment. The things that impressed me were that Betancourt, Munoz, and de

la Torre were aiding DeJoie, and that Castro was active in the under-
taking. In 1961, an invasion of Haiti was attempted with 80 men, and
the poor devils in the force didn't even reach the beaches of Haiti.
They were slaughtered before landing by the Haitian government
forces.

CHAPTER XXXII

After a month in business, in Mexico, I realized that it would be a physical impossibility for me to carry on alone, and discussed my problem with an acquaintance whom I had met in Mexico City. He recommended that I talk to Julio Rothenstreich, an Austrian-Jewish businessman, who sold tool machinery that he bought in the United States. He headed the firm of Doroco, the *Dundish Rothenstreich Company.* Dundish was his brother-in-law and an American citizen living in Mexico. After discussing my problem with him, we decided to combine his company and my printing machinery business. A few weeks after our partnership, I noticed that he was getting visitors who spoke to him in Russian. I was especially surprised to hear Julio speaking in Russian, and my curiosity was aroused as to what was going on. I checked with the secretary who told me that they were from the Soviet embassy, and included Boris Streltzov, chief Soviet engineer, and a Russian named Menshikov, Soviet trade commissioner.

A few weeks later I told Julio that I was preparing to go to New York for my daughter's graduation and would also buy some more machinery. He asked when I was going, and I told him in eight or nine days—the 25th or 26th of June, 1957. He said that there was something he wanted and would discuss it with me the next day. First he would have to "find out something," but wouldn't tell me what it was until later.

The following day, Julio asked me if I was interested in a deal to make some real money. He mentioned that as an American citizen I could freely travel in and out of the United States. Julio did not know my background, so in order to find out what sort of dealings he was involved in, I played along and told him that I was interested.

That afternoon he introduced me to Boris Streltzov, chief engineer of the Soviet Machine Export Division. He was in his early thirties, about five feet, nine inches and 155 pounds, blond and blue-eyed.

Julio must have discussed me with him beforehand because Boris immediately spoke to me in Russian. He told me that there was an opportunity to make a large amount of money.

He showed me a few photographs of a magnetic mine detector being manufactured in Texas, used for identifying underwater objects. Feigning naivete—I knew that it was on the restricted list of items not to be sold to Iron Curtain countries—I asked him why they could not get it themselves. Julio volunteered that it is a restricted item and would have to be bought under a fictitious name and transshipped through Canada and Belgium to Vienna, Austria. From there, Julio's brother would ship it to Russia. Boris stressed the point that it should be done with the utmost secrecy and that money was no object since the detector would be of great value to the Soviet Union.

After this session, Boris proposed that we get together to discuss arrangements for the deal before I left for New York. He left in a car with the diplomatic license plates #39. I took a taxi to the Hotel Reforma, where I entered a telephone booth and called a friend connected with the United States Embassy and asked him to meet me at the hotel bar. Without giving any details, I said that I had something important to discuss with him.

My friend arrived in 20 minutes. I outlined the proposition that Julio and Boris had made me—and that I'd indicated a willingness to play ball with them to find out what their game was. He told me not to give a definite answer and promised to call me at my apartment at 9:00. We parted, and since it was only about 5:00 P.M., I decided to take a walk on the main street, *Insurgentes*, the Broadway of Mexico City. While strolling, I wandered into Sears and Roebuck and ran into Samuel J. Novick, former owner of Wholesale Radio Corporation, Lafayette Radio Corporation, and Electronics Corporation of America in New York City. During the war, he was president of the latter company, which worked on super secret electronics equipment for the United States Navy, with blueprints being sent to the Soviets.

He had skipped to Mexico when the FBI and Senator Joseph McCarthy's Senate Committee wanted to question him about his activities. Among them was his connection with the Arthur Alexandrovich Adams espionage case. It was believed that Novick was Adams' employer and sponsor.

I first met Novick in April 1932 through a Soviet courier, using the name Irving Koenig, who had just arrived from the Soviet Union. An American citizen of Russian birth, Koenig's real name was Israel Koenigsberg. After a few days of acquaintanceship, he told me of his frequent trips to the Soviet Union, and his deals in radio and electronic equipment and that his home was in Chicago.

Shortly thereafter, Koenig signed an affidavit for me for a United States passport when I was notified by the Communist Party that I should prepare to leave for Moscow to receive advanced training at the Lenin School. When we had left the passport office, he said that he would introduce me to a very good friend. We went to 100 Sixth Avenue, near Canal Street, to Wholesale Radio Corporation, where I met Novick. After our first meeting, we saw each other about six or eight times in Communist Party circles. When we faced each other in the Mexico City Department Store, Novick seemed as surprised to meet me as I was to meet him. We stared at each other for a while, but didn't stop or speak. We both knew that we'd chosen opposite sides in the Cold War. I decided to check on Mr. Novick's activity in the near future and walked away from him. After dinner at the Sears Restaurant, I went back to my apartment to rest and wait for my phone call. At 9:00 the telephone rang and my friend from the embassy called and asked me to meet him in 15 minutes near my apartment. I said that it might not be such a good idea to be seen with him near my apartment and suggested that we meet at the entrance of the Palace of Fine Arts on Avenida Juarez. He agreed, and I immediately took a taxi to the appointed place and our timing was just right, because we both arrived there at the same time.

We went into the book shop located in the Palace of Fine Arts, browsed around and exited through the park entrance. We sat down on a bench near the water fountain. He told me that it was a good idea for me to cooperate with Julio and Boris to find out what was behind the whole affair. He had alerted our embassy to their activities, and told me to immediately get in touch with him as soon as I returned to Mexico from New York. We parted company in the park in order not to be seen with one another. The next day, Streltzov and Julio asked me to investigate the possibility of getting the magnetic detector while I was in the United States. I agreed.

Upon my return to New York on June 27, I decided to relax for a few days before looking around for linotype and other printing machines that I needed. In addition, I wanted to check on the firm that made the machine that the Reds wanted. I needed full details on the restrictions by our government, availability, price, etc. My labor was eased when I received a call advising that there were people in Washington who would like to speak to me in regard to some important matters. I agreed, and made arrangements for a meeting. A few days later, I went to Washington and immediately contacted government officials concerned with the problem. Three people met me and began by asking for full details about the requests of Julio and Boris in regard to the magnetic machine. After discussing Doroco and the Russians, I was asked to identify the machine they wanted from a group of photographs from a catalog. They then gave me instructions as to how I should proceed with my further dealing with the Russians: payment in full—$45,000—before I would make any arrangements to get the machine. Further instructions would be given to me after I received the money. Meanwhile I was to carefully try to find out what else they were after. I returned to New York and began making arrangements to purchase and ship machines to Mexico. I also looked into activities on the part of the American Communist Party regarding Cuba* and what the line was concerning the Castro movement.

I spoke to informants within the Party who told me that the instructions were to work with the Castroites, and that Moscow was behind Fidel's revolution in Cuba. The policy was to duplicate the strategy that had worked in China. The immediate aims were to get new Owen Lattimores to popularize the "agrarian reformer" line in order to mislead the American people; to stop all support to the Cuban government, thereby preparing the ground for its downfall; and to arm Castro for a takeover. The picture was clear, and I decided to find out who supported the Cuban Reds with finances and arms in Mexico because I was sure that this was the crucial area for action. The day after returning to Mexico City, I went to the plant to check on my business and to make arrangements to receive the other machines arriving in Vera Cruz from New York. When I inquired from the office girl about Julio's whereabouts, she told me that he had not been in the day before and might have gone on a trip to Monterey with Boris Streltzov. They might be away for a few days.

*See Appendix I, p. 239.

CHAPTER XXXIII

While I was checking invoices of machinery, I noticed large packages of drawings and catalogs marked IMPORTANTE. Being alone in the office, I opened one and found it to contain drawings, catalogs and blueprints of hundreds of industrial plants in Mexico and elsewhere. Included were steel plants in Monterey, the Pittsburgh of Mexico, mining, shipping, railroad, and other installations. I closed the package, as it was before, and decided to check further on Julio, Streltzov, Doroco and Company. Now I was certain that in addition to smuggling, they were also carrying out industrial espionage on a large scale, and started an investigation.

I began by asking Dr. King and others about Julio's background and found out that his wife was a niece of Constantine Umanski, former Soviet Ambassador to Mexico who was killed by a bomb placed by the GPU in Mexico in 1943. Julio, Austrian born, was a naturalized Mexican citizen. A brother, living in Vienna, was an agent of the Soviet government who relayed shipments of goods on the United States embargo list. The Dundish family, Julio's in-laws, are American citizens. The father and sons lived in the United States during the Second World War. They used their citizenship to smuggle iron and steel across the border from the U. S. to sell on the black market. Doroco sold everything in the line of tool and die machinery, trucks, agriculture equipment, electric motors and welding and bronzing equipment. The Mexican government prohibits American motors into Mexico, but the Russians have smuggled them in by the thousands, especially fractional motors such as one-quarter and one-half horsepower. When Julio and Streltzov returned from their trip, they again showed me photos of the magnetic detector they wanted. I told them under what conditions I would try to obtain it. I demanded immediate cash payment and wanted to know the shipping route they would use. Streltzov told me that he would let me know within a few days, but it was the last I heard about it.

One day I learned that as soon as a shipment of machinery arrived, Julio ordered the uncrating of certain machines, identified by some kind of special code mark. He removed small packages wrapped in oil skin, waterproof paper about four by six inches in size, and immediately put them in his safe. As soon as possible, he would remove them and drive away. It appeared as if he was handling diamonds or something of similar value because he was so secretive about it. Once when Julio did not notice me because I was standing behind a large crate, I saw him handling these packages. I was very anxious to find out what they were, but never succeeded.

In the late afternoon or evening, Julio would often go to #19 Saltillo, the headquarters of the Soviet Trade Commission. He would always carry a large briefcase with him.

One morning as I walked into the plant, I heard Julio and Streltzov arguing. It seems that some shipments of tool machinery had arrived and Julio opened certain ones without Boris' permission. Our private offices were separated by glass partitions and I could see them and hear snatches of their conversation. Finally, Julio gave the Russian one package and took another out of the safe. Streltzov put both in a briefcase he carried with him and went out.

I made sure to reach the street before Boris so I would get a chance to talk to him. I made believe I was waiting for a taxi, and when he saw me, he invited me to have a drink with him. We went into a cafe and he quickly ordered. He was very nervous and agitated—and kept repeating *Zhid sobaka*, a Russian derogatory curse meaning "Jew Dog." When I asked him what the trouble was, he ignored my question and asked what I thought about Julio. Playing to his mood, I answered that Julio would do anything for a peso, and that means "anything." "Yes," he answered, "including selling his wife, mother, and father." We were in the cafe about 30 minutes and he kept babbling, *zhidovskaya sobachya morda*, while he kept on drinking. Before we parted, he gave me his telephone number at 19 Saltillo, the Soviet Trade Commission, and told me that when calling I should say "Michael" wanted him. He asked me to call him when I had time for a social evening. He left in his Volvo with diplomatic plate #39.

After that I went out with Streltzov on several occasions, including a week-end at Cuernavaca. He would always drink too much, and usually end up cursing Julio—the *Zhid* who'd "sell his mother for a peso," a phrase he'd repeat over and over.

One day he told me that the Soviets received blueprints of industrial secrets from the French, and that they were able to get much classified material from this source because the USSR had "many friends in the French government."

CHAPTER XXXIV

Fidel Castro arrived in Mexico in June 1954. His brother Raul had proceeded him. Upon Castro's arrival in Mexico, he was immediately placed in contact with General Lazaro Cardenas, and Vincente Lombardo Toledano, who in turn made connections for him with the Soviet Embassy. His closest advisor upon arriving in Mexico was Lazaro Pena, leader of the Cuban Communist Party and chief of the *Confederacion de Trabajadores de America Latina* (CTAL), the Confederation of Latin American Workers. (In 1957, Castro had an apartment at #5 Insurgentes Norte, the same building where Pena lived.) Communist labor leaders such as Vincente Lombardo Toledano were placed in leadership positions of CTAL during World War II by Nelson Rockefeller, the present governor of New York, when he was coordinator of Latin American Affairs for Franklin Delano Roosevelt. Castro was in very close contact with David Siqueros, Mexican artist, who has served a prison term for organizing riots in Mexico, and was one of the conspirators in the assassination of Trotsky. Trapote's studio was a hangout for Spanish Loyalist and Communist exiles. The innocent looking club, *Atenio Espanol,* on Norellos Ave. #26, was one of the relay centers of the Caribbean Department of the Comintern. Other communist centers were the Sea Food restaurant and upstairs apartments at Hamburgo St. #37, the Club Ontillano and the restaurant, *El Gallo Del Oro* on Insurgentes South.

One of the first organizations that served as a Castro front was the *Assistencia Technica,* which had its headquarters in Cuernavaca and had originally been used by the Guatemalan Reds for Soviet espionage. In 1955 it began functioning officially as part of the Castro movement and moved to Calle Amparan #49, Mexico City. A similar group, known as Cesta, was organized in Guatemala in 1954 and later moved to Cuernavaca and Mexico City. Cesta was a secret terrorist organization, similar to the Cheka in Russia, to liquidate all opponents of the regime.

Another organization created and placed at the disposal of Castro was the *Junta de Liberacion Latino Americano* (Supreme Council of Latin American Liberation). One of its leaders was Hipolito Castillo, who later commanded the Castro expedition. The Council consisted of Russians, Germans, Hungarians, Spaniards, Poles and Czechs all trained in guerilla tactics for the coming communist uprising.

These and other fronts, were under the direct supervision and orders of the *Operatsionnoye Upravleniye* (OPU-YE) and *Glavnoye Upravleniye Yuzhnoi Ameriki* (GUJA), Central Administration for South America. Both were sections of the Soviet military intelligence and Latin American secretariat of the Communist Party of the Soviet Union. Upon his arrival in Mexico, Castro immediately began recruiting Cubans and, through Cardenas, was able to rent a large ranch called *Santa Rosa*, about 25 miles from Mexico City in Chalco District. He also acquired the services of Alberto Bayo, a one-eyed Spaniard formerly in the Spanish Air Force, who became a Colonel in the Loyalist Army, trained in Moscow and was an experienced guerilla fighter. The trainees were taught everything; the use of all weapons, infiltration, sabotage, etc. The bibles for these tactics were *China in Arms*, a manual on guerilla warfare, and *El Comite Regional Clandestine Activa*, the Clandestine Regional Committee Acts, printed in Moscow by the GOSIZDAT (State Publishing House), written by the Soviet expert on guerilla warfare and instructor in the Lenin School for foreign students, Alexei Fioderev. Other textbooks were Mao Tse-tung's *Guerilla Warfare* and Chu Teh's *Guerilla Tactics*. During 1955–56, and throughout Castro's stay in Mexico, arms, supplies and funds were supplied by General Lazaro Cardenas and the Soviet Embassy. On June 22, 1956, the Mexican police raided the Santa Rosa camp, arrested the Cuban trainees and confiscated the arms, but they were all released a month later and continued their training in apartment houses, private homes and about 15 places where arms were stored. The Mexican police kept raiding and harassing them and the Fidelistas decided to leave for Cuba. About 80 guerillas loaded and fueled their boat, the *Gramma*, bought with $15,000 cash supplied by former President Carlos Prio Socarres from J. Erickson. It was a 58-foot yacht and sailed from Tuxpan, a Mexican Gulf port, on November 25, 1956. The commander of the *Gramma* and the expedition was Hipolito Castillo, one of the top leaders of the old Comintern and Cominform and one of Moscow's key agents in the Caribbean. He is a Dominican who organized the *Junta de Liberacion Latino Americano*. He is wanted by many governments.

CHAPTER XXXV

The USSR has one of its most powerful weapons in the person of former Mexican president, Lazaro Cardenas. He is one of their mainstays in pushing Soviet intrigue in Mexico and throughout all Latin America. He hates the United States and aids the Russians in their expansion of trade, strengthening the establishment of their base in Mexico and exporting revolution to the Western hemisphere. How does a man like Cardenas—a very rich, powerful, former general and president of Mexico—become a partner in a movement that could, if successful in attaining power, mean his downfall? One answer is vanity. That is why the Kremlin awards peace prizes and endlessly praises Cardenas, the biggest landowner in Mexico, inflating the general's ego by having him head, nominally, the "peace movement." He in turn serves them loyally, directly and by drawing upon the services of others like himself—such as Abelardo Rodriguez, a former general and president of Mexico; who became a big landowner and otherwise enriched himself while in office through graft and corruption, and college professors, journalists and opportunists of all types who look for favors from Cardenas and his clique. While digging into the activities of the Kremlin in Mexico, I nearly always found Cardenas playing a role, so I investigated the general's background and his associations with the Soviets. While he was president from 1934–40, he opened the doors of Mexico to communist refugees from Spain, Italy, Germany and other countries, and allowed Moscow to establish its headquarters for espionage, murder and subversion. Mexico City became a main terminal for Soviet agents:

Egon Erwin Kisch, identified by General Charles Willoughby, director of intelligence for General Douglas MacArthur, as a member of the famous Sorge spy ring in Asia.

Jeanne Garnier, a member of the French Communist Party.

Hannes Meyer, Comintern representative in Mexico and member of the Swiss Communist Party.

"Andre Simon," real name Katz, Comintern agent who worked for the GPU in Spain, member of both the Czech and German Communist Parties. Even though sponsored by Mrs. Eleanor Roosevelt for admittance to the United States, he eventually was ordered deported and skipped to Mexico. He later died from a GPU bullet as did hundreds, and perhaps thousands of others. Cardenas not only allowed European Soviet agents into Mexico, but also helped American communists to find a heaven south of the border. One of them, Maurice Halperin, former officer of the Latin American section of the Office of Strategic Services during World War II, had been an international troubleshooter for the Soviets, travelling throughout the world as needed. In Latin America he has worked in Brazil, Argentina, Venezuela, Peru and Cuba. In Caracas he gave instructions from Moscow and the new line regarding sabotage and guerilla warfare to the Machado Brothers, leaders of the Venezuelan Communist Party.

When he was president, Cardenas said, "The imperialism of the United States is the main obstacle to Latin American development." In 1938, he ordered the confiscation of the United States oil interests. *Cardenasismo* was planted in Mexico and is flourishing to the present day. His record clearly shows where he stood—and still stands. Cardenas' support of our World War II effort was due to the Soviet-American alliance. Immediately after the war, he quickly returned to his anti-Yankee crusade, and followed the line laid down by the Kremlin. In 1948, he attended the Waldorf Peace Conference, in New York. In August 1950, Cardenas was elected as a member of the Presidium of the World Peace Congress at Warsaw, Poland. A year later came the first Mexican Peace Congress in Mexico City: 1955 was a big year. Cardenas was a Vice President of the World Peace Council, Helsinki, Finland, and was awarded the Stalin Peace Prize, which he accepted in Mexico City in May, 1956. That October he was elected vice-president of World Peace Council, Stockholm, Sweden. In 1958, Cardenas made a world tour of Communist countries* in-

---

*Cardenas brought back 55 million dollars of Soviet agriculture and other machinery. Fronting for him in the selling of Soviet shipments was Harry DeSwan, a Dutch citizen of Jewish descent, with a warehouse and showrooms at 29 Rhin Street in Mexico City. The material was unloaded through Tampico and other Mexican ports at night. During World War II, DeSwan sold Japanese and Nazi goods, and smuggled stolen war materials across the border from the U.S.

cluding Red China, the Soviet Union, Czechoslovakia and Hungary, the latter nation still bleeding from the 1956 Soviet attack. He supported demonstrations and riots by the Mexican Communists and front groups, such as the Committee of Action of the Mexican National University faculty, in July 1959, which backed Castro's 26th of July movement.

The Kremlin wanted to publicize Castro more fully and disparage the United States in the eyes of Latin American people in 1961, so they ordered Cardenas to front the Latin American Conference for National Sovereignty, Economic Emancipation and Peace. Boris Kazantzev, the Soviet ambassador to Cuba, helped in the organizing, and the Soviet Embassy in Mexico donated $90,000. plus the cost of printing and other expenses. The conference was held in March at Mexico City. To show that the gathering was representative of all Latin America, they imported an old war horse of the Argentina Communist Party, Sarah Goldberg, as one of Cardenas' assistants. She had been in the Party for a quarter of a century and served as a GPU agent in numerous Latin American countries, especially among the Jewish communities in the various nations. The "U.S. representatives" at that conference included well-known American communists Fred V. Fields, Samuel J. Novick, Albert Maltz and Catherine Cole, a member of the Party in Los Angeles County. Other American traitors hid their identity because they were afraid of being questioned by the authorities upon their return to the United States.

Cardenas monopolized the conference with his ranting against the U. S., demanding the return of Guantanamo Naval Base to Cuba, the internationalization of the Panama Canal, etc. The only thing he did not call for was the return of the country to the Indians. Thus we find Cardenas involved in nearly every anti-American and pro-Soviet activity in Latin America: economic war, bringing Soviet machinery into the hemisphere to compete with American industry—cultural, subverting university students and faculties—political, organizing the famous Moscow ordered peace conferences and pro-Castro congresses—direct military intervention, supplying the Castros with training camps, arms and money to hire mercenaries. Little wonder that Lazaro Cardenas received the Stalin "Peace" prize!

CHAPTER XXXVI

The Soviet Embassy in Mexico is the main headquarters for Kremlin activities throughout the Western Hemisphere. The Soviet Embassy is one of the main suppliers and distributors of communist propaganda in the United States as well as in Latin America. The Embassy, with its huge staff of over 460 Russians, could also call on the services of hundreds of other Iron Curtain countries' representatives in Mexico City. Until recently, they had free rein to travel all over the country and many of them skipped across the border into the United States where they contacted other Soviet agents, including American Communist Party functionaries such as Morris Childs (real name: Chilofsky). He is the Latin American expert of the U.S. Party and makes frequent trips to Mexico—I knew of at least three in 1958–59. Tons and tons of printed material pour from its printing plants in Mexico City and other parts of Mexico. One large plant where the presses run day and night is at #19 Saltillo, the headquarters of the Soviet Trade Mission. Behind fortress-like walls is a large building with a shop containing large presses moored to the floors. They are guarded 24 hours a day.

Others include: *Fondo De Cultura, Editorial Popular, Editorial Atlante, Imprenta Cosmos, Talleres Grafico de Liberia Maderia, Liberia Nacional* and *Popular*—presses of the so-called *Partito Popular,* which print Soviet propaganda.

These tons of propaganda are shipped by trucks to the American borders at Laredo, Baja California and Tijuana, and to Ensenada by truck and boat. The latter, a fishing resort frequented by a large American tourist trade, is 40.3 miles from the U.S.

While in Mexico I learned that besides all its other activities, the Soviet Embassy was putting pressure on former Russian citizens to repatriate to the USSR. Nicolai Menshikov and three other agents of the Soviet Secret Police had paid a visit to Ensenada and Guadalupe, site of a settlement of Russian wine growers, who migrated to Mexico in 1905 from Russia, via California. Known as Old Believers, they left Russia in 1903 because of vicious Czarist religious persecution. The refugees bought land from the Mexican government and settled there. Approximately 500 families developed that section of hilly, desert land into the finest vineyard section in Mexico. The famous *Santo Tomas* and other wines come from the grapes grown there.

These immigrants are still governed, in their own community, by the Russian traditional committee of elders who chose the *Starosta* (chief elder) as their leader. They run their own schools—conducted in Spanish and Russian—and a great many have sent their sons to American universities where they graduated as physicians and engineers.

I read a small article in the *New York Times* about a disturbance that was created by the visit of Soviet agents to Ensenada and the Guadalupe colony and discussed the matter with a senior official at the United States Embassy. We decided that I should take a trip and find out the full details concerning the routes of shipments of Communist printed material into the area, and also Soviet activities among the Russians in the colony. Since there wasn't any air service from Mexico City to Ensenada, or anywhere near it, I took a plane to Los Angeles and a bus to Tijuana. From Tijuana to Ensenada I used three cabs and finally had to rent a car because the taxis kept breaking down.

I checked into the Hotel Plaza, which looked clean and halfway decent, and went out to look over the town. While walking through the main street, passing the shops and fishing tackle stands, I discovered that nearly everyone in town spoke some English—and soon had a hand out for a tip. American money was more acceptable in this town than Mexican. I stopped at a restaurant and was escorted to a table by an English speaking waitress. Looking around the place, I noticed quite a few American tourists, singles, couples and families, but no one of any special interest. After eating, I walked around until I found an open air cafe. It was half filled with American tourists, plus a few natives. While sipping Kahlua, a coffee liquor, I heard two men discussing the local business situation at the next table. They spoke in Russian. One had Semitic features and the other looked like a blond Slav. After listening for a few minutes, I asked if they were Russians and the blond fellow said they were, and invited me to move

213

over to their table. While they were drinking beer, I sipped my liquor. They were both born in Russia, one, a Jew, was from Odessa and the other, a Russian, came from Georgia. The Jew, Kagan, owned a group of motel cottages on the main street, two blocks from where we were. The Russian, Chaifa, was a next door neighbor who owned a fishing supply store and rented small boats to the tourists. They invited me to visit them during my stay.

I asked them about the Russian population in town and was informed that there were only a few families in Ensenada but there was a large colony in Guadalupe about 21.7 miles into the hills. They were mainly wine growers and cattle breeders. I did not want to arouse their curiosity by pressing for further details, so I switched the subject to the local climate and tourist trade. Since the Russian seemed more talkative, I decided that I had to get together with him alone in order to find out more details about the Russian colony. We broke up about 4:00 in the afternoon and I went to my hotel.

I went to my room and read a pocketbook edition about the assassination of Trotsky by the general who was in charge of the investigation of the murder.

I dozed off and didn't awake until after 7:00. I quickly washed, dressed and left the hotel because I was anxious to find out more about the colony. About a block from my hotel on the main street, I saw Chaifa leaving a strip tease joint. He offered to show me the town, and I gladly accepted.

While walking, I asked him in the most indirect way about the political tendencies of the Russians in Guadalupe and whether they were pro-Soviet. He told me that they were not. When I was sure that he was not a communist, I asked about propaganda. He told me that trucks full of printed matter were loaded onto fishing boats and yachts. He has seen the transshipping on many occasions, while he was delivering supplies nearby. These craft came from the U.S. supposedly on pleasure fishing cruises. He informed me that tons of printed material were brought from outside of Ensenada by trucks and stored in a large warehouse. He said the material was printed in English and Spanish. Some cases were marked for other Latin American countries, which meant that the boats probably rendezvoused with ships after they left Ensenada and transferred the material for delivery to other destinations.

Chaifa also said that he once spoke to a Mexican driver of one of these shipments who told him that he and other truckmen drop off some of the loads of printed matter at Tijuana and that it is taken across the border into San Diego and Los Angeles. He told me that he had seen many strangers who didn't look like fishermen land in Ensenada and leave on these boats. I asked if there was much propaganda printed in town and he said that there were only two printers in town, the Mexican newspaper and a small job printer, who did small jobs.

Chaifa showed me a warehouse a half block from the waterfront that was loaded with big bundles covered with sack cloth. Part of this warehouse was the local headquarters of the *Partito Popular* of Vincente Lombardo Toledano, *Confederacion Trabajadores, Latino Americano* (CTAL) and the World Federation of Trade Unions (WFTU). After walking around Ensenada with Chaifa for several hours, we parted after I promised that I'd see him the next day, which was a Saturday, so that he could show me more of the town. I went back to the hotel and made notes on all the things Chaifa had reported and showed me. I decided that early the next morning I would try to get to Guadalupe.

I was up at 7:00 the next morning, took a cold shower, dressed and was in the street before 8:00. The streets were deserted—not even the half-starved dogs, which could nearly always be seen scrounging for food, were to be found. I went back to the hotel lobby and bought a *Los Angeles Times.* I read until 9:30 then went to a restaurant and had coffee. At 10:30, I found a taxi driver who was willing to take me to Guadalupe and back for $35.00 in American money, plus the cost of gas and meals for the trip. If he had to stay overnight, I would have to pay him $10.00 extra. I agreed because there was no other way of getting there.

After three hours of rattling through the hills, we reached a dusty red muddy road going through fields of olive groves and grape vines. The driver explained that this land was exclusively olive and grape country and is cultivated by the "Russian gringos." It stretches for miles and the grapes were the best in the country. After an hour's travel through the fields, we reached the first house. When I saw it, I thought I was dreaming. I remembered seeing the same style house, with a wooden fence around it, in Russia as a child. I told the driver to stop at a store, with kids standing nearby drinking Coca-Cola. Inside, I asked the man behind the counter, in Russian, where

215

I could find Philip Mustafov, the *Starosta*—Chaifa had supplied the name. He dispatched one of the boys to find him, and I bought a few cigars while waiting for the *Starosta* to come. A few minutes later, a six-foot man of about 65, with a large Taras Bulba mustache and weather beaten face, came in and asked who wanted to see him. The storekeeper pointed to me, and I introduced myself as an American newspaper man. I also told him that Chaifa had suggested I see him. He spoke Russian with a strong Caucasian accent, which sounded like a pidgin Russian, but we understood each other. He asked what I wanted, and I said that I was interested in the story of the Soviet embassy's interference in the community, the rumors of forced repatriation, confiscating their land, etc. He took me by the arm and asked me to go to his house so that we could talk more freely. While walking away from the store, I noticed that the driver was sleeping peacefully in the cab. We reached the gate of a wooden picket fence, neatly painted red and blue and a path through a garden of neatly trimmed flower beds, that looked like the cover of a gardening magazine. Behind the colorful flowers was a large, long white house built of beam and mud with a red roof and window frames and blue shutters. The *Starosta* told me that this was the Council House, where the elders meet. Nearby was a round shaped building with a painted dome roof, barns for cattle and, in the field, cows and horses were grazing. A gray haired old woman walked by. She looked weather beaten and strong, wearing a babushka on her head, a long black dress and colored apron around her waist. We sat down on a bench near the house and the *Starosta* began asking me questions about my background—where I lived, where I was born, etc. I told him I was an American born in Russia, and had heard that his community had some difficulties with the Soviet Embassy. He asked me of what interest were his people to the U.S. newspaper. I told him that not only were the papers interested, but that Soviet intrigues were of interest to the American people. He became very friendly as soon as I made it clear that I was not on the side of the Kremlin. The *Starosta* moved a wooden cross-legged table to our bench and went into the house. He returned with a large clay jug filled with pure red wine. He said I had picked a good day to come because in the evening, on Saturdays, there was a meeting of the Council and the weekly town celebration, including a cattle roast. The old man said that I would honor him by being his guest. While we were drinking delicious wine, he told me the story of the colony. In 1903–05, 500 families of their sect, who lived in Georgia and surrounding territories, left Russia because of religious persecution—which increased during the Russo-Japanese War when they were conscientious objectors and would not serve in the Czar's army. They migrated to California, where they continued to use their ancient skills in farming and cattle breeding. In the beginning of 1905, they had an opportunity to buy a large tract of land in Baja, lower California —part of Mexico, where the climate was similar to that in their former homeland. They moved to a desert near Guadalupe, where with back breaking labor, they cleared, irrigated and developed the land. Despite deprivation, they educated their children, and eventually sent many of them to American universities. They became model citizens of Mexico, without a single instance of Mexican courts or police needed for any law violations. Their children were brought up to be loyal Mexicans, both in language and customs—who follow their fathers' religious traditions and life style. The land they cultivated became fine vineyards, producing *Santo Tomas* wines—the best in Mexico. Their olives were of the highest quality and their cattle breeding became famous throughout the country. They never bothered anyone and no one bothered them until after World War II, when they began to receive large amounts of propaganda material from the Soviet Embassy and directly from the USSR. It contained promises of all kinds of golden opportunities for those who returned to the Soviet Union. A land of milk and honey was described, with free land and government grants. This propaganda barrage did not affect them at all and was completely ignored. Since the 1917 revolution and the overthrow of the Czar they had adopted a "neutral" attitude towards the Communist regime and Russia. They didn't care one way or another about the new rulers or their society. The propaganda did not budge even one family to ask for Soviet repatriation. One day in the summer of 1960, the Soviet consulate and three strong arm men arrived in Guadalupe and addressed the Colony Council. He gave the usual propaganda, promising the moon, sun and sky in Russia. The colony turned them down cold—not even one person believed the sweet words.

When the Soviet agents heard their decision, they threatened to put pressure on the Mexican government for their deportation. The colonists took their guns and chased the Red agents out of Guadalupe

—"escorting" them out of the hills toward Ensenada. A short time later, the Soviet Embassy began carrying out their threats of force. They made a deal with their stooge, governor of Baja California, Braulio Maldonado. Known as a corrupt politician, he followed the pro-Soviet line of his friends, General Lazaro Cardenas and Vincente Lombardo Toledano. Maldonado ordered the confiscation of over 250 hectares of vineyards from the colony, with the excuse that it was needed for the settlement of landless Mexican peasants. (The land given to the Mexicans quickly degenerated into a wasteland.) The chief elder said that the colony was not budging from its original position and was waiting for a decision of the Mexican Supreme Court concerning orders to surrender more land. The same Braulio Maldonado, together with communist Emilio Lopez Zamosa, Director of Agriculture, sponsored and directed the Castro-Khrushchev backed Latin American Conference for National Sovereignty, Economic Emancipation and Peace, held at Mexico City on March 6, 7, and 8, 1961. They brought with them to this Kremlin sponsored conference Ramiro Bermudez Algeria, a member of the governing board of the University of Baja California and Sentos Silva Coto, Rector of the same University. These Red stooges are working with the Soviet Embassy in trying to force these peaceful hard working colonists to break up their homes and lives and bend to the will of the Kremlin. This, in spite of the fact that they are all Mexican citizens by birth or naturalization for over a half a century, and in violation of all Mexican laws. After he finished telling me the whole story, the *Starosta* looked me straight in the eyes and said with firm determination: "We will *never* give up what is ours!" We continued drinking, a second jug of wine had been brought to our table, until it started getting dark and people started gathering for the Council meeting and roast. I was invited to sit in on the Council meeting, which was held in the round house, and I went out and told my cab driver that we would stay over until the next morning. It was arranged that he would sleep in the home of one of the colonists. Fifteen middle aged and older people sat in a circle on short wooden benches, some smoking long pipes, others smoking cigars. The *Starosta* opened the meeting by telling who I was and why I had come. He offered his opinion that I was one of them, a friend. They all gave their approval by saying *"Konechno"* (certainly). It seems that the only other business of the meeting were announcements of a post harvest community gathering and the acquisition of a new winery or squashing machine. We disbanded and went into a nearby field where there were men and women sitting on the ground and wooden benches. The women were dressed in colorful blouses and skirts. There were several fires with calves roasting on open spits and barrels of wine propped up on a large tree. Another fire roasted beef and lamb on steel rods with different spices, which they called shashlik. When it was ready, it was transferred to a long wooden stick from which it is eaten. The council members were seated in a circle, the *Starosta* and I with them. I was handed a mug of wine—the beginning of a party that I shall never forget. It lasted until 2:00 A.M. Large chunks of roast calf on wooden sticks were passed out and as soon as you finished one, another was placed in your hand. The young men and women danced wild Caucasian dances, including the famous Russian Cossack dance, the *Kazachok*, to the tune of flutes, accordions and tambourines.

The *Starosta* invited me to stay in his home overnight. In the morning, at 6:30 A.M. we were up and he made an omelet, coffee and fresh baked buns for me. After breakfast, I bid my host *"do svidaniya"* (goodby). He made me promise to return soon and asked that I tell the American people of the infamous deeds of the Kremlin. Outside, my cab driver was ready to take me back. As we drove through town, some of the people waved goodby and called *"Schastlivogo puti"* (good luck) and Bon Voyage. Back in Ensenada, I packed and made ready for the next day's trip back to Tijuana, Los Angeles and back to Mexico City—determined to learn more about the activities of the Soviet embassy.

CHAPTER XXXVII

The first thing I wanted to know was who was really the boss of the Soviet embassy? The ambassador himself, or an underling? Who really gave the orders for espionage, subversion and other activities? The more I investigated, the more I became convinced that it was the ambassador himself. Always joking—frequently kidded about his capitalistic habit of riding in Cadillac limousines—he was always to be found at any party given by the foreign diplomatic corps. This jolly little man from Moscow, Vladimir Bazykin, "former" officer of the Soviet Intelligence Service and former chief of the Latin American section of the Soviet Foreign Service, was 54 years old, 5'6" tall and heavy-set. His wife, daughter and son were in Moscow. She had been an opera singer. Their son was born in the United States while Bazykin was stationed in Washington, D. C. Bazykin's offices were at 204 Tacubaya, a block long, surrounded by a brick and electric wired wall. He had a large staff of spies traveling across the country gathering information, paying large sums of money when necessary. He believed in keeping a very close watch on his staff, having had experience with Igor Gouzenko's defection from the Soviet embassy in Canada, where Bazykin had previously operated. Now he was the director of the Soviet espionage machine for the Western hemisphere. If he needed any help for a job that required an American, he contacted Alexander Kolnay, an American communist who had been in the Hungarian section of the U.S. Party. He had entered the super cloak-and-dagger organization, the OSS, and served in Europe and Italy during World War II. He was in his late 50s, 5'7" and had thinning gray hair. His wife was French and they had a daughter about ten years old.

Kolnay lived on a large, hilly estate in Valle De Bravo, 65 miles from Mexico City and 12 miles from Oxaca. It consisted of a large mansion on top of a hill overlooking the town of Valle de Bravo and a few scattered smaller houses. The main building had 40–50 rooms, with one of the larger housing a powerful short wave radio for sending and receiving messages. The smaller houses had about nine rooms each. According to neighbors and storekeepers, he posed as a real estate operator and had very frequent gatherings of between 50 and 75 people gathering in his home. The cars had license plates from as far away as Canada and different states in the United States.

Kolnay could always call upon his American comrades in Mexico, such as Samuel J. Novick, who is being protected in Mexico by the American industrialist, H. Steele, owner of office supply plants and department stores. He protected Novick by having him entered on his books as an important engineer and intervening with Mexican authorities who investigated Novick. Steele was always present at functions in the American embassy but I doubt very much if Ambassador Robert C. Hill knew about Steele's hobbies. Beside Novick, other American exiles and traitors were available for assignments. One of them, Frederick Vanderbilt Fields, millionaire and former secretary of the Institute of Pacific Relations and other Communist front organizations, who had tired of his American wife, married a Mexican woman to enable him to live in Mexico.

Another American Communist, veteran courier Pauline Rogers, a former section organizer who made numerous trips to the Soviet Union before World War II, became a frequent traveler in and out of Mexico. I've seen her in the Carmel restaurant at #70 Geneve Street and one day followed her to Albert Maltz' apartment at South Yarto #14 (telephone number 48–37–77) and to the Kolnay house at Valle de Bravo. She traveled under the name Sheier, the name of a Jewish poet with whom she had a Communist marriage of convenience.

At Bazykin's call, there were more and more American traitors to do his bidding, especially those who were afraid to show their faces on U.S. soil because they were wanted for questioning about espionage and other crimes committed against the United States. There were 250 to 300 American Communists living in Mexico ready to serve Moscow. One interesting example was Len Adomian (real name Rotewine) a member of the CPUSA, dabbler in jazz music who used this knowledge for the Party. He was formerly married to dancer Edith Siegel who entertained at communist summer camps. When Hans Eisler came to the United States through the sponsorship of Eleanor Roosevelt, and became cultural boss of the Communist Party—while his brother Gerhart was the Moscow agent who directed the American Party—Adomian became his assistant and courier. During World War II, he traveled to U.S. Army camps throughout the country, under the auspices of the War Department, to organize musical entertainment. But his real interest was carrying on the communist program of subversion. When a Senate committee investigated Adomian's record, it was shown that he served with the United States Communist Lincoln Brigade in the Spanish Civil War, and was also a Red courier. A comrade of Adomian in the American Communist Party and the Lincoln Brigade—he was wounded at Bilchette—was Bart Schilling, a courier for the Soviets; he was in exile for the same reasons. A onetime singer with the Federal Theatre Project of the Work Projects Administration during the depression, he publicized himself in Mexico as an artist and portrait painter. Both men are proteges of Margaret Nelkin, whose record in the Red Who's Who reads as follows: Born, Odessa, Russia. Moved to Germany while in her teens. Margaret's first venture in espionage started in World War I when she worked as an agent for the Kaiser's government in Spain and other countries. In 1920 she became a member of the dreaded Cheka (the forerunner of the GPU) under Felix Dzerzhinsky and in 1936–38 was an agent of the GPU in Spain during the Civil War. In 1938 she migrated to Mexico, admittedly with the help of Lazaro Cardenas, and worked with Constantine Umanski when he came to Mexico as Soviet Ambassador. When I last heard of her, she was carrying on her life's work as a Soviet agent in spite of her age and denials.

Margaret's co-worker and comrade, who had as much experience in the espionage trade and intrigue, was Gertrude Dueby, a stubby and unkempt female, wild-haired and dirty. She looked like a Union Square bomb throwing anarchist of the 1920's, but her looks did not reflect her experience as a Soviet agent, posing as an archaeologist. She could usually be found near the borders of Mexico and Guatemala, in the state of Chiapas, or in Baja California. Anytime the Soviets needed a courier or a route to smuggle agents in or out of Mexico, Gertrude was ready to serve.

She was a member of the Communist Party of Switzerland and joined the Swiss Socialist Party and its organizations to subvert them from within until she was uncovered as a Soviet agent and expelled.

But she always called herself a Social Democrat to hide her real identity. Gertrude also came to Mexico under the Cardenas rule.

Another important servant of the Kremlin who reached Mexico through Cardenas was Juan Negrin, the former Premier of Loyalist Spain. He did not come to Mexico emptyhanded. He brought part of the Spanish treasury of gold and jewelry with him, and it was used for propaganda and espionage by Soviet Military Intelligence agents in Mexico through Umanski's office. The gold and jewels were kept in the vaults of Sam Wishniak, president of the Jewish Bank at 59 Venustiana Carranza. A friend of Umanski, he acted as paymaster with the help of R. Bitteta, former secretary-treasurer under former President Miguel Aleman.

To dispose of the smuggled jewels they worked through A. Schildkraut, diamond and jewelry merchant, smuggler extraordinary and gambler. He, too, was a personal friend of Umanski, who, with other Red agents and members of the Soviet embassy staff, spent much time in Schildkraut's home in his walled estate in Cuernavaca, the resort outside of Mexico City. This jeweler, with two establishments on Madero Street, was the fence who turned the jewels into cash for the Soviet espionage machine. Both Schildkraut and Wishniak, who as president of the Jewish Bank had an important voice in the Jewish community, covered up their nefarious activities for the Soviets by making absolutional donations to the United Jewish Appeal and other Jewish agencies. Wishniak has made at least one trip to Israel. These and more, too numerous to mention here, are the people that Bazykin used to serve Moscow, whenever and wherever he needed them.

CHAPTER XXXVIII

By 1962, the Russians were expanding their sphere of influence into practically every field in Mexico, expecially in trade. They were selling agricultural machinery, tractors, trucks, industrial tools, automobiles and many other items. In printing—linotypes, die cutters, guillotines, printing presses, etc.—they cut deeply into my business. I could not afford the long terms and low interest rates that they were giving the Mexicans as incentives to chase Americans out of business.

From home, the news media reports of the chaotic conditions in the United States caused me to worry about my family. Since my children were of school age, one in college and the other in high school, I felt that they needed my guidance. My experience proved to be better than the "education" offered by a great many of their teachers at Brooklyn College and in the New York City school system, who were leftist oriented and twisted the subjects to suit their radical ideology.

The two conditions combined—poor business in Mexico and concerns about home—forced me to sell out and return to the United States. In April, 1962, I liquidated my business in Mexico. During my five and a half years' absence the Kremlin termites had made great strides in the United States. Mass fronts were operating which not only *talked* revolution, but really carried it out in *action*.

The Negro separatist movement, which I, as one of the active forces in the Communist Party for over 20 years, had helped to develop on orders from the Communist International—beginning with the resolutions of the Sixth World Congress of the C.I. held at Moscow in April–May, 1928—was flourishing.

During the 1920's and '30's the Communist Party had been unable to attract any great number of Negroes to its policies despite all the beautiful slogans of equal rights and self-determination. The great majority of black people were patriotic, loyal Americans who did not accept us or our Leninist slogans of splitting the United States.

The Party had used every approach to ensnare the Negroes. Those willing to go along were showered with praises and bribes with whatever tempted them. Some, men like James W. Ford and Harry Haywood, were sent to the Lenin School and other Communist universities. They returned as Kremlin mercenaries to "lead" the Negroes into following Communist directives to further Moscow's interests. They failed almost completely.

The Communists did manage to get some cooperation from a few black leaders, such as A. Philip Randolph, president of the Brotherhood of Sleeping Car Porters, who followed the Party line through numerous front organizations like the phony National Negro Labor Congress. And the Reds made good use of such issues as the Scottsboro Case. I know: I helped set them up.

It usually took quite some time, but when it became obvious that an organization was a Communist front, led by the Kremlin, some black dupes—like Randolph—left. As a result, the Communist Party once again operated with only a handful of black front men—W. E. B. Dubois, Ralph Bunche and a few others—without any Negroes to follow them. Ralph Bunche, of Howard University, finally pulled out of open Party activities and built up his national and international stature to play a larger role in the struggle for the minds of the Negro masses. Later, United States government hearings on his status as a security risk were quickly hushed up and a whitewash report issued overnight. Despite repeated failures among black Americans, the Party always kept the front machinery in reserve for the opportune moment when it would be needed. Starting before the Second World War they have carried out a systematic penetration of Negro organizations. The Student Non-Violent Coordinating Committee, the Southern Christian Leadership Conference and many more were targets. Training and guidance was given to some of the black church leaders and the effort paid off by getting Martin Luther King, Ralph Abernathy and others working together with the Communist Party's Moscow-trained Negro mercenaries like James Jackson, Harry Winston and Claude Lightfoot. These men have been publicized and sometimes financed with funds from Moscow's treasury.

Martin Luther King, whom J. Edgar Hoover characterized as a "habitual liar," learned the technique of starting demonstrations from the Communists. He started many so-called peaceful demonstrations, then did a vanishing act before the riots began. Despite his open advocacy of selective lawbreaking, King was given the Nobel Peace Prize and praised by three of our Presidents.

The groundwork for the present anarchy and civil strife was laid in the 1920's and 30's by the Communists with the creation of various Party organizations and fronts. The Reds realized that the only way to weaken our country is by dividing it through anarchy and chaos. I am sure that with Moscow's unlimited finances, and its agents, including the American Communist Party, more and more revolutionary organizations will be created. What I saw upon my return to the United States, and the bombings, riots and other guerilla warfare activities throughout the country today—and the people leading them—remind me, with shame, that I was one of those who helped to create these forces and the plans for the destruction of our nation through the creation of a Red guerilla army. I rededicated myself to do everything in my power to defend the United States.

Today the Communist Party leadership includes experienced military men trained in Moscow, such as Harry Winston, who received military training in the United States Army during World War II and at the Lenin School. As a rehearsal they showed their strength at the Peekskill Riot in 1949, where they confronted the State Police and surrounding law-enforcement agencies. In its activities, the United States Communist Party has been guided by instructions given to it by the Communist International:

> In view of the extraordinary importance of the counterrevolutionary shock troops, the Communist Party through its nuclei in the unions, devotes special attention to this question, arranging a thoroughgoing educational and communication service (espionage) which shall keep under constant observation the military organs and forces of the enemy, his headquarters, his arsenals, the connection between these headquarters, and the police, the Press, and the political parties, and work out all the necessary details of defense and counter attack.
>
> —Third World Congress of the Communist
> International, July, 1921

These and other orders of a similar nature were given to us continuously by the Kremlin and the result is the W. E. B. Dubois Clubs, Black Panthers, Young Lords and other terrorist groups—the Fifth Column in our midst.

The Reds have a complete battle plan—military strategy, creating riots and anarchy, destroying the police and military by subversion and assassination, etc. This is their main objective according to my own experience in the Communist Party through the schooling and training given to me. Agents are provided with manuals in the schools for espionage and sabotage agents conducted in the Soviet Union, Czechoslovakia, Poland and Hungary. The diagrams of one such publication were obtained in Europe by the Central Intelligence Agency and presented to a Congressional committee. Two key instructions are: Make investigations and reports on the activities of the police and security services. Investigate and repress those security organizations which support the government.

Make no mistake about it, we are at War.

EPILOG

I firmly believe that our country is the best in history. We have the greatest system yet devised by man. No one power or combination of powers is capable of destroying us, if we remain united behind our government, which we freely elect. We can disagree on problems and their solutions, but we must keep these disputes "within the family." Outside our land, our motto must be, "Our country, may it always be in the right, but right or wrong, it is our country."

APPENDIX I

Desiderata

Expropriatsia and criminal experience became both a memory and a recurring theme for the remainder of my childhood and throughout much of my adult life. Not only in Russia, but even in the United States, the Communist Party considered this a perfectly acceptable means of raising funds when the Party was operating underground.

The first time it was used in the United States was in 1929, when a Party functionary, Barney Mass, held up a bank in Boston, Massachusetts. He did a very amateurish job, was caught, and the Party disavowed any knowledge of it. Then a large counterfeiting job was done by Alexander Burton, a lieutenant of Jay Lovestone, general secretary of the Communist Party. Bogus hundred-dollar bills were distributed by the Mafia, with whom the American Bolsheviks had an agreement for such undertakings. Burton served fifteen years at Lewisburg Federal Prison in Lewisburg, Pennsylvania, and after his release was given a job by Lovestone and Dave Dubinsky as medical coordinator of the International Ladies Garment Workers Union on 25th Street and 7th Avenue, New York City.

Expropriatsia is now an everyday international practice by Communist Parties; for example, it was practiced in Cuba by Castro and Company during the Batista regime, in Peru, Venezuela, Colombia and throughout Latin America. This is in keeping with Lenin's instructions in *Left Wing Communism*, "Communists are to be ready to cheat, lie, perjure and do everything possible to gain their ends. We must be able to withstand all this, to agree to any sacrifices, even if need be to resort to all sorts of stratagems, artifices, illegal methods, evasions and subterfuges."*

Iosif Dzhugashvili, alias Stalin, was the main brigand. In 1907,

Left Wing Communism, Vol. 30, Int. Publishers.

he first made it "fashionable" for the Bolsheviks to carry out these assignments when he led a gang that robbed a payroll and murdered the bank messenger, two guards and the driver in Tiflis, Georgia.

The terminology comparing their enemies to mad dogs was used by the Bolsheviks for years, and I heard it many times during my life in the Communist movement. During the Moscow purge trials, Vishinsky, when he was prosecuting Zinoviev, Kamenev and other of Lenin's co-workers, called them mad dogs. When I was called before the Central Control Commission of the U.S. Communist Party on various charges, I became a mad dog myself.

George Ashkenudze, one of the leaders of the Russian Socialist Left Wing Federation, told me that on other occasions the Soviet government sent some of the imperial Russian crown jewels to finance the Soviet Government Trade Delegation* in Washington, and the rest were used to set up an American Communist Party. I had also heard this same story from Alexander Stoklitsky—that over 1,000,000 rubles'** worth of diamonds were sent there with Borodin. Part of the jewels was given to Frank Boland, representative of Eamon DeValera (the future president of Ireland), in New York. The gems were reclaimed in 1948 through a conference in London between the Soviet Representative in England and a representative of the DeValera government.

Michael Borodin, whose real name was Michael Gruzenberg (Father, Rabi), was born in Yanovichi, Vitebsk, in Byelorussia. He joined the Jewish Bund Social Democratic organization, then quit the Bund and joined the Bolsheviks in 1903. He arrived in the United States between 1907 and 1908 and changed his name to Berg. He studied at Valparaiso University in Indiana. Berg ran a radical prep school until 1917 when he returned to Russia.

*The Produce Exchange Corporation, succeeded by Amtorg Trading Corporation.
**The ruble was worth 50¢, American money.

Borodin was notified by Nuorteva that Sandburg was in Oslo and told to contact him in regard to some missions that Sandburg agreed to carry out. Borodin and Sandburg met at the Grand Hotel in Oslo, Norway, and discussed their mutual interest in getting money and propaganda into the United States. It was arranged that Sandburg would carry out one of these missions. According to the story told me by Alexander Stoklitsky, a member of the Russian Bureau of the Russian Federation of the S.P., Borodin gave Sandburg four checks of $10,000 each and $80,000 in English pounds. But this information contradicts other stories, including Theodore Draper's in *Roots of American Communism,* page 237.

The truth is that Sandburg hid the money in a money belt on his waist, and the checks were hidden on his person. One check for $10,000 was found on him when he was searched at Customs, and a trunkful of propaganda and important coded documents were confiscated. The rest of the money and bank drafts were handed over to Nuorteva, including a manuscript, *A Letter to American Workers,* by Lenin. This was later published in the *Revolutionary Age* and the *Liberator,* of which Sandburg was a co-editor.

Isidor Blankstein was born in Russia in 1895. He came to the United States in 1912 and became a member of the Socialist Party, Russian Branch. In 1918–19 he worked on the staff of L.C.K. Martens; he was arrested and held as an alien radical in 1919. He was arrested in New York on a deportation warrant by the U.S. Immigration and Naturalization Service. From the time he vanished in 1923 until 1943, he worked as a Soviet courier and agent until he was apprehended by the U.S. Department of Justice, Immigration and Naturalization Service in 1953. He was ordered deported, but is still here, thanks to the Warren decisions of the Supreme Court nullifying most of these cases.

Martens lived long enough to preside as judge over his former leaders and comrades during the Stalin purges of 1936–37, and to sentence to death Zinoviev and Kamenev and others, all former co-workers of Lenin. Nuorteva was sent to Siberia and eventually liquidated as an absconder of funds that he could not account for in the United States, and as an American Secret Service agent from evidence supplied by Louis C. Fraina and other informants.

Santeri Nuorteva was born of peasant parents in 1879 on a farm outside Helsinki, formerly Helsingfors. He attended engineering school in St. Petersburg and at the turn of the century came to the United States. In 1911, while working at different occupations for small engineering firms in Minnesota, he joined the Finnish group of the Socialist Party. In 1914, at the beginning of World War I in Europe, he bought a controlling interest in the *Raivaaja*, the official organ of the Finnish Federation of the Socialist Party.

On February 19, 1918, he received a cablegram from Y. Sirolo, the Provisional Premier of the short-lived Finnish Soviet Republic, appointing him representative of the Finnish Peoples' Republic in the United States.

He immediately set up an office of the Finnish Information Bureau at 299 Broadway, New York City. The money for this came from the sale of some of the Imperial Crown Jewels brought in by couriers, and from donations by some American Soviet apologists and do-gooders, not unlike the present-day Cyrus Eaton (American millionaire and Soviet supporter). Nuorteva and Ludwig C. A. K. Martens, the unrecognized Soviet ambassador, were both declared personae non grata and deported to Moscow.

Information found in the files of Robert MacLeod Hodgson, former British ambassador to Russia, revealed that Nuorteva had worked for U. S. Military Intelligence—the L. C. Fraina spy case was one instance, and there was evidence of others. In 1922 he was sent to Siberia where he died of "lead poisoning" in the form of a bullet from the GPU (Soviet Secret Police).

Three visitors from Moscow had just arrived and were introduced to us as Comrade Brooks (his real name was Professor Valetski) alias Walecki, H. Brooks Michaelson (also real name Max Hourwitz), who had the full power to act in the name of the C.I.; John Pepper, former member of the Socialist Labor Party of Boston, Mass., who came to take charge of reorganizing the Hungarian Federation; and Davidson (real name Boris Reinstein) who came as representative of the Profintern (RILU). But Valetski spoke with full authority of the ECCI and Davidson spoke for the Profintern. Brooks spoke on the unity of all factions of the Party and the preparation for the coming National Convention of the Party.

Boris Reinstein during his report congratulated me on my methods, etc.

Schneider and Potash were both ordered deported from the United States many years later—Schneider was deferred under deportation proceedings and died in 1960, and Potash is still here.

Potash was deported to Poland in 1955, but smuggled himself back into the country years later. He was allowed to stay because no other country would accept him.

Anna Louise Strong was born in the United States, the daughter of a Congregational minister. She went to Russia early in 1920 after the Bolshevik revolution.

She shuttled between the United States and the USSR, as a Soviet agent, reporting to Alexander Trachtenberg. Trachtenberg headed International Publishers, and was a member of both the National Executive Committee of the Communist Party U.S.A. and the Party's Espionage Control Commission. She worked with Agnes B. Smedley and Edgar Snow in the Richard Sorge spy ring, and was also a member of the 4th Department of Soviet Military Intelligence.

Tomorrow's China and *I Change Worlds* were but two of the many propaganda books she authored for the Soviets.

Because of her sympathies for Mao Tse-tung and the Chinese, the Soviets arrested her on February 4, 1949 and she spent five days in the famous G.P.U. Lubyanka prison. Accused of espionage, she was expelled from the country. (See articles in *New York Herald Tribune*, March 27, 1949.)

She remained in America until 1950 or 1951, when she returned to her roost in Peking, China, writing for the Communist regime.

In the United States she was a top member of the Friends of the Soviet Union, the National Council of Soviet American Friendship, was Director of the Communist Front Committee for a Democratic

Far Eastern Policy, and editor of *Far East Spotlight,* its publication. She died February 26, 1970, in Communist China.

Davidson is the present secretary of the Liberal Party in New York. He has never to my knowledge condemned the Communists or officially condemned international Communism, either through testimony under oath or by helping the government agencies.

Mandel was research director of the Senate Internal Security subcommittee until his retirement in the 1960's. He remains a personal friend of Jay Lovestone who, while working on Internal Security, visited Lovestone every week or so to give him full information on most of the Senate committee's investigative and security matters. He could never stand Gitlow, Kornfeder or me because we knew of his connections with Lovestone.

"I hereby sentence you, Maurice Malkin, to 2½ to 5 years of hard labor at Sing Sing Prison."

When Judge Lewis E. Smith pronounced this sentence upon me, I stood beside my attorney, Edgar F. Hazelton, as though I were paralyzed. I never believed it would come to this. I did not even turn my face to see the reactions of the most innocent of all—Leo Franklin or Basoff, who did not know Communism or its meaning.

I remembered my father's prophecy that by following other gods, especially Marxism and atheism, trouble would surely follow us.

At the same time, I thought of the unscrupulous means the Party had always used to gain its ends—the deliberate frame-ups, the scapegoats—the relentless sacrificing and devouring of its own.

I was awakened to reality when the deputy sheriff led us back to the jail. After sentence was passed, all bail was canceled until a new appeal was set.

William Kruse was supposed to have been expelled in 1929 as a member of the Jay Lovestone faction but secretly he remained a Communist Party member and was active in the Communist Party fronts while holding down the job of educational supervisor for Bell and Howell, the firm headed by Senator Charles Percy. When I called his office in 1951 while working for the Immigration and Naturalization Service, he refused to see me. He sent out word that he would not have dealings with police spies and stool pigeons.

Trachtenberg joined the C.P. from the Socialist Party in 1921. He was a member of the National Committee of the C.P., a member of the Central Control Commission (court and jury) and the head of International Publishers, the C.P. publishing firm. He was convicted and sentenced in 1951 to five years in a federal penitentiary under the Smith Act.

Moissaye Olgin was a member of the National Committee of the C.P. and editor of the *Morning Freiheit* (Jewish Communist daily).

Jack Stachel joined the C.P. in 1923. He was a former patent-medicine salesman who rose to the position of membership on the National Committee because he knew how to follow orders. He was always on the winning side.

Goldfrank was a person looking for a career and recommended by Corliss Lamont.

Santos later became assistant to Quill and was deported to Hungary in 1948. After the 1956 revolt, he escaped from Hungary and told the House Committee on Un-American Activities about the conditions under Communism.

Curran apparently broke with the Party after World War II, although he has never to my knowledge testified about anything that went on while he was a member. The break came when the Party prepared to ditch Curran and elevate Harry Bridges, the West Coast longshoreman boss, to rule over all Communist-controlled transport unions. Violence broke out in late 1949 between the Communists and the Curran forces over possession of the N.M.U.'s six-story building on West 17th Street. Curran won.

Frederick Vanderbilt Fields, famous in the Institute of Pacific Relations, millionaire related to the Vanderbilt and Marshall Fields families, now in exile in Mexico.

A curious note on Mrs. Burnham. In an exclusive story on January 21, 1928, the *New York World* startled the town and set tongues to wagging when it reported that "old friends of Mrs. Grace Mailhouse Burnham, an attractive woman of thirty-seven (and a widow of several years), were surprised to learn, a few days ago, that she had given birth, January 10, to a daughter, whom she named Vera, meaning 'truth.' " The father of the "eugenic baby" was a carefully kept secret. A Russian circus strongman claimed months later he was the father, but this was hotly denied by the widow. In Party circles, Mrs. Burnham's child was known as the "William Weinstone eugenic baby."

On April 1, 1930, newspapers reported she had picked up a $100,-000 unsecured loan on the Communist cooperative housing project, Workers' Colony, Inc., which the Party had started in 1927 on property overlooking Bronx Park at Allerton Avenue. Mrs. Burnham announced, through her attorney, that she would expect no interest on the loan.

General Krivitsky was mysteriously shot to death February 10, 1941, in a room of the Bellevue Hotel in Washington. Though he was listed a suicide, I am certain myself that he was murdered by Soviet agents.

Gold was brought into court on charges of assault and other crimes, but was able to escape punishment because the Communist Party and its front, the American Labor Party, were able to make political deals to get him and others off the hook, especially when Thomas E. Dewey was district attorney of New York during 1936–37.

Potash became a national figure in the Communist Party because he carried out orders like a robot. Only once did he deviate. That was in 1927–28 when he and Gold were on the verge of expulsion for following "right-wing opportunism while supporting Jay Lovestone when he was general secretary of the Communist Party. They were saved because Jay Lovestone was temporarily in the majority. William Z. Foster told me in 1927, when I was released from Mineola County Jail on bond, that Gold and Potash are "two cheap opportunists" and their days in the Party were numbered. But they both were saved and eventually became members of the National Committee of the Communist Party and survived all purges. Gold dropped by the wayside after his 1953 conviction in Washington, D.C. for perjury in violation of the Taft-Hartley Act and was sentenced to three years in the federal penitentiary. I helped prepare the case for his conviction, which ended his activities in the Furriers' Union—or any other union—and he is not even mentioned in Party circles. He now lives on his wife's inheritance. Potash was indicted under the Smith Act in 1951 and served five years in the federal penitentiary for advocating the overthrow of our government by force and violence. He was later deported to Poland as an alien who had never been naturalized. He liked communism so much that a few years later he smuggled himself back into this country and served another year for illegal entry into the U.S. He now teaches in a Communist school at 80 East 11th Street and gets paid by the Communist Party for creating spies and saboteurs in the land that gives him a chance to live like a human being instead of a derelict robot. [See also Appendix II.]

Gerhart Eisler was resident agent of the Soviet government in the U.S. and a representative of the Communist International. After conviction in the U.S. he skipped bail and escaped on the Polish ship SS *Batory*. He was a very good friend of Eleanor Roosevelt, who also sponsored Hans Eisler, Gerhart's brother, to legalize his entry into the U.S. Gerhart Eisler died in 1968 in East Germany.

Whittaker Chambers went to Adolph Berle, Assistant Secretary of State, and informed him that Alger Hiss was a spy and was giving information to the Soviet government. Berle gave the information to Roosevelt.

Kurt Rosenfeld was the leader of the short-lived Bavarian Red Government of 1919. He came here in 1934 and worked through the offices of Arthur Garfield Hays, chief counsel of the American Civil Liberties Union, while carrying out Moscow's bidding.

Ambrogio Donini was an exile from Italy, and an international Soviet spy. I exposed him in my testimony, but he was allowed to remain in the U.S. and carry on Soviet espionage thanks to protection from such people as Mrs. Roosevelt, Joseph Lash and from the National Student Union. In 1945–46 he returned to Italy, and later was exposed by the DeCasperi government as a Soviet agent.

Sex as a weapon was fully introduced by the so-called mother of the German C.P. Clara Zetkin after World War I. Some of the largest cities and seaports in Germany were rampant with prostitution and revolutionists, and Communists found the red-light districts among the prostitutes a good place for collecting funds and a haven from the police. It is a known fact that these elements along with their pimps were never on good terms with the police, and the Communists always used the underworld with all its machinery for their own purposes—whether it was distribution of narcotics, counterfeit money or false documents, or execution. These unsavory elements were able to supply them with their services, especially around the seaports of Hamburg, Bremen, etc. Clara Zetkin even wrote articles in the *Rohte Fohne* (official Communist newspaper in Germany) and proposed to Lenin to organize the prostitutes into a trade union. At first Lenin scorned this idea. After thinking it over, he saw an opportunity where they could be of great use to the Party.

Another person in the Bolshevik limelight was Alexandra Kollentai (later Soviet ambassador to Sweden and Mexico), who was the author of a book called *Red Love and Free Love*. During the heat of the fighting in October, 1917, while everyone was out in the streets fighting the counterrevolution, Lenin found her busy on a mattress in Smolny Institute (the Bolshevik Headquarters) with a young sailor, Dubenko (the leader of the Red naval forces). Since then, every Communist Party in the world has used the young girls in the Young Communist League and the C.P. to work the waterfront to entice longshoremen and sailors to come to Communist affairs, and to propagandize for the Party. Girls would always also be found in the Communist summer camps doing the Party's bidding plus offering a little enjoyment on the side. The Party believes that the only laws and morals are Communist morals; there are no bourgeois morals or capitalist morals. Therefore, Communists do not believe in family institutions or morals—so everything is free.

Ambassador Robert C. Hill was one of the most experienced diplomats in Latin America. He served as ambassador to El Salvador, Costa Rica and in other parts of the world prior to his post in Mexico from May, 1957 to January, 1961, the period in which Castro was making his coup in Cuba.

Ambassador Hill, a credit to our diplomatic corps and country, was respected and loved by all Americans in Mexico. He was honored and respected by the Mexicans. It was my pleasure to be present at a few functions and receptions given in honor of this great representative of the United States and to witness the honors and esteem that were shown. As soon as Hill took his post in May, 1957, I checked and secured some of the information, which I relayed to a senior official of the U. S. embassy in Mexico and to one of his aides. I am sure that all the reports gathered by sources in Mexico concerning the activities of the Fidelistas were relayed to the State Department. But that information was ignored by those in the pro-left group in the department such as William Wieland. Ambassador Hill said of him: "I was warned by members of the foreign service about Mr. Wieland, that he was an opportunist and a dilettante and that I should be very careful in my dealings with him" (Committee of the Judiciary, U.S. Senate Report, June 12, 1961). Wieland ignored these reports, but did take to heart the words of people like himself, Herbert Matthews of the *New York Times* among them.

Everyone got into the act of making Castro a savior of humanity, including Ed Sullivan, a journalist turned showman. Sullivan turned up in Castro's mountain camp and asked Fidel if he was a Communist. Such naïveté almost borders on idiocy.

Another entertainer, Jack Paar, who had a TV show on the NBC network said that Castro was a very nice guy, apparently because one of Fidel's relatives is friendly with Paar's daughter. Besides, he was sure that Castro was not a Communist. Paar was very good at summing up people on his program and making instant analyses of complex world problems, but couldn't see Castro as a Communist.

These were some of the State Department's "advisors" on the Castro Soviet takeover. This old "Yenan Line," swallowed by the gullible during the New Deal of Roosevelt and the Fair Deal of Truman, which the Lattimore-Hiss gang was able to put over with slogans about Mao's "agrarian reformers," cost us the loss of China to the Reds. The same tactic was used again about Castro—"the George Washington of Cuba"—misleading our country and our government into helping establish a Communist base 90 miles from our shores. Leading personalities and publications, such as the *New York Times*, unwittingly assisted the Kremlin in Castro's takeover of Cuba.

APPENDIX II

_____

Irving Potash

Irving Potash, a former inmate at the penitentiary in Elmira, never did a stitch of useful work in his life. He was a former apprentice dental mechanic and an ex-convict friend of Little Augie Pisano.* Potash robbed the dental mechanics during their organization strike in the early 20s and was placed in the Furriers' Union by the Party when we captured the union in New York in 1925. He was one of the leaders who promised me during our trip to Mineola, where I surrendered on January 10, 1929, that he would see that my old parents did not suffer economically during my absence. However, when my 71-year-old mother came to the union to get transportation to visit me, he told her that they did not know me, in spite of the fact that my name and imprisonment were being used in all appeals for funds in my behalf as a martyr for the cause.

Later, Potash was convicted in 1951 under the Smith Act, served in a federal penitentiary and was later deported to Poland. Two years after his deportation, he hated capitalist, blood-sucking America so much that he escaped from the workers' paradise, Communist Poland, stowed away and came back to the U.S. to suffer in a steam-heated apartment, clean clothes and human conditions.

I was employed by the Department of Justice as an expert analyst and consultant, when I was tipped off that his wife, Gita Potash, whom I had recruited in 1922 or 1923 when she arrived in the United States from Russia, had some important information. After a little talk with the chief of the Anti-subversive Section, we decided to send an investigator named Stapp to see her. After seeing her, he reported that she would make a deal with us. If we would not file cancellation proceedings against her for claiming non-Communist

_____

*Later convicted in Washington, D.C. for violation of the Taft-Hartley Act and for perjury.

status when she obtained her citizenship, she would give us some important information in return. We told her that we did not make deals but that we would give it some thought. It all depended on what aid she could be to the government. A few days later, she called us and wanted to see someone again. After seeing her, she told the investigator that Potash was back and that he could be apprehended in a restaurant in Bronxville, New York, where he was actually caught. He was later convicted for illegal entry. After serving his sentence, he was released. No country wanted him and the U.S. government was powerless to deport him. However, if the Justice Department really wanted to enforce the law, there are over 15,000 such cases involving potential fifth columnists, spies and traitors who are walking the streets and leading demonstrations, riots, lootings and disorders.

Over 20,000 cancellation cases could be enforced under the law and could be interned or deported. But the defenders of Communists, the American Civil Liberties Union and other pseudo-liberals, are always quick to come to their aid, always swift to raise the hue and cry about curtailment of civil liberties.

APPENDIX III

POLICY OF THE C.I. ON BORING FROM WITHIN

George Dimitrov

General Secretary of the C.I.

Our program must be to gain our ends through our friends, sympathizers and allies, while keeping ourselves in the background. As Soviet power grows, there will be a greater aversion to Communist Parties everywhere. So we must practice the techniques of withdrawal—never appearing in the foreground—letting our friends do the work. We must always remember that one sympathizer is generally worth more than a dozen militant Communists; a university professor who, though not a Party member, lends himself to the interest of the Soviet Union, is worth more than 500 poor devils who don't know any better than to get themselves beaten up by the police.

Each man has his value, his merit: the writer who, without being a Party member, defends the Soviet Union—the union leader who is outside our ranks but defends the Soviet International policy—these people are worth more than a thousand party members.

Those who are not marked as Communists enjoy a greater freedom of action. This dissimulated activity which arouses no resistance is much more effective than a frontal attack by the Communists.

The Communist Parties of the whole world must learn the lesson of the Spanish War—where the efficacy of the Fifth Column was proved. Our friends must confuse the adversary for us, carry out our major directives and mobilize in favor of our campaigns people who do not think as we do, and whom we could never reach.

In this tactic we must use everyone who comes near us—and their number grows every day.

Particularly, we must use ambitious politicians who need support —men who want to rise to the limelight but lack the ladder, and who realize that we Communists—through publicity—can provide that ladder.

We will provide the ladder today, and take it away the moment it suits us!

APPENDIX IV

The Communist Party U.S.A. and the Mafia

The Communist Party of the United States has had an agreement with the Mafia since 1924, with the arrival in the United States of Eneo Sormenti, alias Vidali Contreras Victorio. Eneo arrived here as a stowaway from Trieste in 1923. Upon his arrival he reestablished the understanding between the Mafia and the Communists that was made in Italy by Bordiga, a leader of the Italian Communist Party, and by Ercoli Palmieri Togliatti, alias Ercoli.

The agreement called for the Mafia to do work for the Communist International, such as murdering opponents, distributing counterfeit currency and dope, stealing government documents such as seals and stamps for foreign passports, and other jobs which Communist agents could not carry out, but which the Mafia and its connections could.

In the United States, Sormenti strengthened the ties with the Mafiosi. Their first jobs were the fur strike and the cloak strike of 1926, for which gangsters were used.

In 1927–28 when Sormenti was on Ellis Island awaiting deportation, he was visited by Dr. Abraham Markoff, a dentist who spoke Italian and was a Communist Party member of the National Committee, and Joseph Brodsky, an attorney for the Communist Party, to whom Eneo gave the contracts with the Mafiosi.

In 1929 when Federico Alpi, alias Morigni, alias Fred Brown, arrived with instructions as a Communist International representative to the Communist Party U.S.A., he also had instructions from Ercoli from Moscow on the Mafia–Communist Party pact.

And in 1929–30 American bills in denominations of $100 and $50 were being printed in Moscow in Spassky near Teatralny Ploshchad (theater square). The counterfeit bills were first tried out in Central

245

America, Cuba and the Panama Canal Zone by sailors. The bills were brought there by Harry Kweit, Communist courier, and also by members of the newly formed Marine Workers League and the Marine Workers Industrial Union (Communist Seamen's Union) led by the well-known George Mink. After successfully passing as real American currency, the bills were shipped here to Nicholas Dozenberg, a charter member of the Party who had been working as a Soviet agent since 1927. Nicholas had known Dr. Valentin G. Burton in the Communist Party in New York, where Burton maintained an office as M.D. He was an all-round jolly fellow, and a good mixer with everyone he met (I also knew him as Alexander Burton). He was always ready to undertake risky adventures—and not averse to performing a few abortions!

Nick persuaded Burton to get someone to help in distributing the counterfeit bills, convincing him that the Soviet Union needed American dollars (real ones) to buy machinery, etc., for its first Five-Year Plan. Burton contacted a private detective, J. Smiley, in Chicago, and Abraham Markoff and the Mafia in New York; Smiley contacted the Mafia in Cicero, a suburb of Chicago, and got a group of venturesome Mafiosi to distribute the bills. The split was 25 percent for them, with the remainder to be sent to Moscow by courier for Burton, Nicholas Dozenberg, Abraham Markoff and Alpi.

The Chicago police caught one of the passers, who began talking and involved Dr. Burton's friend and collaborator, E. Dachow Von Bulow. Von Bulow was a former German army officer who worked with Burton for the Communist Party on a few smuggling deals on orders from J. Lovestone, then general secretary of the Communist Party.

In May 1934 Von Bulow testified for the prosecution and implicated his pal. Doc Burton, adhering to the code of the Communist Party and the Mafiosi, remained silent. As a result, Burton's physician's license was revoked and, on May 25, 1934, he was sentenced to fifteen years in prison. He was released after serving ten years and was then given a job by his friends Jay Lovestone and Dave Dubinsky, as medical coordinator in the I.L.G.W.U. at 7th Avenue and 26th Street in New York City. Dr. Burton kept quiet for two reasons —the Party code, and his contact with the Mafiosi.

In 1934 one of the chief Soviet intelligence agents in the United States, Valentin Markin, who was getting out of line with the Soviet hierarchy, was fatally injured in a West 52nd Street hallway in New York. In 1937, Juliet Stuart Poyntz, an American Party leader and a Soviet agent, broke with them. She was lured from her room at the West Side Women's Club on West 57th Street, New York City, by her former sweatheart, Shachno Epstein, and with the help of New York Mafia was taken on board the Soviet freighter *Kim*. She was either killed and thrown overboard or taken to Russia and killed there.

In 1943, an opponent of the Communist Party, Carlo Tresca, was killed on 15th Street and 5th Avenue by the Mafiosi, one named Pagano, of the Luchese mob, under the leadership of Eneo Sormenti who knew Carlo from the old days.

These are only a few of the numerous jobs done by the Mafiosi for the American Communist Party, and they do such jobs for all other Communist Parties in accordance with their pact.

Since the death of Abraham Markoff and Alpi's escape from the United States, there is no one in the Party leadership who can be trusted with the contract. There have been so many disenchantments and splits within the Party that Moscow cannot take the chance of having someone reveal the connection between Moscow and the Mafia.

INDEX

249

254